North Carolina
and World War II

ALSO BY ANITA PRICE DAVIS

The Margaret Mitchell Encyclopedia (2013)

New Deal Art in Virginia: The Oils, Murals, Reliefs and Frescoes and Their Creators (2009)

New Deal Art in North Carolina: The Murals, Sculptures, Reliefs, Paintings, Oils and Frescoes and Their Creators (2009)

Anita Price Davis *and* Marla J. Selvidge
Women Nobel Peace Prize Winners (2006)

COMPILED BY ANITA PRICE DAVIS

Georgia During the Great Depression: A Documentary Portrait of a Decade (2008)

North Carolina During the Great Depression: A Documentary Portrait of a Decade (2003)

ALL FROM MCFARLAND

North Carolina and World War II
A Documentary Portrait

ANITA PRICE DAVIS

McFarland & Company, Inc., Publishers
Jefferson, North Carolina

LIBRARY OF CONGRESS CATALOGUING-IN-PUBLICATION DATA

Davis, Anita Price.
　　North Carolina and World War II : a documentary portrait / Anita Price Davis.
　　　　p.　　cm.
　　Includes bibliographical references and index.

　　ISBN 978-0-7864-7984-9 (softcover : acid free paper) ♾
　　ISBN 978-1-4766-1992-7 (ebook)

　　1. World War, 1939–1945—North Carolina.　2. Military bases—North Carolina—History—20th century.　3. Prisoner-of-war camps—North Carolina—History—20th century.　4. World War, 1939–1945—North Carolina—Prisoners and prisons.　5. Historic sites—North Carolina.　6. North Carolina—History, Military—20th century.　I. Title.

D769.85.N8D38 2015
940.53'756—dc23   2014041583

BRITISH LIBRARY CATALOGUING DATA ARE AVAILABLE

© 2015 Anita Price Davis. All rights reserved

No part of this book may be reproduced or transmitted in any form or by any means, electronic or mechanical, including photocopying or recording, or by any information storage and retrieval system, without permission in writing from the publisher.

On the cover: A metal drive in Forest City, North Carolina, commands: "Let's stop Hitler. Put old aluminum here" (courtesy of David Daniel, Forest City, North Carolina)

Printed in the United States of America

McFarland & Company, Inc., Publishers
　Box 611, Jefferson, North Carolina 28640
　　www.mcfarlandpub.com

North Carolina and World War II is my salute to the North Carolinians (in service and on the home front) who did their part in World War II. I was a product of that war, and herein I record the story of North Carolina's role in it.

In particular, I dedicate this volume to my merchant grandfather Plato Rollins Price, who sent three sons to war. One of these "boys"—my father—would not return. Mother and I lived with P. R. Price and my grandmother when my father answered his draft summons and even for a while after my father's death at the Battle of the Bulge.

My grandfather carried me on his hip as he served his patrons and always introduced me the same way: "This is the Toodle," he would say. "Her father was killed in service." He swallowed hard after the words, and he paused for a moment to allow the customer to ponder the meaning of what he had said. Somehow I knew that thinking about my father's death made Pop sad, but I knew also that he was proud of him—and of me.

My grandfather P. R. Price operated a filling station while his sons were in the service. He knew rationing and redeeming ration stamps (author's family album).

Acknowledgments

North Carolina and World War II tells the story in both words and pictures of the Tarheel State during the 1940s. Readers will find that North Carolina experienced intensely the hardships of the decade and yet gave generously to the cause.

In this book readers will see the settings, the events, the artifacts, and the people of the era. They will read the words of the time from recordings, letters, diaries, interviews, and manuscripts.

This book is not the work of one person. Many people deserve credit—especially those who served and sacrificed at home and in battle.

Especially deserving of thanks is my twelve-year-old grandson, Robert, who helped edit and print photographs for the volume. He worked uncomplainingly and was a joyful colleague. My six-year-old granddaughter Marie helped me select images for the book.

The Mickel Library at Converse College was of great assistance to me. Wade Woodward, Dell Morgan, Mark Collier, and Becky Poole were always a source of help and encouragement.

Matthew Clark, publisher of the *Daily Courier*, gave me permission to use photographs and to quote freely from the *Courier*, the *Spindale Sun*, and the *Rutherford County News*. His graciousness and his help will never be forgotten.

Brigadier General Ed. Y. Hall collaborated with me on this work from its beginning. He is an editor and a friend.

People from all over the state shared their stories, their photographs, and their memorabilia generously with me.

My gratitude goes to my loving son Robbie, my wonderful daughter-in-law Stacey, my two grands (Robert and Marie), and my husband of fifty-one years, Buren. They are always accepting of my projects and my work. Without their help, I could not have completed this task. I give them my thanks and my love—always.

Table of Contents

Acknowledgments vi

Preface 1

1. The Beginning of World War II in Europe — 5
2. The Beginning of America's Direct Involvement in the War — 8
3. Some Immediate Effects of the War on North Carolina (December 1941–August 1942) — 14
4. Other Effects of the War on the State and the Nation — 22
5. National Cemeteries in North Carolina — 27
6. Sites in the Mountain Region — 35
7. Sites in the Piedmont Region — 56
8. Sites in the Western Coastal Plain — 77
9. The Southern Tidewater Subregion of the Coastal Region — 100
10. The Central Tidewater Subregion of the Coastal Region — 135
11. The Three Capes of North Carolina — 145
12. The Northern Tidewater Subregion: Nags Head, Manteo, Edenton, Elizabeth City, Weeksville, Vultee — 159
13. The Incalculable Costs of World War I and the Great Depression to the World, the Nation and the State Before World War II — 175

14. The Incalculable Costs of World War II	177
15. The Medal of Honor	179
16. The Home Front	188
Bibliography	197
Index	209

Preface

December 6, 1941, was a typical Saturday morning for most North Carolinians. Many residents woke early, retrieved their daily newspaper from their porch, and prepared to read the news of the day.

The Charlotte temperature was warm for a December day—even in the South. The overnight low had been 51°. The high for December 6 in Charlotte was forecast as 56° and the low as 37°. No precipitation would occur on this Saturday—the day before the long-remembered December 7, 1941: the date that President Franklin Delano Roosevelt declared to be "the date that would live in infamy" (Wunderground.com, "Weather History for Charlotte, NC").

The news headline on the *Daily Times-News* for Burlington, North Carolina, for December 6 hinted at an upcoming tragedy for the following day. The Saturday headlines read: "Far East Crisis Hangs in Balance Today" (Bolden 1995, 2).

The United States and Japan had been engaging in negotiations since November. The two countries appeared to be in a deadlock. On December 6, President Roosevelt sent a personal appeal for peace to Emperor Hirohito of Japan and waited for an answer. Emperor Hirohito's answer would come on December 7, 1941, but it would not be in the form of a written reply (Chitwood et al. 1949, 816).

Many North Carolinians sat in their kitchens on this Saturday morning and listened to the radio as the women prepared breakfasts for the families. Radio programming of particular interest to Carolina listeners included the local and national news, farm reports, and on-the-air performances by area musicians.

Children were already begging to be allowed to listen to *Let's Pretend*, which would be broadcast later that morning. This radio show—sponsored by Cream of Wheat—featured stories and fairy tales that enthralled young listeners. Most young people could sing all the words of the catchy Cream of Wheat jingle:

> Cream of Wheat is so good to eat
> As we have it every day.
> It makes us strong as we sing this song,
> And it makes us shout, "Hooray!"
> It's good for growing children
> And grownups, too, to eat.
> For all the family's breakfasts,
> You can't beat Cream of Wheat [lyrics].

There were other amusements besides the radio in the early 1940s. Morella reports that most Americans attended two movies per week. Some fathers began checking the newspapers for show times, prices, and line-ups. The children hoped a double feature might be playing this Saturday night (Morella 2012).

Movies with Charlotte native Randolph Scott (1898–1986) were always favorites in North Carolina. Between 1928 and 1953, Scott made over 100 films—six in 1940 and 1941 alone; these recent movies included the Westerns *When the Daltons Rode* (1940), *Belle Star* (1941), and *Western Union* (1941).

Other movies popular with young people in 1941 included Walt Disney's animated *Dumbo*, *Tarzan's Secret Treasure* (starring Johnny Weissmuller), the horror film *Wolf Man* (starring Lon Chaney, Jr.), and shorts with the Three Stooges. Popular with adults were *The Maltese Falcon* (with Humphrey Bogart and with John Huston as director), *Red River Valley* (a Western with Roy Rogers), and *Sergeant York* (with Gary Cooper in the title role).

With the Great Depression only recently having begun to recede, however, many North Carolinians still did not have the money for such extravagances as "shows." Harmonizing around a piano with family and friends on a Saturday night was often a more economical choice.

Reading a volume borrowed from the bookmobile was another inexpensive, alternate option for a Saturday night. Some of the popular recent novels were *The Yearling* by Marjorie Kinnan Rawlings (1939 Pulitzer Prize winner), *Gone with the Wind* by Margaret Mitchell (1937 Pulitzer Prize winner), and *The Grapes of Wrath* by John Steinbeck (1940 Pulitzer Prize winner). There had been no Pulitzer Prize for fiction in 1941 after the controversy over Ernest Hemingway's *For Whom the Bell Tolls,* but this discussion only seemed to generate more interest in the novel.

Many Carolinians planned to read in detail, *later*, the newspaper article that discussed the tensions between the Far East and the United States. President Roosevelt seemed to be attempting negotiations with Japan. Most Americans did not foresee the hesitancy of Japan to respond promptly as an immediate preamble to war—but December 7, 1941, would prove that it was.

The nation would lose 2,403 of its finest the very next day. The attack prompted America's entry into the war.

North Carolina was a unique state during World War II. The state trained more troops than any other. This volume focuses on the 20+ military sites within the state during World War II, these locations as they exist today, the home front during World War II, and those who served. North Carolina gave freely—even sacrificially.

North Carolina and World War II tells the story of the state in wartime through the voices of those who remember, through the eyes of those who share their images, through the mementos of the time, through the citations of the Medal of Honor Winners from North Carolina, and through the documents that record the events for posterity. Markers for the 8,500 North Carolinians who gave their lives remain in various places, at home and abroad. Memories of those who knew them still linger and should not be forgotten.

The uniqueness and the sacrifices of the state remain. *North Carolina and World War II* will help ensure this preservation.

Chapter 1

The Beginning of World War II in Europe

World War II officially began on September 1, 1939, when Nazi troops invaded Poland. Germany's justification for the troop invasion was that Poland had not accepted Germany's offered territorial adjustments.

Germany had demanded the annexation of Danzig, a free city protected by the League of Nations. Danzig connected Poland with the Baltic Sea and served as Poland's seaport. This annexation by Germany might prevent Poland from trading with others.

Spreading of War in Europe. In order to demonstrate their support of Poland, both France and Great Britain declared war on Germany two days later: September 3, 1939. Nevertheless, Germany "had its way" with Poland; Russia and Germany divided the land of Poland between them.

Russia seized Latvia, Lithuania, and Estonia. In December of 1939, Russia attacked Finland. Although Finland defended its independence, the Finns finally had to yield in March of 1940.

Since the September 1939 declaration of war, little fighting had occurred—except in Finland. Then in April of 1940, Germany occupied both Denmark and Norway; by the end of June in 1940, Hitler—with Italy—had claimed France, Belgium, and Holland. War seemed close for Americans.

Responses of the United States to War in Europe. The decade of the 1930s and its accompanying Great Depression had brought economic hardship to North Carolina, to the nation, and to the world. The nation had just begun recovering from the many problems of the thirties when war began abroad. The war was beginning to spread from nation to nation like an uncontrolled forest fire. Public opinion within the United States varied as to whether America should take sides or try to remain neutral. President Franklin Delano Roosevelt and Congress began to take some actions.

The United States froze assets that were within the United States and that belonged to conquered countries. The rationale was that this action would prevent the Axis powers from obtaining and using those funds.

President Roosevelt—without the vote of Congress—gave 50 destroyers to Great Britain in return for a lease of 99 years on eight bases from British Guiana to Newfoundland. After the occupation of two-thirds of France by the Germans in June of 1940, the United States began to strengthen its national defense by allocating $4 billion for defense and by enacting the first military conscription law in peacetime.

The Lend-Lease Act (March 11, 1941) encouraged the production of war equipment and supplies for the Allies. This production would help to ensure the assistance of the Allied Powers in the event that the United States needed it and would help to provide employment for U.S. labor and U.S. industries (Chitwood et al. 1949, 807–11).

The Lend-Lease Act (HR 1776, Section 3a) also enabled the president to "authorize the Secretary of War, the Secretary of the Navy, or the head of any other department or agency of the Government" (HR 1776, Section 3a-2) "to sell, transfer title to, exchange, lease, lend, or otherwise dispose of, to any such government any defense article" (OurDocuments.gov, "Transcript of Lend-Lease Act [1941]").

The United States froze German and Italian assets in the United States in May, seized Axis and Axis-controlled ships in American ports, imprisoned for attempted sabotage nearly a thousand seamen, and prepared a list of those Axis and pro–Axis firms with which it would not trade. In addition the U.S. forces took over the defense of Iceland, Greenland, and Dutch Guiana (July–November 1941).

President Roosevelt and Prime Minister Winston Churchill signed the Atlantic Charter in August 1941. This action, which expressed the desire for the eradication of "Nazi tyranny," made the United States a "co-belligerent" even though it had not issued a formal war declaration.

Relations Between Japan and the United States in 1940 and 1941. The U.S. government recognized the brutality of the Japanese surprise invasion of China in the summer of 1941. Some Americans even began to boycott Japanese goods.

In November of 1941 Japan and the United States continued their talks. Japan made several demands on the United States. Japan proposed that the United States stop all aid to China, furnish Japan with all the oil Japan needed, and release any frozen Japanese assets.

On December 6, 1941, President Roosevelt sent a personal message to

1. The Beginning of World War II in Europe

Emperor Hirohito. The president asked for peace and the withdrawal of Japanese troops from Indochina. The *News and Observer* (Raleigh, North Carolina) announced this appeal as its December 7, 1941, headline: "President Sends Personal Appeal for Peace to Japanese Emperor."

A conference with envoys from Japan and Secretary Hull was on the agenda for that day. Before the meeting, however, the Japanese attacked Pearl Harbor (Chitwood et al. 1949, 812–17).

Chapter 2

The Beginning of America's Direct Involvement in the War

On Sunday, December 7, 1941, two hundred Japanese aircraft made a surprise attack upon the unsuspecting American fleet at Pearl Harbor. Also prey to the attack were the unwary United States Army and United Navy bases near Pearl Harbor. Although the United States had remained apart from the fighting that had gripped other countries since the 1930s, Japan had successfully drawn the United States into the hostilities.

Immediate Results of the Aggression in American Deaths and Casualties

The aggression on December 7, 1941, resulted immediately in 2,403 American deaths: 2,335 military personnel and 68 civilians. The wounded—both civilian and military workers—resulted in an additional 1,178 American victims. Many of the wounded and dead were North Carolinians. The count of dead and wounded would have likely been much higher had the attack occurred on a weekday, instead of a Sunday when many of the military were on shore leave.

American aircraft losses included 188 destroyed airplanes and 159 damaged planes. Most of the destruction occurred while the U.S. planes were still on the ground.

Damage to the U.S. Pacific Fleet on December 7, 1941

The U.S. Pacific Fleet suffered 21 sunk or damaged ships. Three of these vessels—the USS *Arizona*, the USS *Oklahoma*, and the USS *Utah*—were beyond repair.

2. The Beginning of America's Involvement in the War

***The USS* Arizona *(BB-39)*.** At 8:10 a.m. on December 7, 1941, the USS *Arizona* (BB-39) endured the greatest loss of life of any ship at Pearl Harbor that day. An armor-piercing bomb ignited the ship's ammunition magazine in the forward part of the ship; the *Arizona* sank during the aggression. Almost half of the 2,403 Americans killed by the Japanese during the 110-minute attack on Pearl Harbor were sailors and Marines aboard the *Arizona*, numbering 1,177 (Anderson).

North Carolina began its sacrifices on day one of World War II. Six of the casualties from the explosion and fire on the USS *Arizona* were from North Carolina; a seventh casualty may have been a North Carolinian (Pearl Harbor: Remembered; Military.com, "Pearl Harbor: Day"—see note at end of chapter).

1. Durham, William Teasdale   S1c   USN   NC
2. Leigh, Malcolm Hedrick   GM3c   USN   NC
3. Pinkham, Albert Wesley   S2c   USN   NC
4. Rhodes, Mark Alexander   S1c   USN   NC
5. Stallings, Kermit Braxton   F1c   USN   NC
6. Tussey, Lloyd Harold   EM3c   USN   NC

This photograph from Pearl Harbor on December 7, 1941, shows the USS *Arizona* (BB-39) as it lists and burns furiously as a result of the attack by the Japanese. Of the 1,177 sailors who died aboard the *Arizona*, 1,102 still remain on the ship (postcard by Ray Helbig's Hawaiian Service).

Today—more than seventy years after the sinking of the USS *Arizona*—one can still sometimes see drops of oil that have leaked from the sunken vessel and risen from the wreckage to the surface of the water. Many locals refer to this residue as "the tears of the *Arizona*" or "the *Arizona*'s black tears." This name seems especially appropriate because of the bodies that remain on the vessel (Tritten 2003).

***The USS* Oklahoma *(BB-37)*.** A second naval catastrophe occurred on December 7, 1941. The USS *Oklahoma* "turned turtle" and sank during the Pearl Harbor attack.

A North Carolinian who had received assignment to the *Oklahoma* was William Edgar Green (November 12, 1918–June 17, 2004) of the United States Navy. Green was on detached leave in the 14th Naval District Headquarters in Pearl Harbor when the December 7 attack occurred. He survived the attack. Green recalled "running outside when I heard the noise. I remember that one

The USS *Oklahoma* capsized as a result of the fire from the attack on Pearl Harbor on December 7, 1941, and 429 men lost their lives (U.S. Navy).

plane was so close that I could see the teeth of the pilot. I remember drawing my .45 and beginning to fire at the plane" (interview by the author, December 2000; Davis and Walker 2003, 10–11).

The military set up a first-aid station on the pier at Ford Island, the destination of those taken from the water. Green recalled working to help the injured and dying from Sunday at about 8:00 a.m. (Hawaiian-Aleutian Time) until Wednesday at 4:00 a.m. During the approximately 45-hour period, the North Carolina native stopped only long enough to eat one bologna sandwich.

Green served 22 years in the navy and retired to North Carolina (his birth state) and later to Florida. He died shortly after his interview with the author (Price and Walker 2003, 11).

The USS *Oklahoma* Memorial stands on the shores of Ford Island and is next to the former berth of the *Oklahoma*. The memorial lists the name, the military branch, and the rank or rate of each man who lost his life aboard the *Oklahoma* on Pearl Harbor Day. Salvage and repair attempts failed, and on May 17, 1947, the vessel sank 540 miles northeast of the Hawaiian islands while being towed toward San Francisco Bay.

Of the 429 sailors and marines who died on the USS *Oklahoma* on December 7, 1941, only 36 have been identified positively. The 393 remaining victims are missing in action (MIA); 380 of these are honored in graves with the marking "Unknown" in "The Punchbowl" (the National Cemetery of the Pacific, Honolulu, Hawaii). Thirteen bodies were never recovered (Phister 2008, 179).

Brothers William Edgar Green (left) and Dwight Joseph ("Buck") Green both served in the U.S. Navy. Edgar (November 12, 1918–June 17, 2004) served on the USS *Oklahoma* and survived the attack on Pearl Harbor; Dwight (May 26, 1926–October 21, 2006) served on the USS *Biloxi* throughout the war (courtesy Margaret Green).

The USS **Utah *(BB-31)*.** The attack on Pearl Harbor resulted in the sinking of a third American vessel. The USS *Utah* (BB-31) claimed the lives of 58 members of the United States Navy. None of the victims of the *Utah* were North Carolinians.

Although the USS *Utah* was later righted, the fates of 58 sailors are still uncertain. The place of interment of some of these victims is still unknown. The remains of some of those who died on the *Utah* may remain in the water. Some may be in unmarked graves on the Island of Oahu in the Cemetery of the Pacific, also known as the Punchbowl.

Many of these graves in the Punchbowl bear the label "Unknown." The United States Navy offers a DNA kit to female relatives and descendants of these unidentified men, many of whom may have been on the USS *Utah*. These kits may help to identify the remains of these men who died on December 7, 1941 (USS *Utah*).

The surprise Japanese attack astounded the United States and all the world. Many North Carolinians had arrived home from church and had turned on their radios. It was then—at 12:55 p.m. EST, or thereafter—that they heard the news of the attack on Pearl Harbor for the first time.

"A Date Which Will Live in Infamy"

In his speech broadcast on December 8, 1941, President Franklin D. Roosevelt declared that December 7 was "a date which will live in infamy." His words remain true.

Those who are old enough to remember the attack on Pearl Harbor often recall exactly what they were doing when they received the news of the surprise assault. Eight-year-old Jerrell Bedford remembered being with family and friends on the playground at Ellenboro School just before learning of the attack; the group of Woodmen of the World Insurance Members was being photographed, and no one knew the news at that time.

Deaths and Devastation on December 7, 1941. The time period from 7:55 a.m. until 9:45 a.m. Hawaiian-Aleutian Time (12:55 p.m. until 2:45 EST) on December 7, 1941, resulted in the immediate deaths of 2,403 Americans. The Japanese, on the other hand, had only one soldier captured and 65 members of their military killed in action (Rosenberg).

The Pearl Harbor Medal. By the Defense Authorization Act of Congress for the Fiscal Year 1991, the Pearl Harbor Medal commemorated employees of

2. The Beginning of America's Involvement in the War

the army and navy and members of the military who survived the December 7, 1941, Pearl Harbor attack. The act authorized a bronze medal for each survivor.

Pictured on the obverse side of the 1.5-inch bronze Pearl Harbor medallion are naval vessels under attack. Above the view of the battle scene are the words "Remember Pearl Harbor." Below the scene are the words "December 7, 1941." Three lines indicate "Act of/Congress/1990."

The reverse side of the Pearl Harbor Medal shows the American eagle holding an olive branch. On the medal is a quotation from President Roosevelt's speech on December 8, 1941: "A date which will live in infamy." Below the eagle is a three-line inscription: "For/Those Who/Served" (Foxfall Medals).

Note

Robert Lewis Carroll was a casualty on the USS *Arizona*. His state of residence, however, is debatable. Because of this quandary, one cannot be sure whether North Carolina lost six—or seven—aboard the *Arizona*. The "USS *Arizona* Casualty List" (Pearl Harbor: Remembered) assigns no place of residence to Robert Lewis Carroll.

PearlHarbor.org gives Carroll's state as North Carolina. Carroll's state of residence on "The Alphabetical USS *Arizona* Casualty List," however, is Washington (USSArizona.org).

Find-a-Grave.com indicates that Carroll entered service from the state of North Carolina, that his name is on the USS *Arizona* Memorial, and that he is listed also on the Honolulu Memorial Courts of the Missing within the National Memorial Cemetery of the Pacific, often called the Punchbowl (an extinct volcano). On the memorial tablet are the names of missing Americans from World War II; Carroll's name is among these who do not have actual grave markers because the victims are MIA, lost, or buried at sea.

CHAPTER 3

Some Immediate Effects of the War on North Carolina (December 1941–August 1942)

The United States formally declared war against the Empire of Japan after President Roosevelt's December 8, 1941, speech. On December 11, 1941—three days after declaring war on Japan—the United States pronounced war on Germany also. The whole world held its breath and waited to see the effects of these declarations of war.

North Carolina was immediately affected by these assertions of war. Whereas some areas did not feel the impact for quite some time, North Carolina experienced two direct consequences before the end of the month.

Naval Warfare Begins off the Carolina Coast (1941–1942)

After America's declaration of war against Germany, German Admiral Karl Dönitz immediately began establishing the details for plan *Paukenschlag*; *Paukenschlag* was the German codename for Operation Drumbeat, or Timpani Beat. The focus of this operation was the use of German long-range submarines to strike American coastal waters.

On December 18, 1941, five Type IX submarines left Lorient, France. The German Operation *Paukenschlag* had begun (Chen).

On December 31, some fishing boats spotted a periscope in the waters near Cushing Island, Maine, and near Ram Island, Connecticut. Naval warfare had officially begun.

Torpedo Alley. In 1942—the year following the start of the German Operation Paukenschlag—German U-boats turned the shipping lanes off North Carolina's coast into a deadly alley: Torpedo Alley. The German submarines sank

259 ships from January 11, 1942, until August 1, 1942; the Atlantic Ocean near the coastline was at times littered with "cargo and bodies." Astonished civilians sometimes witnessed from North Carolina beaches the sight of explosions from the "deadliest fleet of submarines ever launched. Never was Germany closer to winning the war ... a war we had to win—because this one hit terrifyingly close to home" (Hickam 1989, back cover).

The United States was sending most of its battleships to Europe and to the Pacific during these early days of World War II. This left the East Coast largely unprotected.

The Protection of America's East Coast. The United States began to avert the problem of U-boat attacks by installing deck guns on fishing boats and private yachts. These simple weapons converted these crafts into protection vessels; another means of protection was the use of anti-submarine vessels.

Only one anti-submarine vessel received the assignment to combat the German U-boats off the coast of North Carolina. This ship was the *Dione*, a United States Coast Guard cutter (National Geographic).

The launch date of the cutter *Dione* was June 30, 1934; its commissioning was on October 5, 1934. The name *Dione* came from the mother of Aphrodite in Greek mythology.

The Manitowoc Shipbuilding Corporation in Manitowoc, Wisconsin, built the Coast Guard cutter *Dione,* which served the East Coast, especially in 1942. Her decommissioning came on February 8, 1963 (U.S. Coast Guard, "The Dione").

The Battle of the Atlantic (1939–1945), in which the *Dione* participated, was the deadliest naval conflict in history. The local newspapers, however, did not publicize the extent of Germany's success off the East Coast of the United States. News items usually indicated only that a couple of medium-sized Allied ships had sunk in the Atlantic. In actuality, in 1942 alone, Germany sank an average of 33 Allied ships each week.

Merchant Mariners. An important fact that the media did not publicize during World War II was that a greater percentage of merchant mariners died in service than any other kinds of service personnel in the United States. One in every 26 mariners died in the line of duty—many in the Atlantic and off the coast of North Carolina.

The German U-boats traveled at a surface speed of 18 knots and outmatched their targets. The merchant ships and Coast Guard patrol boats off the East Coast—Germany's prey—traveled at only seven knots. The German referred to these attacks on American vessels as "The Great American Turkey Shoot." North Carolinians on the coast became accustomed to blackouts each night and were often aware of the dangers, the lights, and the sounds from Torpedo Alley (National Geographic).

North Carolina, then, felt the brunt of World War II earlier than some other states. Homer Hickam in his *Torpedo Junction* gives an account of attacks on Allied shipping by German U-boats from January 1942 to August 1942 and the locations of such attacks. He also documents German U-boats sunk, dates, and locations. There is no doubt that North Carolina entered the fray quickly and furiously (Hickam 1989, 328–42).

Coast Guard Seaman 1st Class Billy Sutton's experiences included patrolling Wilmington's beaches—a part of Torpedo Alley—during World War II. The North Carolina seaman rode horseback on the seashore to watch for German submarines. Sutton had joined the Coast Guard (with parental permission) at age 17; if he had waited to be drafted, he would not have had choice in his assignment (Sutton, interview with the author November 12, 2013).

The January 1, 1942, Tournament of Roses (a Nationwide Celebration), World War II, and North Carolina

The public remained eager for news after the December 7, 1941, attack on Pearl Harbor. The declaration of war against Japan by the United States on December 8 further heightened interest among Americans and throughout the world.

President Roosevelt created even more concern in his Fireside Chat broadcast on Tuesday, December 9, 1941—two days after the attack. He warned his listeners: "The attack at Pearl Harbor can be repeated at any one of many points in both oceans and along both our coastlines and against all the rest of the hemisphere" (Roosevelt [1941]).

Football fans across the country and residents of Pasadena, California, especially began immediately to wonder about the fate of the Tournament of Roses Parade and the Rose Bowl Game. These events had become synonymous with America's New Year's elebrations.

The Rose Bowl Game is the oldest bowl game. It bears the nickname "The Granddaddy of Them All." First played in 1902, the Rose Bowl Game had been played annually since 1916 on the afternoon of New Year's Day ("Rose Bowl Game" 2013, 296–302).

3. Some Immediate Effects of the War on North Carolina   17

Football fans began to wonder if the game would transpire in 1942. Even some of the most devout fans, however, pondered if these celebratory events should still be a concern during a time of national emergency. Many citizens questioned the use of resources for festivities in wartime; other people noted the tempting situation created for Pacific enemies with Americans congregating on the West Coast of America on January 1, 1942—just days after the attack on Pearl Harbor.

On December 13, 1941 (less than a week after the Pearl Harbor attack), Lieutenant General John DeWitt, the commander of the United States Fourth Army and the person in charge of the West Coast military, settled the Pasadena Rose Bowl Game issue. Lieutenant General DeWitt ordered the Tournament of Roses Parade and the Rose Bowl Game cancelled because of national defense concerns and because of the urgency of enhancing civilian protection.

California Governor Culbert Olson concurred with Lieutenant General DeWitt's decision to abandon plans for the 1942 Pasadena Rose Bowl activities. The California governor stated to the media: "The congestion of the state highways over a large area, incident to this tournament and football game and its serious obstruction to their use in defense work, the concentration there of a large police force, now needed for defense services, the unusually large gathering of people known to the enemy, exposing them to the dangers now threatening, requires that plans for the holding of this tournament and football game be abandoned" (Sumner).

Oregon State was eligible for competition in the 1942 Rose Bowl Game. Many at Oregon State were eager to play in the Rose Bowl Game. They wanted to demonstrate their team for the first time in the Rose Bowl Tournament. Bud Forrester, the athletic spokesperson for Oregon State, openly questioned the decision of Lieutenant General John DeWitt: "I wonder if General Dewitt intends to lock up all the department stores where people might gather, or restaurants, churches and all the public meetings" (Sumner).

Percy Locey—the athletic director of Oregon State—drove to San Francisco with other college officials to meet with Lieutenant General John DeWitt. DeWitt, however, was not willing to reconsider the decision to cancel the Rose Bowl; he told Locey emphatically that if necessary he would "call out the troops to stop it" (Sumner).

Suggestions for re-locating the game—often in conjunction with raising funds for the war effort—began to fill the media. Archie Ward, the sports editor of the *Chicago Tribune*, volunteered to host the game in Soldier Field; however, the difficulties that a Midwestern winter might impose on transportation, on the attendees, and on the game itself resulted in an almost immediate rejection of the proposal. Cities such as Memphis and the nation's capital offered to sponsor the game, but they were ultimately rejected.

Another entity, however, was working quietly in the background to bring the game to the pleasant climate of North Carolina. This prospective host-to-be was a Southern contestant in the Rose Bowl Tournament: Duke University. Both Duke University and Durham, North Carolina, were eager to invite guests to the area and to the Duke University Stadium, which had been completed in 1928 (Sumner).

The Duke football coach in 1941 was Wallace Wade. Wade was no stranger to the Rose Bowl Games. On January 1, 1926, as head coach of the University of Alabama's Crimson Tide football team, Wallace Wade and the Alabama team had gone to the Pasadena Rose Bowl and had won against the Washington Huskies with a score of 20 to 19. The Crimson Tide and Wallace Wade returned to the Rose Bowl against Stanford on January 1, 1927; the game was a tie (7–7). Wallace Wade's last Rose Bowl appearance with the Alabama team was against the Washington State Cougars on January 1, 1931; the Cougars won with a final score of 24–0 (Wikipedia, "List of Alabama Crimson Tide Bowl Games").

In 1931, Wallace Wade—at the age of 39—left the University of Alabama to coach at Duke University, a private college with little football glamor at the time. Wade helped lead the Iron Dukes football team to the Southern Conference Championships in 1933, 1935, 1936, and 1938.

On January 1, 1939, Duke had met Southern California in the Pasadena Rose Bowl game. The results were disappointing for Iron Dukes fans. Southern Cal took home a 7–3 win. Coach Wade had created controversy when he refused to shake hands with the Southern California players until after he shook hands with the Southern Cal coach (Penn 2011).

Before Duke could request the right to serve as host for the 1942 Rose Bowl game during wartime, Coach Wade and other Duke officials took two initial steps: conferring with officials of Oregon State University for their opinions and contacting North Carolina governor J. Melvin Broughton for his approval. Governor Broughton was not opposed to the plan to bring the Rose Bowl game to Durham; he saw no reason that the game would hamper military preparedness or present a safety concern for the attendees or for the state. The governor even agreed to help with the effort.

On December 14—one week after the attack on Pearl Harbor—Duke University formally presented to Oregon State University its request to host the 1942 Rose Bowl game. Oregon State, the United States Army, and

3. Some Immediate Effects of the War on North Carolina

the Rose Bowl Committee readily endorsed the plan. Duke now had less than three weeks to perform a task that ordinarily would take months to complete.

An important first step in preparing for the Duke Rose Bowl was increasing the seating capacity of the Duke stadium; its seating capacity at the time was 35,000. Pasadena had had 60,000 in attendance at the 1931 bowl game in 1931—a decade before. More seats would be a welcome addition for the Rose Bowl.

Duke's design was to use borrowed bleachers to close the open end of the horseshoe-shaped stadium and to add additional bleachers at the top of the stadium. The end result would be a stadium that would seat 56,000—21,000 spaces more than its usual capacity. Even after the advertisements announced a sell-out game, however, and even in the era of 1940s segregation, Duke provided 140 tickets for African Americans in the Durham community.

Duke ensured generous facilities for the media, including five newsreel companies that planned to film the game for national distribution. NBC—with announcer Bill Stern—would broadcast the game. The Carolina Inn—the historic hotel located on the campus of the University of North Carolina in nearby Chapel Hill—agreed to provide housing for the Oregon State team.

Another major task Duke had to consider was the printing, selling, and distribution of more than 56,000 tickets in about a two-week time period. There were, of course, no Web page, online ordering, or credit cards to speed the process of securing and requesting a ticket.

The tickets printed are collectors' items. They announce the date of the game: Thursday, January 1, 1942, at 2:00 p.m. They also list the price; one ticket, for example, sold for $4.40: $3.89 admission, $.39 federal tax, and $.12 state tax. The tickets indicated where the ticket holder should enter the Duke stadium to locate the specified seat number on the ticket. An interesting historical fact appears at the bottom of the ticket: "Transferred this year to Durham, North Carolina, from the Pasadena Rose Bowl in California."

The 1942 Rose Bowl game tickets went on sale December 16 from the Duke University box office. The tickets sold for $4.40, the same price as the tickets to the Pasadena Rose Bowl game the previous year. Scalpers, however, were charging—and getting—$25 for seats between the 40-yard lines.

Working through the box office, using the mail, and receiving telegraphic money orders, Duke was able to sell the entire print run of tickets within two days. Durham's hotels and roads were full for days before the event. Governor Broughton accommodated the working press by turning his roofed seat over to them.

The Oregon State entourage left Oregon on December 19, 1941, by train; they arrived in Durham on December 24, 1941. Oregon State coach Lon Stiner teased that Duke used its Southern hospitality—parties, receptions, tours, and barbecues—to weaken the team before the big game on January 1, 1942.

Game day brought chilling rain, fog, and temperatures in the '40s. Duke—although it was currently undefeated for the season, was the second highest scoring team in the nation for 1941, and was on its own home field—lost the game 16 to 20; the team suffered seven turnovers.

There were several ironies in the event. Johnny Prothro, Duke's starting quarterback, went on to serve well as Oregon State's head coach (1955–1964). Shortly after the game, the Iron Dukes Team lost its coach (Sumner).

Duke Coach Wallace Wade in World War II

After the end of the football season of 1941–1942, 49-year-old Coach Wade surprised the football world by resigning from Duke University and re-enlisting in the United States Army as a foot soldier. (He had served during World War I as cavalry captain of the 117th Infantry.)

Wade's first obligation was to report to Fort Bragg, North Carolina. His duty assignment was to the 272nd Field Artillery. Wade led the battalion in the Invasion of Normandy (June 6, 1944), the Siegfried Line Break (October–December 1944), the Battle of the Bulge (December 16, 1944–January 25, 1945), and the Crossing of the Rhine (March 1945).

For his service, Wade earned the Bronze Star medal,

Legendary football coach Wallace Wade helped to relocate the 1942 Rose Bowl football game to Duke University after the attack on Pearl Harbor. He was later awarded a Bronze Star for his service during the war. In 1967 Duke renamed their football stadium in his honor. Wade lived in North Carolina until his death in 1986. Franklin Creech sculpted this bronze bust, which is on display at Duke (courtesy Garry Thompson).

the rank of lieutenant colonel, and four battle stars. The French government presented him with the Croix de Guerre ("the Cross of War"); this medal for heroism was a high honor (Fravel).

After World War II, Wade returned to Duke in 1945 as director of athletics. In 1946, he again served as the football coach of the Iron Dukes. In 1950 Wade became the commissioner of the Southern Conference. His experiences in football made him well qualified for the post. In addition to coaching for the University of Alabama and Vanderbilt, Wade had coached the Iron Dukes from 1931 to 1941 and again from 1946 to 1950.

In 1967, 38 years after the construction of the Duke University stadium, the school decided to name the stadium after Wade. Wade stated many times after the re-naming of the stadium that having the stadium bear his name was his greatest honor in life.

Wade remained on his farm in Durham until he died at the age of 94. Duke president Terry Sanford—later North Carolina governor—delivered the eulogy for Wade (June 15, 1892–October 7, 1986). Sanford described Wade as one who "held presence, commanded attention and demanded excellence" (King 1997).

The Duke Department of Athletics commissioned Franklin Creech to prepare a bronze bust of Wallace Wade. Creech (AB, Duke Class of 1964) attended Duke on a football scholarship. Creech taught in public schools, colleges, and universities—including Duke University. He established a foundry in Smithfield, North Carolina, where he produced many works; his sculptures are numerous on the Duke Campus (King 1997).

Chapter 4

Other Effects of the War on the State and the Nation

Although the United States did not officially declare war on Japan until December 8, 1941, President Roosevelt endorsed the Burke-Wadsworth Bill for conscription in 1940. Passed by the Congress of the United States on September 6, 1940, the Selective Training and Service Act (STSA) provided for the first peacetime draft in America's history. The STSA of 1940 required that men of ages 21 to 35 register with local draft boards; this age range would later become 18 to 65.

Conscription Acts and Their Results

Roosevelt believed that both the expanding hostilities among nations and the increasing conflicts throughout the world necessitated the adoption of America's first peacetime conscription act. The original STSA specified that no more than 900,000 men would be training at a time; the act limited—at first—the service for draftees to a period of 12 months (Infoplease, "Selective Service").

The Burke-Wadsworth Bill and the 1940 Selective Training and Service Act. Unlike the conscription acts of World War I that did not detail the provisions for conscientious objectors, the 1940 Selective Training and Service Act made it possible both to draft personnel and to provide service opportunities for those who were conscientious objectors. The Burke-Wadsworth Bill did not require combatant training for the land and naval forces for those who were conscientiously opposed—because of religious belief or training—to participation in any form of war (Ohio History Central). If the conscientious objector received induction into the land or naval forces, according to the 1940 act, the inductee would receive assignment to noncombatant service as defined by the president. If the objector was opposed to participation in noncombat-

4. Other Effects of the War on the State and the Nation

ant service because of beliefs or training, the person would receive assignment to work of national importance under civilian direction (Selective Service 2013).

Other Selective Training and Service Acts of the 1940s. Early summer of 1941 found President Roosevelt again addressing the United States Congress about selective service. The president asked that Congress extend the term of duty for the draftees beyond the current twelve months. The bill passed.

Congress did not pass the bill without debate, however. The *New York Times* on August 13, 1941, reported that the bill narrowly passed, 203 to 202. The vote was 182 Democrats and 21 Republicans to enact the bill; there were 133 Republicans, 65 Democrats, and 4 others who voted against the measure (Wikipedia, "Selective Training and Service Act of 1940").

Many men readily enlisted in service after the bombing of Pearl Harbor and after the United States declared war on Japan on December 8, 1941. Such enlistment often gave the men more choice in their duty assignment.

John Franklin Anderson of Cleveland County, North Carolina, for instance, joined the U.S. Army Air Forces on December 13, 1941—less than a week after the United States declared war on Japan. Anderson's stations included Denver, Colorado; Barksdale Field in Shreveport, Louisiana; Foster Field in Texas; Matagora Peninsula; Salt Lake City, Utah; Hawaii; and finally Fort Stewart in Georgia. Anderson received his honorable discharge in January 1946, after more than five years in service (Davis and Walker 2005, 19).

Some new selective service acts of the wartime 1940s expanded the age range of men required to register for the draft. The STSA during World War II extended the ages of those who must register to men aged 18 to 65; the wartime STSAs specified, however, that only men aged 18 to 45 were liable for military service.

The length of service time changed during World War II. Draftees would serve not just one year or eighteen months; rather, they would serve a term to extend six months after the end of World War II.

Between the October 1940 peacetime draft registration and the November–December 1943 draft conscriptions were five other registrations: July 1941 (which required males 21–36 to register), February 1942, April 1942, June 1942, and December 1942. Between the 1940 draft registration and the October 1946 draft registration after the end of the war, more than 10 million men in America registered for the draft (Chacha 2013).

The draft cards that the registrants completed contained personal information, including complete name, date of birth, place of birth, residence, information about employment, the name and address of a person who would be able to provide the whereabouts of the registrant, and a physical description (race, height, weight, eye and hair colors, and complexion) of the person signing up for the draft. Many of these completed draft cards from many states are still available for viewing (Ancestry.com).

These records were available for several decades at the National Personnel Records Center (NPRC) in St. Louis, Missouri. On July 12, 1973, however, a fire at the NPRC resulted in the destruction of 16–18 million Official Military Personnel Files (OMPF).

Both army and air force records received damage. About 80 percent of the army personnel records for those discharged from November 1, 1912, to January 1, 1960, burned. Seventy-five percent of the air force records for those discharged between September 25, 1947, and January 1, 1964, and for those whose names came after "Hubbard, James E." burned. The NPRC continues to try to reconstruct basic service information for the many who served from North Carolina and the nation (National Archives, "The 1973 Fire").

James Montgomery Flagg's Poster "Uncle Sam Wants You." James Montgomery Flagg (1877–1960) first published the poster "Uncle Sam Wants You" in 1916. In 1917 and 1918 alone, the United States printed over four million copies of this work.

Although Flagg prepared 46 different posters to support the war effort, "Uncle Sam Wants You" was and is the most frequently displayed. The poster was important during both World War I and World War II.

In creating what he referred to as "the most famous poster in the world," James Montgomery Flagg said he used his own likeness to create the image of Uncle Sam (Library of Congress).

4. Other Effects of the War on the State and the Nation 25

Flagg himself delivered a copy of the poster to President Roosevelt in the 1940s. Flagg's "Uncle Sam" is still a popular personification of the United States (Library of Congress).

"Uncle Sam" encouraged joining the military even after the end of World War II. In 1948 a newly passed selective training and service act required the registration of all men from 18 to 26. The act provided that men from ages 19 to 26 could be liable for induction; the term of duty for the selectees would be 21 months of service, to be followed by 5 years of reserve duty (Infoplease).

Honoring Those Who Served

By the end of the war, the nation had recruited 16,112,566 citizens to serve its military needs. Taking the number of Americans who served in World War II (16,112,566) and dividing that number by 48 (the number of states in the United States at that time) yields an average of 335,678 recruits per state. Instead of contributing 335,678 enlisted personnel, however, North Carolina supplied 362,500 of its finest; this number was 26,823 more persons (7 percent more) than the recruits expected from the "Old North State." Of these 362,500 who served from North Carolina, 7,000 were women and 69,000 were African Americans (Powell 2006, 1230–34; North Carolina Museum of History). North Carolina's total population according to the 1940 census was 3,571,623. The state's contribution of individuals to the war effort was more than 10 percent of its total populace.

Medal of Honor Winners from North Carolina. One evidence of the distinguished service of North Carolinians is the number of recipients of the Medal of Honor. The Medal of Honor is the highest military decoration presented to a member of the U.S. armed forces. The United States presented only 464 such decorations during World War II; with 48 states at the time, this meant each state averaged only nine decorations.

Seven recipients had their place of attribution as North Carolina:

Name	Service Branch	Place of Birth	Place of Attribution
Eubanks, Ray E.	Army	Snow Hill, NC	LaGrange, NC
Halyburton, William David, Jr.	Navy	Canton, NC	NC
Herring, Rufus Geddie	Navy	Roseboro, NC	Roseboro, NC
Murray, Charles Patrick	Army	Baltimore, MD	Wilmington, NC
Thompson, Max	Army	Bethel, NC	Canton, NC
Urban, Matt Louis	Army	Buffalo, NY	Fort Bragg, NC
Warner, Henry F.	Army	Troy, NC	Troy, NC

The citation of each North Carolina Medal of Honor winner is contained in this volume. Fourteen additional recipients of the Medal of Honor had been born in North Carolina but had moved to another state. This increases the ranks of North Carolina even further (Sterner).

Deaths and Burials of Those Who Served During World War II. Of the 16,112,566 Americans who served in World War II, 405,399 died during their military service. This meant that the average number of military deaths per state was 8,445.

North Carolina sacrificially gave 9,458—1,013 more than the expected sacrifice per state. North Carolina gave 7 percent more than the expected average of 8,445 (Powell 2006, 1230–34).

A number of these North Carolinians remain buried abroad. Others are in unmarked graves or received burial at sea; some are in marked graves in cemeteries abroad. Still others are on the vessels that claimed their lives. The families of others of these heroes elected to have the bodies returned to the United States after the war.

Many of the distinguished North Carolina heroes found rest in a local cemetery that their families chose or in Arlington National Cemetery. Four national cemeteries in the State of North Carolina became the resting places for others who served; they are an important way within the state to honor those who sacrificed for their country. These four national cemeteries in North Carolina are—in alphabetical order—New Bern, Raleigh, Salisbury, and Wilmington. An examination of each burial ground is in order.

Chapter 5

National Cemeteries in North Carolina

The purpose of the first national cemeteries in the United States was to bury the Union dead from the battlefields, from the prisons, from mass graves, and from the general hospitals near training camps for troops. Four of these national cemeteries had their locations in North Carolina: New Bern, Raleigh, Salisbury, and Wilmington.

These four North Carolina national cemeteries—like national cemeteries throughout the United States—originally limited their interments to Union dead. After the Civil War searches uncovered more Union dead near battlefields, churchyards, farms, prisons, or railroads, these bodies received burial wherever possible—some in national cemeteries.

An act of Congress (1873) extended the right of burial in a national cemetery to Union veterans who had not died in service but who had earned an honorable discharge and later died. The national cemeteries did not admit the Confederate dead, however.

By 1898 those Americans who died abroad in the Spanish-American War and whose disinterred bodies received shipment to the United States could have burial in a national cemetery in the United States. Four of these national cemeteries, of course, were in North Carolina.

When the cemeteries began to fill to capacity, especially after World War II, the United States Department of Veterans Affairs (DVA) decided not to establish new national cemeteries or to enlarge existing national cemeteries. Instead, the DVA established a grant program to states that had an interest in building and operating cemeteries for veterans.

Today, the DVA maintains four national cemeteries in North Carolina. These cemeteries are still in New Bern, Raleigh, Salisbury, and Wilmington (National Cemetery Administration, "New Bern National Cemetery").

This postcard shows the American flag in the center of the walkway of New Bern National Cemetery. The monument on the right is the 9th New Jersey Regular Volunteer Infantry Memorial and the statue on the left is the Rhode Island Monument (Genuine Curteich-Chicago Postcard Company).

The New Bern National Cemetery (Craven County)

The New Bern National Cemetery is at 1711 National Avenue in New Bern (Craven County), North Carolina. This coastal location contains 7.7 acres of land. The National Park Service numbers the graves in the New Bern National Cemetery at more than 6,500, with some 1,000 unidentified bodies. The New Bern National Cemetery is on the National Register of Historic Places. In 1996 the cemetery closed its gates to any new interments (National Park Service, "New Bern National Cemetery, New Bern, North Carolina").

New Bern National Cemetery was established February 1, 1867. New Bern had fallen to the Union early in the Civil War and had served as a base of operations to the Union army throughout the war. The establishment of a cemetery in New Bern was advantageous to the Union. The New Bern National Cemetery contains Union dead brought in from throughout New Bern, Beaufort, Morehead City, Kinston, Hatteras, Roanoke Island, and the surrounding coastal areas. Four special monuments commemorate Union servicemen from Connecticut (1898), New Jersey (1905), Massachusetts (1908), and Rhode Island (1909).

North Carolina had left the Union on May 20, 1861. It supplied more men and materials to the Southern army than any other state. North Carolina endured more losses of men than any other Southern state. Confederate dead, however, are not in national cemeteries (National Cemetery Administration, "New Bern National Cemetery").

In 1898 and after, burial was available in the New Bern National Cemetery—and in other national cemeteries—to those who died on foreign soil and whose disinterred bodies arrived in the United States. Many who served in other wars and in World War II have their resting place here (National Cemetery Administration, "New Bern National Cemetery").

New Bern National Cemetery does not currently accept new interments. Only subsequent interments for veterans or eligible family members in an existing gravesite are allowable. If a burial space should become available because of a disinterment or canceled reservation, another eligible veteran may use the site on a first-come, first-served basis (National Cemetery Administration, "Department of Veteran Affairs National Cemeteries").

Raleigh National Cemetery (Wake County)

The establishment of the Raleigh National Cemetery at 501 Rock Quarry Road dates from 1865 and from General William T. Sherman's and his army's

An identifying feature of the Raleigh National Cemetery (which dates from 1865) is the masonry wall surrounding it. Within the cemetery is the distinctive Artillery Monument (late 1890s): a black, wrought iron cannon mounted on a cement pedestal (United States Department of Veterans Administration).

occupation of Raleigh. The Raleigh National Cemetery in the Piedmont section of North Carolina was originally at the Union military post called Camp Green.

The remains of Union veterans from Goldsboro, Henderson, Franklin, and other areas are interred in the site; veterans from later wars are also honored there. In the year 2005 the seven-acre cemetery contained more than 5,900 military personnel from the Civil War and from more recent wars (National Cemetery Administration, "Raleigh National Cemetery").

The Raleigh National Cemetery is in a relatively isolated area of the city, which is the capital of the state. The memorial park is easily recognizable by the masonry wall that encloses the burial ground. Within the confines of the cemetery is a large Georgian Revival lodge. The National Register of Historic Places included the Raleigh National Cemetery in 1997 (National Cemetery Administration, "Raleigh National Cemetery").

The Raleigh National Cemetery, of course, accepted those who died in

World War II and veterans of World War II who died after the war—as long as criteria for burial and space were met. The Raleigh National Cemetery, however, no longer accepts new interments. Only subsequent interments for veterans or eligible family members in an existing gravesite are allowable. If a burial space should become available because of a disinterment or canceled reservation, another eligible veteran may use the site on a first-come, first-served basis (National Cemetery Administration, "Department of Veteran Affairs National Cemeteries").

Salisbury National Cemetery (Rowan County)

The original Salisbury National Cemetery is at 202 Government Road. Although not designated as a national cemetery until 1865, this 15-acre cemetery in Rowan County has been the final resting place of some Union prisoners of war since 1863.

Because of Salisbury's proximity to a railway center that could facilitate prisoner exchange and because Salisbury was one of the largest cities in the area, it seemed an ideal site for housing a Confederate prison. There were some exchanges of prisoners when the Civil War first began, but by 1864 the Salisbury facility in the Piedmont region of North Carolina held 10,000 prisoners. This population necessitated burial sites.

During the winter of 1864, 5,000 Union prisoners died from disease and starvation. More than 11,000 men died during 1864 and 1865; these men lie in 18 trenches, each of which is 240 feet long. After the end of the war, 412 additional remains from Lexington, Charlotte, Morganton, and other sites came to rest in Salisbury. On the 12.5 acres are 15,800 graves (National Cemetery Administration, "Salisbury National Cemetery").

Salisbury National Cemetery on Government Road received the remains of veterans from later wars—including World War II. John Henry Bradley, who had participated in the best-known flag raising on Iwo Jima, remarked, "The real heroes ... are the guys who didn't come back" (Bradley 2000, 4). Salisbury accepted the heroes and all those who honored the nation with their service.

One of the "real heroes" interred at Salisbury National Cemetery is Corporal Arthur Fred Price, the father of the author. Cpl. Price trained at Camp Breckinridge, Kentucky, before receiving orders for Belgium in 1944.

Twenty-year-old Corporal Price was the victim of a landmine outside of Liege, Belgium, on December 28, 1944. Cpl. Price's original interment abroad was in the Margraten Cemetery in Holland, Plot P, Row 1, Grave 20. His brother Sergeant Falls W. Price, Company C, 423rd Infantry Regiment, 106th Infantry Division ("Golden Lion"), visited Margraten in 1945 while his unit was stationed in the area (Davis 2005, 56–57).

In 1949 the remains of Cpl. Arthur F. Price—along with 90 other North Carolinians—returned to the United States aboard the *Haiti Victory*. Corporal Price's April 27, 1949, burial was in Section B, Gravesite 886, of the original Salisbury National Cemetery (Davis 2002, 214–15).

When the Salisbury National Cemetery on Government Road began to fill to capacity, in 1999 veterans and representatives of Rowan County and of the Salisbury National Cemetery traveled to Washington, D.C., to ask for help in securing both additional cemetery acreage and funds to improve the services of the existing Salisbury National Cemetery. On Memorial Day of 1999, the Veterans Administration announced it was donating 40 acres (from the W. G. "Bill" Hefner VA Medical Center) to the Salisbury National Cemetery. Included in the acreage was the Brookdale Golf Course, which Samuel C. Hart had donated for the use of the hospital in 1953; the course was in use until the late 1980s. The additional acquisition would provide 20,000 burial spaces for

The elaborate ornamental cast-iron gates shown on this postcard are open and invite the visitor to enter the Salisbury National Cemetery. The postcard is from the 1940s, but the gates, which connect with a stone wall perimeter, remain in good condition (C. T. American Art Colored, Asheville Post Card Company).

veterans and family members; by all estimates this supplemental property would suffice for the next 50 to 75 years.

On Pearl Harbor Day of 1999 the groundbreaking ceremony celebrated the annexation of the addition to the cemetery. The address of the Cemetery Annex is 501 Statesville Boulevard, Salisbury, North Carolina. In March 2000 the Salisbury National Cemetery Annex performed its first burial.

In 2001 an expansion on the 31 acres of the former golf course provided an additional 12,000 burial spaces. The estimated cost for this expansion was $2.8 million.

Because the existing columbarium for the storage of cinerary urns had almost reached capacity, the construction of a new columbarium to accommodate 1,000 urns began in the Salisbury National Cemetery Annex on November 14, 2011. This facility should be adequate for at least ten years. The addition of 2,400 crypts, which are in-ground and pre-placed, would allow for 1,500—not the usual 700 burials—per acre.

By Memorial Day of 2012, the original Salisbury National Cemetery had 7,000 markers. This original cemetery was closed to all new burials except for some subsequent burials.

As of 2013, the Salisbury National Cemetery Annex—with its 4,000 markers—is the only national cemetery in North Carolina open to new burials. The other three national cemeteries in the state—New Bern, Wilmington, and Raleigh National—are not open to new interments (Wikipedia, "Salisbury National Cemetery").

The Salisbury National Cemetery Annex has space available and is currently (2013) able to accommodate both full casket interments and in-ground cremated interments. The annex has a columbarium available for cremated remains and claims a new administrative office and a new maintenance shop (National Cemetery Administration, "Salisbury National Cemetery").

Wilmington National Cemetery (New Hanover County)

A fourth national cemetery in North Carolina is that in Wilmington. Wilmington is in New Hanover County, which is in the coastal area of the state. The Wilmington National Cemetery at 2011 Market Street encompasses 5.1 acres; it honors 6,171 persons (2005). On January 31, 1997, the National Register of Historic Places listed Wilmington National Cemetery in its ranks.

Two major Civil War battles at Fort Fisher (about 28 miles from Wilmington) necessitated a national cemetery in the Wilmington area. These two engagements left many Union servicemen dead in December 1864 and January 1865. Other deaths occurred during the march of the Union servicemen from Fort Fisher to Wilmington, during the occupation of Wilmington, during the fall of Wilmington in February of 1865, and during the imprisonment of many Union servicemen by the Confederates.

The purchase of the land for the Wilmington National Cemetery dates from 1867 and 1877. The original interments in the cemetery were from Wilmington, the Lutheran churchyard in Wilmington, Fort Fisher, Fort Johnson, Fayetteville, Smithville (Southport), and a 12-mile stretch along both the Wilmington and Weldon Railroad and the Wilmington and Manchester Railroad (National Cemetery Administration, "Wilmington National Cemetery").

The Wilmington National Cemetery was on 5 acres of land about a mile east of downtown. Originally 2,000 Union troops lay in the cemetery. Some of the 1,300 unidentified graves had the marking "U.S.C.T.," which meant "United States Colored Troops"; some of the other markings were U.S.Col.Inf. (United States Colored Infantry) (Gorman-Fancy et al. 2010, 193–94).

The Wilmington National Cemetery honors some veterans of later wars also. The Wilmington National Cemetery, however, does not currently accept new interments. Only subsequent interments for veterans or eligible family members in an existing gravesite are allowable. Periodically, burial space may become available because of a canceled reservation or when a disinterment has been completed. When either of these two situations occurs, the gravesite is made available to another eligible veteran on a first-come, first-served basis (National Cemetery Administration, "Wilmington National Cemetery").

The Wilmington National Cemetery holds also the remains of those who served in World War II. The cemetery and its staff honor those who served. The site itself is on the National Register of Historic Places, and its staff serve those who call or visit.

CHAPTER 6

Sites in the Mountain Region

Measuring from Murphy in the west to Manteo in the east, North Carolina is 560 miles wide. North Carolina is the longest state east of the Mississippi.

The Atlantic Ocean borders North Carolina on the east. Tennessee borders the state on the west, and South Carolina and Georgia border it to the south. Virginia borders North Carolina to the north.

North Carolina has three distinct geographic regions, all of which maintained military sites during World War II. The Mountain Region was useful to the nation during World War II because of its inland location, its facilities, and its populace. The Mountain Region is the subject of this chapter. The Piedmont Region occupies the central section of the State of North Carolina. This middle region, which encompasses one-half of the state, was vital to the war effort. It is the subject of the Chapter Seven. The Coastal Region has harbors and two coastlines—an inner coast that the Albemarle and Pamlico sounds indent and an outer coast formed by a chain of sand reefs, from which Cape Fear, Cape Lookout, and Cape Hatteras protrude. The Coastal Region is the subject of Chapters Eight through Twelve (Compton 1948, 155).

North Carolina supported the war effort in many ways. North Carolina's public schools won national recognition for their sales and purchases of $43,000,000 during eight victory and war drives. North Carolinians entering the various armed services during World War II, included 13,000 in the Marines, 90,000 in the navy, and 258,000 in the army. Lefler notes more than 100 army, navy, Marine, and coast-guard stations in the state during World War II (Lefler and Newsome 1959, 444–45).

More than 70 major military sites occupied North Carolina in its mountains, its Piedmont Region, and its Coastal Region during World War II.

World War II Contributions of the Mountain Region City of Asheville in Buncombe County: Vital Asheville Hotels

One might assume that North Carolina's Mountain Region was an isolated area that would not be able to assist in the war effort. That assumption would be in error. The Mountain Region and its sites had many services to render. The United States government used Buncombe County, the mountain city of Asheville, the Asheville tourist facilities, building structures, and Asheville citizens in several ways.

The United States Army used four of the largest hotels in Asheville to house some of the service personnel who were completing an assignment. In these luxury hotels, some returning combat veterans found rest and relaxation before their new obligations (Osborne 2007, 180). These hotels at times also housed enemy non-combatants.

Asheville's Grove Park Inn. One of the first uses of Asheville tourist facilities was the U.S. government's leasing of the Grove Park Inn; this luxury facility had housed President Roosevelt on September 9, 1936. Advertised as "the finest Resort Hotel in the world," the manor served the nation and the world before and during the early days of World War II (Davis 2003, 42, 43).

In April of 1942 the U.S. government leased the luxury Grove Park Inn to house diplomats, who often needed temporary facilities. Asheville was a location far from the Washington, D.C., area; this distance suggested increased safety for the occupants.

Quartered in the Grove Park Inn were Hungarian, Bulgarian, and Italian diplomats; these officials often brought with them their families, servants, pets, and private possessions. Axis diplomats from Cuba, from Mexico, and from El Salvador also had housing here. On June 11, 1942, the last of these diplomats began their trips home.

Interestingly, the government housed some Japanese diplomats at the Grove Park Inn for a short time. The Greenbrier Inn in West Virginia received these diplomats after their transfer from North Carolina.

In October 1942 the U.S. Navy leased the Grove. The exclusive resort became a rest and rehabilitation facility primarily for naval officers.

Manuel L. Quezon (president of the Philippines) and his staff were residents of the Grove Park Inn for about a month in 1944. The Grove served also as the temporary headquarters of the exiled Philippine government during that month.

6. Sites in the Mountain Region

The original Grove Park Inn had walls that were four feet thick. Edwin Grove had instructed that no cut edges of the stone should show (The Omni Grove Park Inn, photograph by Charley Akers Photography).

The United States Army leased the Grove Park Inn from July 1944 until September 1945. After a 21-day furlough at home with their families, many returning combat veterans received 10–14 days at the Grove Park Inn—or another facility—for a period of rest and rehabilitation; some of these veterans could bring a spouse if they elected to do so.

Asheville-Biltmore Hotel. The United States government used hotels in downtown Asheville to house its returning soldiers. One of the hotels that served the military was the Asheville-Biltmore Hotel.

The Asheville-Biltmore Hotel at 76 North Market Street was the work of L. B. Jackson and some other investors. The brick building contained 100 rooms in its eight stories. The Asheville-Biltmore Hotel is now the Altamont Apartments (Bishir et al. 1999, 269).

Asheville's Battery Park Hotel. The Army Redistribution Station (ARS) rented the Battery Park Hotel on Haywood Street in Asheville during the 1940s. The ARS used the mezzanine level of the Battery Park to house its headquarters. The roof of the hotel housed a club for enlisted men.

Asheville-Biltmore Hotel, Asheville, North Carolina

The Asheville-Biltmore Hotel served as a relocation center for returning military personnel to enjoy several weeks of rest and relaxation and to boost their morale before their next assignment (Graycraft Card Company, Danville, Virginia).

6. Sites in the Mountain Region 39

N-404 BATTERY PARK HOTEL, ASHEVILLE, N. C.

The Queen Anne style architecture of the Battery Park Hotel is still a dominating feature in downtown Asheville. The hotel featured a roof garden and a grand dining room in its prime (Asheville Post Card Company, Asheville, North Carolina).

Edwin W. Grove, who had developed the Grove Park Inn, had erected the brick-faced, terra cotta–trimmed Battery Park Hotel in 1924. The 14-floor, 220-room Battery Park Hotel—designed by W. L. Stoddart of New York—replaced the 1886 Battery Park Hotel, a Queen Anne style hotel. Grove died at the Battery Park Hotel on January 27, 1927.

In the 1980s, the Battery Park Hotel became an apartment house for senior citizens. The first floor still houses businesses (National Park Service, "Travel Itinerary: Asheville").

Asheville's George Washington Vanderbilt Hotel. W. L. Stoddart, who designed Asheville's Battery Park Hotel, also designed the George Washington Vanderbilt Hotel for the industrialist George Vanderbilt; it was ready for occupancy in 1924. Vanderbilt also built the famous Biltmore Estate within the city (National Park Service, "Travel Itinerary: Asheville").

The Vanderbilt Hotel at 75 Haywood Street has held apartments for the elderly since March 1970. The skyline, therefore, has not changed drastically at the Haywood Street location (Emporis).

Soldiers could find clergy of the Catholic, Jewish, and Protestant faith on the ground floor of the Vanderbilt Hotel (Curteich-Chicago "C. T. Art Colortone" Post Card, collection of Harry N. Martin).

6. Sites in the Mountain Region

World War II Contributions of the Mountain Region City of Asheville: Asheville Facilities Crucial to the War Effort

Asheville was crucial to the war efforts of both World War I and World War II. The mountain city provided—among other things—personnel, residential facilities for the military personnel of the nation, housing for enemy non-combatants, airfields, and medical care. The Kenilworth Inn in Asheville served in a variety of ways both before and after its reconstruction; the Asheville City Building and the Asheville-Henderson Airport/Airfield were also essential to the military during World War II especially.

Kenilworth Inn (Appalachian Hall Convalescent Center). Designed by the Philadelphia architects Francis and William Price, the original Kenilworth Inn dates from 1891. Bishir et al. write that the majestic, luxurious resort was a "concoction of Tudor and other motifs." In 1909, however, fire destroyed the inn (1999, 262, 285).

James "Jake" Madison Chiles—who owned the acreage of the original Kenilworth Inn—was determined to see a new, 500-room inn rise from the ashes of the old resort. The new hotel he envisioned was of Tudor Revival style, with stone masonry, stucco, half timbers, half-hipped roof, covered and open porches, terraces, ballrooms, billiard parlors, and tea rooms. Because of the 1916 flood and other complications, however, the "new" Kenilworth was not complete until January of 1918.

In February of 1918 the U.S. government leased the completed facility and used it as a hospital during World War I. The hospital carried various names: the U.S. General Hospital No. 12, the U.S. Army Convalescence Hospital No. 12, and the Biltmore Hospital.

During World War I, 3,000 German aliens occupied a Madison County internment camp in Hot Springs, North Carolina. As a result of a typhoid outbreak, 180 received treatment in Army Convalescence Hospital No. 12 in Asheville. These treated civilian prisoners were not under military control, but they were under governmental control.

Jake Chiles regained control of the Kenilworth Inn in 1923. The Kenilworth profited as a luxury hotel until the 1929 market crash. Chiles sold the structure, which remained vacant for one year. Two doctors—William Ray Griffin, Sr., and his brother Mark Griffin—reopened it as a mental health facility: Appalachian Hall.

Appalachian Hall. The United States government found that many of those participating in World War II would need to convalesce, as had personnel in World War I. In February 1943, the United States Navy leased Appalachian Hall, renamed the U.S. Navy Convalescent Hospital, Kenilworth Park. The U.S. Navy Convalescent Hospital included rest, relaxation, and recreation; the navy added recreational facilities—like a motion picture facility and bowling alley—for its convalescents; events such as dances, picnics, stage shows, and dining were often open to the public to boost morale.

After the war, the Griffin brothers regained the facility and continued to practice medicine in the facility. In 1999 a realty company sold Appalachian Hall/Kenilworth Inn; it became an apartment building.

The National Register of Historic Places includes this facility, which served 7,000 patients during the government's tenure. The Kenilworth Apartments at 60 Caledonia Road are still in operation. The centennial of the Kenilworth Inn is 2018 (Wikipedia, "The Kenilworth Inn").

The Asheville City Building for the U.S. Headquarters of Weather Wing of the Flight Control Command (Later Called the Army Air Force Weather Service) and for the Army Airways Communication System. Because it was attempting to spread out its headquarters in case of enemy attack, the U.S. government found the inland town of Asheville ideal for its purposes. Lt. Gen. William O. Senter, who was a commander of the Weather Wing of the Flight Control Command of the Army Air Force Weather Service, said that the officers in charge were "trying to get everybody out of Washington." Senter remembered coming to Asheville in 1943 to try to find suitable quarters (Chapman and Miles 2006, 30).

The ideal site for the quarters of the Weather Wing of the Flight Control Command (later called the Army Air Force Weather Service) seemed to be the Asheville City Building. The government rented one half of the building (four floors) for the Weather Service and the other half for the Army Airways Communication System.

Architect Douglas D. Ellington came to Asheville in the mid–1920s. He planned the First Baptist Church, the S and W Cafeteria, and the Asheville High School.

One of Ellington's most important works was designing the Asheville City Building. Ellington chose building materials for the city hall that presented the pink shades of the Asheville clay. He used "pink Georgia marble piers." Between the piers are "precise vertical rows of ornamental green and gold feather motifs" (National Park Service, "Asheville City Hall").

6. Sites in the Mountain Region 43

The Asheville City Hall is at 70 Court Plaza and houses—among other city offices—the Office of the Mayor. Its importance during World War II, however, is still not diminished.

Grove Arcade in Asheville. Edwin W. Grove—the builder of the Grove Park Inn (1915) and the Asheville Battery Park Hotel (1924)—was a self-made millionaire. He had developed Grove's Tasteless Chill Tonic for malaria and moved to Asheville in 1910 (Davis 2003, 147–49).

The Grove Park Inn brought visitors from across the nation. Grove had further plans for Asheville. He wanted to develop "the most elegant building in America." When he died in 1927, the 269,000-square-foot building was two years from completion. The Grove Arcade held offices, candy and cigar stores, beauty and barber shops, bookstores, groceries, a haberdashery, a public stenography office, fruit stands, millinery shops, and a photography center. It was the "center of commercial and civic life in Western North Carolina" for 13 years (Grove Arcade, "History").

The Postal Accounts Division of the United States Post Office moved from Washington to the Grove Arcade in Asheville during World War II. The United States government considered the location in Asheville to be a remote place and the Grove Arcade to be of satisfactory size (Langley and Langley 1975, 115).

The federal government required the 74 shops and 127 offices to vacate the Grove Arcade. The tenants had less than one month's notice of eviction. The federal government continued its ownership of the building after the war and headquartered the National Climatic Data Center in the Grove Arcade. The public, however, began to clamor for the Arcade to revert to its original use even though the government planned to enlarge the facility in the 1980s. The government announced plans to build a new facility for the Climatic Data Center. By 1995 the new Federal Building was complete.

The Grove Arcade became a part of the National Register of Historic Places in the mid–1980s. The Grove Arcade Public Market Foundation—a not-for-profit, 501(c)3 corporation—began working to restore the Grove Arcade to its original form and function.

Under the National Monument Act, the City of Asheville acquired title to the Grove Arcade in 1997. Asheville signed a 198-year lease with the Grove Arcade Market Foundation. The restored Grove Arcade, with its shops, restaurants, offices and 42 luxury apartments, has continued to be vibrant since 2002 (Grove Arcade, "History").

Asheville-Hendersonville Airport. To transport enlisted men and officers efficiently to and from Asheville in the Mountain Region of North Carolina, the Asheville-Hendersonville Airport (also called the Asheville-Henderson Airport) was vital. In April of 1944 the United States Army/Navy Director of Airfields noted that the runway had 4,000 feet of hard surface; both the U.S. Army and the U.S. Navy conducted flight operations from the Buncombe County field (Freeman, "Western North Carolina").

The Army Air Force, the United States Navy, and the Coast Guard used the local airport during World War II. The Asheville-Henderson Airport was under the command of the AAF commanding general; the airport served as an office for the Army Air Communication System and as a wing of the AAF Weather. The navy used the field primarily for air transport (Osborne 2007, 180).

Commercial airline service at the Asheville-Henderson Airport did not begin until after World War II. Delta Airlines, Capital Airlines, and Piedmont Airlines all used the Asheville-Henderson Airport for a while.

In January 1961 the Asheville Regional Airport opened 3 miles to the west of the Asheville-Henderson Airport. The newer Asheville Regional Airport included a longer runway than had the Asheville-Henderson Airport; this longer expanse was more conducive to the flights of modern airlines. Other modernization was also apparent.

Sometime between 1961 and 1963 the Asheville-Hendersonville Airport closed. The Charlotte Sectional Chart (May 1963) labels the Asheville-Henderson Airport as an "abandoned airport." The airport, however, had served its nation well—particularly during World War II (Freeman, "Western North Carolina").

World War II Contributions of the Mountain Region of North Carolina: Crucial Efforts of Montreat (Buncombe County), of Chaplain Charles Burrington Long's Work with German Prisoners of War, of Lake Lure and the Lake Lure Inn Rest and Rehabilitation Facility (Rutherford County), of Swannanoa (Buncombe County), and of the Moore General Hospital (Buncombe County)

In Buncombe County, about 18 miles east of Asheville in the Mountain Region of North Carolina, is another North Carolina site that the U.S. government was able to use to advantage during World War II. The sparsely settled mountain area of Montreat proved valuable to the war effort.

Montreat and the Assembly Inn that Housed Non-Combatant Enemies. In 1907 J. R. Howerton of Charlotte, North Carolina, had acted for the Presbyterian Church to help in the purchase of the Montreat Retreat Association. This organization had provided libraries, education, and facilities for conventions in the area since 1897.

In 1913, Dr. Robert Campbell Anderson (1864–1955), president of the Mountain Retreat Association, advanced the idea of using the grounds and facilities for a school. It was one of these campus buildings—the Assembly Inn—that the United States State Department found ideal for use during World War II (Montreat College, "About Us").

The Assembly Inn was the center of Montreat College. After the previous structure burned in 1922, President Robert Anderson made sure that the new Assembly Inn was fireproof. The stone walls and columns in the lobby are aglitter with mica, often used for insulation. Wood is in use only for the doors. Three-story round pillars separate the arched windows of the "massive, river rock and quarried stone structure" overlooking Lake Susan (Bishir et al. 1999, 305–06).

In 1942 a representative of the United States State Department approached Montreat president Anderson about using the Assembly Inn to house some of the non-combatant enemies of the United States. Specifically, these non-combatants included some Japanese and German civilians. These Japanese and Germans moved into the Assembly Inn on October 29, 1942, for six months. Of the 264 non-combatants relocated to the Assembly Inn, 152 were children.

Many of the new Montreat residents were families of businessmen who worked in Central and South America. The Immigration and Naturalization Service (INS) took these groups into custody in 1941 when the United States entered World War II.

The Germans lived on one floor of the Assembly; the Japanese lived on another floor. Interaction between the two groups was discouraged by the INS. The INS eventually sent the Japanese men to an internment camp in Texas.

The Assembly Inn, which was a part of the Presbyterian Church, treated these internees humanely. The Presbyterian Church and the Assembly Inn furnished Bibles printed in Japanese and in German to all the residents.

When Christmas of 1942 began approaching, the Assembly Inn allowed

The primary building material of the Assembly Inn of 1923 was Montreat stone. There was no contractor; native labor constructed the inn (Asheville Post Card Company, Asheville, North Carolina).

the detainees to choose whether they wanted trees. The Presbyterian Church and the Assembly Inn, however, surprised the children with Christmas gifts.

Dr. Robert Campbell Anderson, who was directing the Assembly Inn during Christmas of 1942, often spoke of a memorable moment in the celebrations. On one floor of the Assembly Inn, the Germans began singing Christmas carols. On another floor the Japanese began singing also. Local residents came to the inn; from outside they joined in the singing. All the windows of the lobby and the sun parlor opened, and all the voices joined in singing the same carols—albeit in different languages.

During the six months that the Assembly Inn housed the German and Japanese detainees, according to Dr. Anderson, the Internment Camp "cleared" $75,000. At this time in history, this was enough to cover all the debt incurred by the camp, put in sidewalks, and still have a substantial capital account (Center for Diversity Education).

Chaplain Charles Burrington Long's Work with German Prisoners. Even after the end of World War II, the work of North Carolinians continued to help the nation on the road to recovery. One North Carolina resident of the

6. Sites in the Mountain Region

After World War II, North Carolinian chaplain Charles Burrington Long remained stationed in Kassell and Schwabish Hall, Germany. His family joined him. The Long family is (from left to right) son George, wife Bernice Burns Long, husband Charles Burrington Long, and son Siegby Long (courtesy Clara Long and Kristy Long).

Mountain Region (Ellenboro, NC; Rutherford County) who worked to bring about peace and healing during and after World War II was Chaplain Charles Burrington Long.

Stationed in Kassell and Schwabish Hall, Germany, after the war, Chaplain Long's duties included counseling hospitalized American military personnel. During the transition of some German prisoners to their eventual freedom, a few received permission to work with Chaplain Long, who had brought his family—his wife Bernice and their sons Siegby and George—with him.

One German prisoner by the name of Salzberger had been an artist; his duty was to assist Chaplain Long. Salzberger longed to paint, but he had no supplies. Chaplain Long wrote to his wife Bernice's sisters—one of whom was a professional artist—about the need. The sisters sent painting supplies from North Carolina to Long, who gave them to Salzberger; this is another instance of North Carolina's efforts to promote peace. Salzberger gave six of his paintings of his remembered German scenes to Chaplain Long and Long's family.

Painting by German prisoner of war R. Salzberger The canvas was taken from an army pup tent and the painting now hangs in the home of Clara Long, daughter-in-law of Charles and Bernice Long (courtesy Clara Long and Kristy Long).

Charles Burrington Long remained in the National Guard after he left his active duty military status; he continued to serve the Methodist Church in North Carolina. Charles Burrington Long (1902–1960) and Bernice Burns Long (1901–1981) rest in Westview Cemetery in Kinston, North Carolina.

On November 22, 1963, widow Bernice Long received a recognition of service award in honor of Charles Burrington Long; President John F. Kennedy issued and signed the tribute for "devoted and selfless consecration to the service of our country." Bernice received the envelope the day of President Kennedy's assassination; the postmark was on November 20, 1963. This was one of the last things that President Kennedy signed (Long, Clara and Kristy).

The mountain region of North Carolina served on behalf of the fine arts in various ways. In 1942 George and Edith Vanderbilt agreed to hide and store 62 of the nation's most prized works of art. In January 1942 pieces by Vermeer, Van Dyck, Gilbert Stuart, Goya, and Rembrandt arrived in their Biltmore

House. These works—and others—remained in Asheville until 1944 when the war began to wane (Mims 2014, pp. 40–47).

Lake Lure and the Lake Lure Inn Rest and Rehabilitation Center in Rutherford County. Construction work on the Lake Lure Inn began in February of 1925. The Rutherford County facility was a $400,000 investment. On September 10, 1936, President Roosevelt and his party lunched at the three-story, stuccoed building with the red-tiled roof. The Carolina mountains are clearly visible from the Lake Lure Inn.

The Army Air Force (AAF) established the Lake Lure Rest and Redistribution (R&R) Center in Rutherford County in July 1943. The center provided 10 to 20 days of rest and relaxation for combat aviators and their wives. The AAF employed and used some adjacent properties also. Lake Lure, North Carolina, became the nation's first R&R center.

R&R helped both to deter combat fatigue and to prepare military personnel for their next assignments. While in the Lake Lure Inn facility for R&R, the airmen received examinations by military doctors, by surgeons, and by psychiatrists to ensure the fitness of the servicemen for further assignments.

During the two years (July 1943 until October 1945) that Lake Lure and the Lake Lure Inn served as an R&R center, more than 5,000 servicemen were able to profit from this assistance. Rutherford County was especially supportive of these servicemen who transitioned through the Lake Lure Inn. Such organizations as the Rutherford County Chapter of the American Red Cross and

The Lake Lure Inn (Curteich-Chicago Postcard Company).

the Rutherford County Library helped to provide books, services, and equipment to the returnees housed in the county.

The Lake Lure R&R Center officially closed on November 1, 1945. The buildings reverted to their original owners and uses (Davis and Walker 2003, 34; Davis and Hambright 2002, 21–28).

Remembrances of a Former Resident of the Lake Lure R&R Center. Technical Sergeant Forrest S. Clark, in a 2002 interview with the author, remembered that he was a radioman-gunner on a B-24 of the 44th Bomb Group, 8th Air Force. The 44th Bomb Group (whose insignia was a flying eight-ball) was stationed at AAF115, Shipdham, England.

Clark's plane had suffered battle damage on a bombing mission over Lichfeld, Germany, on April 13, 1944. Clark's internment was in Switzerland. He escaped with the help of the French underground and passed the French border in December 1944.

By March 1945 Forrest Clark had been repatriated to the United States and had received orders to the Lake Lure Inn. In 2003 Clark wrote about his internment:

> The value of the Lake Lure Rest and Rehabilitation Center was that it reaffirmed faith for many battle-shocked combat veterans. We had religious services that reinforced our spiritual faith as well as prepared us for re-entry to civilian life, marriage, and careers. There is no doubt in my mind and spirit that it had a lifelong effect on me. I think there is an important unwritten story here about the part of Lake Lure in World War II. I learned to pray in the service, and I learned the value of a spiritual dimension to my life [Davis and Walker 2003, 34; interview with Forrest Clark].

Swannanoa and the Moore General Hospital; Oteen Veteran's Administration Hospital. Swannanoa is eleven miles from Asheville but is part of the Asheville Metropolitan Statistical Area. The town of Swannanoa took its name from the Swannanoa River, which flows through its boundaries. One of its facilities is Moore General Hospital.

During World War II, a general army hospital for treating sick and wounded military personnel was essential for the Mountain Region of North Carolina. In May of 1942 construction began in Swannanoa of a hospital com-

Opposite, top: Oteen's Veteran Administration Hospital (Post Card Company, Asheville, North Carolina). *Bottom:* Convoy transporting equipment and military personnel through the mountains (Roger Wesley Goodwin and Meg Goodwin Cooksey; author's collection).

442:—ADMINISTRATION BLDG. AND U. S. VETERANS' HOSPITAL NO. 60, OTEEN, N. C.

plex with many buildings, 1,520 beds, and 1,500 employees. The hospital took its name from the surgeon general of the Confederacy: Samuel Preston Moore of Charleston, South Carolina. Moore Hospital began admitting patients in November of 1942.

The Moore Complex served as a center for training medical corps personnel during World War II. There were 36 structures in use to house these trainees. The 28th General Hospital was the first training unit to receive assignment to the Moore Complex. German prisoners of war occupied a separate camp on the north section of the Moore Hospital grounds beginning in May of 1945. These detainees provided labor and maintenance services for the complex.

After the end of World War II, the status of Moore General Hospital changed to a surplus facility in September 1946 by decree of the U.S. War Department. The Veterans Administration used the buildings for several years. The Moore General Hospital's new title was the Swannanoa Rehabilitation Center.

The Oteen Veterans Administration Hospital is at 1100 Tunnel Road in Asheville, North Carolina. As a veterans hospital, it is not open to the general public (National Park Service, "Oteen").

The Mountain Region of North Carolina and Its Contributions to World War II: Mines, Minerals, Mica, and Miners (Avery, Yancey, and Mitchell Counties)

A little-known fact is that the Mountain Region of North Carolina was an important mining area, during World War II especially. The region produced iron and was a leading producer of the vital mineral mica.

North Carolina Mica. North Carolina produced three-fourths of all the mica in the world during World War II. This is a staggering amount of the important material, and most of it came from the Mountain Region.

Uses of Mica in World War II. Mica was vital to the war effort because it was heat and flame resistant. Mica was an important insulator.

Mica was essential in the manufacture of airplanes. It was indispensible in electrical equipment and in stoves and heaters.

Mica was useful for lanterns for servicemen during the war years. Each army—French, British, and American—had its own lantern design. The United States had a lantern design with four squares; it added an extra mica sheet behind the reflector of the lantern. The French had a delicate design for their lanterns. The British lanterns had nickel plating (Innovateus).

Ground mica had a special use during wartime. During World War II, aircraft runways were critical—even in the deserts and jungles of the world. For the United States to construct asphalt plants in these remote areas would have been a difficult, time-consuming, and expensive proposition.

Instead a central production plant processed the asphalt into thin strips; the plant rolled these thin strips into enormous rolls. These strips of asphalt could easily adhere together before their long journeys were complete; they could even meld together into one mass. To prevent this sticking, plant employees inserted ground mica between the layers. Upon the arrival at its destination, the workers placed the asphalt on "stamp lickers" and rolled out the surface.

Mica Miners and Sheeters. During World War II 1,500 people worked with "sheeting and trimming" mica in the North Carolina mountain counties. Most of the mica sheeters were in the Toe River Valley and in Plumtree, North Carolina, where the author's grandparents lived and worked in mining for many years. The mountain counties of Yancey, Mitchell, and Avery had about 2,200 miners during the war period (Presnell 2005, 40, 41, 51, 153).

World War II Contributions of the North Carolina Mountain and Piedmont Regions: Textile Mills, Their Workers, and Their Participation in the War Effort

The rivers in the Mountain Region often ran with great force and were able to power textile mills; many factories sprang up. These factories often changed their products to supply the needs generated by World War II.

Textile Workers' Contributions to the War Effort. Nell Daves Price (later Burns)—the author's mother—worked for a while at the Queen Ann Mill in Ellenboro, North Carolina. She later became assistant register of deeds for Rutherford County. After the beginning of World War II, the Queen Ann Mill where Nell worked began to produce mattress covers for the military barracks in North Carolina and the nation. Nell Price was North Carolina's version of Rosie the Riveter in the Mountain Region. Nell Price aided the war effort further. She even gave up her beloved husband and the father of her child to the draft and the war. His grave site is in the Salisbury National Cemetery. (See Chapter 5 for more information on the Salisbury National Cemetery and on Corporal Arthur Fred Price.)

Rationing. North Carolinians contributed to the war effort in many other ways. Nell Price remembered the rationing stamps and the difficulty in securing sugar, gasoline, and other items.

The ration book had certain directions on the back cover:

1. This book is valuable. Do not lose it.
2. Each stamp authorizes you to purchase rationed good in the quantities and at the times designated by the Office of Price Administration. Without the stamps you will be unable to purchase these goods.
3. Detailed instructions concerning the use of the book and the stamps will be issued. Watch for those instructions so that you will know how to use your book and stamps. Your Local War Price and Rationing Board can give you full information.
4. Do not throw this book away when all of the stamps have been used, or when the time for their use has expired. You may be required to present this book when you apply for subsequent books.

    Rationing is a vital part of your country's war effort. Any attempt to violate the rules is an effort to deny someone his share and will create hardship and help the enemy.

    This book in your Government's assurance of your fair share of certain goods made scarce by war. Price ceilings have also been established for your protection. Dealers must post these prices conspicuously. Don't pay more.

    Give your whole support to rationing and thereby conserve our vital goods. Be guided by the rule:

    "If you don't need it, DON'T BUY IT" [U.S. Office of Price Administration 1942].

    When you have used your ration, salvage the Tin Cans and WASTE FATS. They are needed to make munitions for our fighting men. Cooperate with your Salvage Committee [U.S. Office of Price Administration 1943].

P. R. Price—the author's grandfather and Nell Price's father-in-law—ran a gasoline station with groceries at the Rutherford-Cleveland County Line on Highway 74. He was aware of the hardships that those on the home front were enduring to help the war effort. Coffee, gasoline, sugar, and evaporated milk were some of the rationed items that he had to monitor carefully.

The North Carolina textile workers contributed to the war effort by their products. Nell Daves Price (Burns) recalled several Rutherford County mills changing their products to aviator scarves, tents, and bandages to meet the military needs across the nation.

The Office of Civil Defense appointed some air raid wardens. This service was another way that North Carolinians served. Elijah Hamrick's home was at the highest point in the town of Ellenboro; his daughter Evelyn often made the morning call to A. B. Bushong, the air raid warden for Ellenboro. Her call had to include the code words "Bacon 28." A typical call from Evelyn might have been: "Bacon 28 reporting. Sighted 3 planes, flying low, two engines, flying east from the north" (Davis and Walker 2003, 118).

North Carolina, then, did its part in World War II in many ways. The Mountain Region excelled in its contributions.

Chapter 7

Sites in the North Carolina Piedmont Region and Their Vital Contributions to World War II and the War Effort

Of the three regions in North Carolina, the most westerly one is the Mountain Region. The reader has already explored—in Chapter Six—the many contributions of that region to the war effort.

The region of North Carolina that borders the Mountain Region to the east is the Piedmont. The word *Piedmont* comes from the French language and means "foot of the mountain"; many people, in fact, refer to the Piedmont Region as "the foothills."

Although the Piedmont is one of three divisions, it covers more than one-half of the state. The elevation ranges from 300 feet above sea level on the east to 1,500 feet above sea level on the west. The Piedmont was essential to the war effort. The counties in the Piedmont that had notable military sites included Mecklenburg, Union, Guilford, and Granville. A consideration of each county is in order.

World War II Contributions of the Piedmont Region of North Carolina: Mecklenburg County

Mecklenburg is the most densely populated—and the most populated—county in the Piedmont and in the state of North Carolina. Charlotte is both its largest city and its county seat (Wikipedia, "Mecklenburg County").

The Piedmont quickly converted its people and its industries from peacetime goods to wartime products. A notable example was the "shell plant" near Charlotte, North Carolina.

The Charlotte "Shell Plant." On June 1, 1942, the Department of the Navy proposed a contract with the United States Rubber Company for the construction of a shell loading and assembly plant. The envisioned facilities for the production of 40-mm shells and other ammunition would initially occupy 249 individual buildings, from 6' × 6' to 870' × 500'; most of the buildings would have wooden frames and concrete-block foundations.

The projected site of the shell plant was ten miles south of Charlotte on 2,260 designated acres. These acres were near what is now Highway 49, or the southeast corner of the intersection of Westinghouse Boulevard and South Tryon. The property would contain 13 miles of railroad tracks and 8 miles of gravel roads. Five boilers would provide heat for the various buildings; water would come from Charlotte. Prescribed for the plant was sewage disposal and a sewerage system—unusual at the time.

On December 12, 1942, the first casings received their test loads at the Charlotte plant. Loading for line one was in operation on December 17, 1942 (Department of the Navy).

Several thousand people worked for the U.S. Rubber Company ("The Shell Plant") in Charlotte. During World War II, the main function of the Shell Plant became the production of 75-mm anti-aircraft shells for the navy (Charlotte-Mecklenburg Story, "The Shell Plant").

Many of the employees at the Shell Plant were women. They usually earned about $25 per week; these salaries were more than the typical salaries that women could make as sales clerks.

The Shell Plant employed both men and women as security guards. These patrols carried guns at their side as they walked or drove around the premises. The plant was open around the clock, and three eight-hour shifts ensured work continued.

With its explosives, the plant was an extremely dangerous place to work. There were regular air raid drills during which employees reported to the cafeteria to wait for the "all clear." Employees had to wear steel-toed shoes for protection; uniforms—navy blue skirts or slacks and light blue shirts—and identification photos ensured that only employees would be on the premises.

North Carolinian Mary Wilson Tucker (Arrowood) was one of some 10,000 people who worked in the Shell Plant. Her job was helping to load the powder into the shell casings. Mary remembers how her hands often became red, sore, and rough after working with the powder for the shells (Mary Wilson Tucker Arrowood, interview by author, 2003; Davis and Walker 2004, 112).

Mary Wilson Tucker Arrowood moved in with her parents-in-law after her marriage to Dan Ray Arrowood. She left the Shell Plant and took another job closer to their home (Second Lieutenant Dan Ray Arrowood, interview by author, 2003; Davis and Walker 2004, 25).

The Shell Plant continued to progress. The plant moved from loading the casings by hand to producing the ammunition on an assembly line. The speed and safety records for the Charlotte-based plant were good.

The Shell Plant in Charlotte received the army-navy "E" award of excellence in April 1944—and two other times before its production ended. On December 6, 1944, the Shell Plant reached its "peak day." It produced 213,143 rounds in 24 hours.

The United States government and the U.S. Rubber Company cancelled their contract two days after Japan surrendered. The employees of the plant received termination.

The Shell Plant became a naval ammunition depot. Some of the frame structures became Marine barracks; the employment building became apartments (Charlotte-Mecklenburg Story, "Shell Plant").

Mary Wilson Tucker (later Arrowood) was an employee of the Shell Plant in Charlotte until her marriage to Second Lieutenant Dan Arrowood, a North Carolinian who piloted a B-24 with the 400th Squadron, 90th Bomb Group, 5th Air Force (courtesy of Mary Wilson Tucker Arrowood).

The Charlotte Quartermaster Depot. During its first full year of operation as an assembly plant (1915), the Ford plant on 222 North Tryon Street in Charlotte assembled 6,850 Model T Fords. Plant workers paired their constructions with frameworks shipped from Michigan.

In 1916 the Tryon Street operation relocated to 210 East Sixth Street in Charlotte. Parts for the Model T's arrived at the Charlotte location primarily by rail from across the country. Workers continued to assemble vehicles at the Charlotte site on East Sixth Street through 1924.

The successful Ford Motor Company began building a new manufacturing plant on Statesville Avenue in Charlotte in 1924. Designed by the internationally recognized architect Albert Kahn, the 240,000-square-foot facility on Statesville Avenue cost Ford $2,000,000, or $25,000,000 in today's currency. The new facility had easy access to the Southern Railway (now Norfolk Southern) line (Charlotte Motor Speedway).

Production in the new plant began on September 14, 1924. Five hundred workers reported to the plant. In 1925, the Charlotte plant produced 60,032 vehicles. The plant in Charlotte changed to Model A's in 1928.

Before it closed as a production plant, the Ford Motor Company Assem-

7. Sites in the Piedmont Region

A warehouse at the Charlotte Quartermaster Depot suggests the enormous size of the facility (photograph no. H_2000_01_417_22; courtesy of the Robinson-Spangler Carolina Room-Public Library of Charlotte and Mecklenburg County).

bly Plant in Charlotte produced a total of 231,068 vehicles: cars and trucks. The work of the plant itself was not complete, however (Charlotte Motor Speedway).

On May 15, 1941, Lieutenant Colonel Clare W. Woodward, three army officers, and 32 civilians established an office in the south wing of the old assembly plant of the Ford Motor Company. The new purpose of the plant was to serve as the Charlotte Quartermaster Depot, a part of the Quartermaster Corps of the United States Army.

The original charge of the Charlotte Quartermaster Depot was to supply Carolina military installations with the necessary provisions that they had requisitioned. Everything from toothpicks to M1 Garand rifles could cycle through the Charlotte Quartermaster Depot. The Charlotte Quartermaster Depot eventually sent supplies to other states, including Virginia, West Virginia, and South Carolina. It also sent requisitions overseas in emergency situations.

Even though the original, primary purpose of the Charlotte Quartermaster Depot was to handle requisitions within the states, in January 1944 it sent 745 tons of materials abroad. By November 1944, the total was 5,941 tons.

The Charlotte Quartermaster Depot and its grounds were immense. The site encompassed 72 acres. The warehouses had 1.2 million square feet of space.

The Charlotte Quartermaster Depot brought employment to the area. In addition to the 80 military employees, the depot hired more than 2,500 residents. The monthly payroll was about $300,000.

The Charlotte Quartermaster Depot performed a vital role for the military even after World War II. A unit of the American Graves Registration Service (AGRS) moved into the former Charlotte Quartermaster Depot. The AGRS identified and returned the remains of 5,170 deceased military personnel to families in Southern states, including North Carolina, South Carolina, Virginia, Tennessee, and Georgia. The escort personnel necessary to perform these services included 144 representatives from the army, 22 representatives from the air force, 10 representatives from the navy, and 30 representatives from the Marines. The final deactivation of the Charlotte Quartermaster Depot came in January of 1949 (Charlotte-Mecklenburg Story, "Charlotte Quartermaster Depot").

Charlotte Municipal Airport/Charlotte Army Air Base/Morris Field. In the 1930s Charlotte mayor Ben E. Douglas urged the creation of a major municipal airport for Charlotte. He believed commercial flights and airmail service were essential because the city could not grow "without water and transportation."

The Charlotte city manager—at the urging of Mayor Douglas and the Charlotte City Council—filed an application with the Works Progress Administration (WPA) on September 3, 1935, for the construction of an airport. The WPA was a federal work program that provided income and work—not handouts—to Americans during the Great Depression of the 1930s.

After the proposal for the Charlotte airport received approval on November 13, 1935, the council diverted funds for the purchase of land for the airport site and for the repayment of the transfers after the sale of bonds for the airport. On March 1, 1936, the sale of the airport bonds was complete.

In 1936–1937 the WPA erected the Douglas Airport Hangar at the airport in Charlotte. The Charlotte airport project was the largest project in allotted funds—until that point. The City of Charlotte invested $57,703; the WPA funds amounted to $323,889. Salaries from these funds to site workers amounted to $143,334.

The construction of the hangar was an important part of the WPA project. The hangar was in use for many years (Charlotte-Mecklenburg Historic Landmark Commission).

The United States Army rented the municipal airport in Charlotte,

7. Sites in the Piedmont Region

This postcard shows the hangar built by the Works Progress Administration in 1935–1937 at the municipal airport in Charlotte (Dixie News Company, Charlotte, North Carolina).

North Carolina, in April 1941—about eight months before the December 7, 1941, Japanese attack on Pearl Harbor. Present at the dedication ceremony of the Charlotte Army Air Base on April 21, 1941, was North Carolina governor James M. Broughton and Fiorello H. La Guardia, the mayor of New York City.

About 10,000 people visited the Charlotte Army Air Base. Many listened as Mayor La Guardia spoke; some were surprised when they heard his warning of an emerging contest: "We are challenged by Adolf Hitler now." His remarks foreshadowed what was to come for the base and for its service personnel before the year's end. The next day (January 22, 1942)—in honor of the late Major William Colb Morris of Harrisburg, North Carolina—the name of the airport became Morris Field. Morris (1891–1939) had been a flier and instructor during World War I (Home Front).

From two short runways, Morris Field and the Charlotte Army Air Base would expand to several hundred acres with a control tower, 100 buildings, and even water, sewer, and electric services. Training combat-ready troops was an important assignment for Morris Field and the Charlotte Army Air Base.

The former municipal air field changed drastically in 1941. A fence around the perimeter of the base restricted entering and exiting the area. There were even wartime restrictions on the news on the base; the base intelligence officer reviewed news stories of military and non-military events before publication.

Troop training at the base began in August 1941. Before the construction of the 100 buildings, tents were necessary as troops poured into Charlotte for field service and duty training. "Tent cities" around the base helped provide housing initially.

The crews at the base worked around the clock. Each month wounded veterans, women, and mechanics were able to repair about 100 planes.

Blackout cloths over the windows prevented light from interfering with crews at rest; the blackout cloths over windows where crews were at work helped to hide information from outsiders. Protecting workers and maintaining security were of prime importance.

To turn the base into a pilot training base, the federal government spent $6 million. The base was operational for five years.

On May 14, 1946, the government turned over the air base to local officials. The airport took a new name: the Charlotte Municipal Airport. The Charlotte Housing Authority converted some of the buildings into apartments; these renovations helped relieve the postwar housing shortage in the Mecklenburg area.

The municipal airport that was once Morris Field is still functional. In 2013 it bears the name Charlotte/Douglas International Airport. Its contributions to World War II were many (Home Front).

World War II Contributions of the Piedmont Region of North Carolina: Union County

The western boundary of Union County, North Carolina, joins the eastern boundary of Mecklenburg County, North Carolina. Both counties gave to the nation and state during World War II.

Camp Sutton as a Military Camp in Union County. Camp Sutton was an important facility within Union County, North Carolina, during World War II. The camp received its name from Frank Howie Sutton (July 15, 1917–December 7, 1941); Sutton was the first war casualty from Monroe, North Carolina, in World War II.

Sutton died at Tobruk (over Libya), the same day as the Pearl Harbor bombing in 1941. Pilot Sutton had been on duty with the Royal Canadian Air Force in North Africa when his death occurred. Few details on his demise are available.

7. Sites in the Piedmont Region

The United States War Department officially named Camp Sutton on February 9, 1942. The War Department General Order Number 10 of February 24, 1942, first publicized the name of the facility for others to see (Shute, "Monroe").

From the time of the construction of the camp in 1942 until the end of World War II in 1945, Camp Sutton served the state and nation well. In addition to training troops, the camp attracted new people to Monroe; these people filled every available house and apartment in Monroe and contributed to the economy of Monroe and Union County. By securing building permits, property owners were able to add to their houses and construct even more houses and apartments in the area for the increasing population.

Camp Sutton served as a training site for the U.S. Army Corps of Engineers. Its official dedication date was March 7, 1942. As early as the spring of 1942, Camp Sutton served as a "tent" camp.

Camp Sutton was on U.S. Highway 74 and was three miles east of Monroe, North Carolina. It covered 2,296 acres; a railroad line serviced the camp (Shute, "Camp Sutton").

J. Ray Shute, during an oral history symposium presented to the Old Monroe Neighborhood Association on August 17, 1980, talked about Camp Sutton and the tents, among other things. He recalled:

> Well, they started to hiring carpenters by the thousands I reckon. You'd go out to that area [in the early part of 1942] and you couldn't hear anything but hammers building floors for the tents, you know.... The only thing wooden was the floor and the framework around it [Shute, "Oral History Symposium," 6–7].

During the 1940s—an era of racial segregation—Camp Sutton separated its troops by race. The first major unit to train there was the 73rd Field Artillery Brigade. New concept units such as Tank Destroyers Battalions also had stations at Camp Sutton for a while.

Camp Sutton supported and helped stage the 1942 Carolina Maneuvers. The area that would became Camp Sutton in 1942 was an important area for the 1941 maneuvers (Union County Public Library).

A main purpose of Camp Sutton was preparing troops for duty overseas.

Camp Sutton was one of the state's largest military training facilities during World War II. There were 49 units and 16,000 men who trained at Camp Sutton.

An important goal for Camp Sutton was training troops for the U.S. Army Corps of Engineers. Those trained in engineering at Camp Sutton received instruction in constructing both pontoon bridges and fixed bridges.

Tents used for housing troops and equipment storage at Camp Sutton, 1942 (courtesy Carolinas Genealogical Society and the Historical Society in cooperation with the Union County Heritage Room).

Richardson's Creek, which divided Camp Sutton in half, served as an ideal site for practicing fixed bridge construction.

The southern boundary of Union County—where Camp Sutton was situated—was the boundary of South Carolina. The Catawba River in South Carolina was easily accessible from the camp. The Catawba was ideal for instructions in crossing rivers and in erecting pontoon bridges.

Camp Sutton trained depot companies, base equipment companies, dump truck companies, utilities detachments, general service regiments, graves registration companies, and construction battalions. Camp Sutton also functioned as a prisoner of war camp.

Camp Sutton as a Prisoner of War Camp. There were, in fact, more than 10,000 prisoners in North Carolina between 1943 and 1945. German POWs from the Africa Corps and later from Normandy were predominant at Camp Sutton.

There were few problems with the POWs at Camp Sutton. The inmates received humane treatment and maintained discipline among themselves. The prisoners enjoyed many comforts at the prison and worked hard at many tasks; some even received coupons for payment. For the most dependable inmates, the offer of employment by local farmers and tree cutters was an option.

The POWs at Camp Sutton could attend religious services. The German Red Cross ensured that they had a library of books in German. The prisoners even had time for recreation: Ping-Pong, soccer, volleyball, and other games and sports.

There were, however, some tensions among the prisoners; not all German inmates supported the Nazi regime. The Union Library in its excellent review and summation of Camp Sutton was able to report, "Most of the inmates viewed their overall experience as positive, given the circumstance of captivity" (Shute, "Monroe").

Camp Sutton trained about 3,500 former prisoners of war in engineering. These Italian workers would assist in the construction and repair of the damages caused by war after their return to Europe (Union County Library).

The Deactivation of Camp Sutton. The deactivation of Camp Sutton came in January of 1945. The last German POW, however, did not leave until the spring of 1946—nearly a year after the end of the war. The buildings and property that had once been Camp Sutton served in another capacity after the war. Polio patients found housing in the buildings that had once been a part of Camp Sutton; they came to the area for treatment particularly after the epidemics of the late 1940s and early 1950s (Shute, "Monroe").

The area where Camp Sutton once served the state and the nation now has mostly commercial uses. Few of the original Camp Sutton buildings remain. Immediately after the deactivation, however, the improvements—such as roads, bridges, sewer lines and the beginnings of a modern hospital—that Camp Sutton left behind benefitted Monroe.

World War II Contributions of the Piedmont Region of North Carolina: Alamance County

On February 18, 1942, Alamance County residents read in their newspapers of the approval of a $3,000,000 investment and an agreement between the government, Fairchild Aircraft, the Huffman Field, and Burlington. The transaction was part of the war effort.

Fairchild Aircraft Company. Fairchild Aircraft launched an aircraft industry to begin producing training planes for the military in the old Burlington Rayon Plant located between Burlington and the Haw River. The transaction included the enlarging of the Burlington Rayon Plant. There would be an estimated 4,000 to 5,000 employees at Fairchild Aircraft (Bolden 1995, 8).

A Fairchild AT-21 Gunner Trainer. A manufacturing plant for these training aircraft was located in Burlington, North Carolina (Grogan Photograph Company, Danville, Illinois).

Burlington was eager to accommodate those moving to the area for employment at the Fairchild Plant. Some of the buildings to house these new workers resembled barracks. The new housing area took the name Fairchild Heights.

"Plastified wood" was used for the construction of the AT-21. This training plane had one machine gun in its nose. The AT-21 resembled a small bomber. Intended for training crews in the use of flexibly mounted guns and power gun turrets, the AT-21 also provided opportunities for trainees to learn to work as crew members.

The first AT-21 came off the Burlington production line in 1943. There were 104 others that followed before the use of the plasticized trainers ended in 1944. Training examples of actual aircraft followed the trainers and replaced the AT-21 trainers produced at the Fairchild Plant. Fairchild Aircraft vacated the Burlington facility after its production work on the AT-21 was complete (Ellis, 273).

Another company moved into the old Burlington Rayon Plant/Fairchild Aircraft Plant. The new company in the Burlington facility was the Firestone Company. In North Carolina Firestone had the charge to produce 90-mm guns for the military (Bolden 1995, 9, 95).

After the end of World War II, the plant had a new tenant. In April 1946, the Western Electric Corporation (later AT&T) moved into the plant. Western Electric manufactured electronic equipment; much of its equipment at the time went to Bell Telephone Company and the U.S. government (Ellis, 273).

The Fairchild building was still government-owned and available in the 1980s. It continued to operate as an Western Electric/AT&T facility until AT&T moved to the Rock Creek Industrial Park in 1992.

Western Electric Burlington had produced many electronics for the government; it also built the guidance system for the Titan missile. After the plant closed in 1992, it sat idle until 2005; at that time a local business executive bought the plant for manufacturing (Wikipedia, "Alamance County").

Fairchild Field. Included in the $3 million transaction with the government, Fairfield Aircraft, and Burlington in 1942 was the purchase of Huffman Field, a commercial airfield. Huffman Field, which had opened on July 3–4, 1933, received some improvements as a result of the investment. The upgrades to the airfield included new hangars and a concrete runway. Huffman Field, which became Fairchild Field, was able to serve as a test ground for the planes made at Fairchild Aircraft during the brief time that Fairchild Aircraft was in operation (Bolden 1995, 9, 95).

Huffman Field was directly across the street from the Fairchild plant. With the funding of $3,000,000, some monies were available for the construction of a concrete runway and hangars.

Before the improvements, Huffman Field had a single asphalt runway on a 227-acre property. The two new hangers included one that was 90' × 40'. During 1942 the field was "described as being owned by the Defense Plant Corporation ... and operated by private interests" (Freeman, "Greensboro Area").

Its name became Fairchild Field. After the end of World War II, the Fairchild Field continued as a civil airport.

The Closing of Fairchild Field. Fairchild Field closed sometime between 1966 and 1972. Commercial constructions now occupy the field. The original site was at what is now Route 70 and North Graham Hopedale Road. John Hunter notes, "The remains of the runway are still visible if one knows what to look for" (Freeman, "Greensboro Area").

In 2000 Alamance County had two flying services. Both services used trained instructors to teach student pilots. These teachers also were able to make commercial flights throughout the nation.

One of the services was the Burlington Flying Service, located at Municipal Airport. The other service, the Alamance Aviation Service, was on the old Fairchild Field; this remnant of World War II and North Carolina remained (Ellis).

World War II Contributions of the Piedmont Region of North Carolina: Guilford County

Guilford County is located in the Piedmont Region of North Carolina. It adjoins Alamance County, which was the home of Fairchild Aircraft and Fairchild Field, discussed above.

Greensboro Army Air Force Basic Training Center No. 10 (BTC-10). Greensboro—located in Guilford County—is in the north-central portion of North Carolina. After the advent of World War II in 1941, the United States Army Air Force (AAF) needed a training center for many new recruits.

Considering the interest expressed by Greensboro City officials in hosting a training center and after examining the area, the AAF determined that the Greensboro area would indeed be ideal as a training center. The city had a strategic location; the necessary transportation and the essential support facil-

7. Sites in the Piedmont Region

Most residents of Greensboro were familiar with Main Gate No. 1 of Basic Training Center No. 10 in Greensboro, North Carolina (Southern Bell Telephone and Telegraph Company).

ities were available in Greensboro. In addition, the city officials expressed a willingness to develop the large tracts of land needed for the AAF project: a training center to train and mobilize tens of thousands of new personnel for the air war in Europe and in Asia. In 1942 the United States awarded Greensboro the AAF Basic Training Center No. 10. The 652 acres for Basic Training Center No. 10 were near Summit and Bessemer avenues. BTC-10 opened on March 1, 1943; the center gave military personnel four to six weeks of basic training in combat skills and was able to send trained companies to the front (Digital NC).

Greensboro Overseas Replacement Depot (Greensboro ORD). Osborne states that the BTC-10 trained 87,000 new recruits before changing its identity in 1944. In that year it became the only overseas replacement depot (ORD) in the eastern United States and one of only six ORDs in the United States.

The Greensboro ORD was a place for—among other things—processing individuals, reassigning military personnel to new duties, and shipping AAF personnel to transfers overseas. The Greensboro ORD, at its peak, had 900 buildings, housed 30,000 people, and included a large hospital for the region (Osborne 2007, 186).

Most people came to know the Greensboro facility through its second identity: ORD. The military base newspaper estimated that more than 330,000 military personnel came through and/or trained in Greensboro between 1943 and 1946. They filled the railroad depot during their arrivals and departures (Digital NC).

With the end of World War II, the Greensboro ORD in August 1945 became a separation facility. Called AAF Redistribution Station No. 5, it reassigned returning soldiers to other posts. The station finally closed in September 1946 (Craven and Cate, "Redeployment and Demobilization").

The Bessemer Improvement Company purchased many of the buildings and much of the Greensboro ORD acreage. Bessemer focused most of its newly purchased land on residential development (City of Greensboro).

Some of the remaining land went to the State of North Carolina. North Carolina Agricultural and Technical State University made use of some of the buildings and acreage. Other buildings and items connected with the ORD sold at auction (Osborne 2007, 186–87).

Major George E. Preddy. Greensboro contributed to the war effort in still another way. Major George E. Preddy, Jr.—who would be a member of the 352nd Fighter Group, Eighth Air Force—was born in Greensboro. The pilot called his first plane Tarheel. Before his death on Christmas Day in 1944, he shot down 32 enemy aircraft (O'Keefe 1977, 81).

Greensboro–High Point Municipal Airport. Lindley Field was a civil airport located eight miles northwest of Greensboro. When World War II began, the airport helped the war

Greensboro native Major George E. Preddy, Jr., was killed by Allied ground fire on December 25, 1944. His total score was 26.83 air-to-air victories. He was the top Air Force ace from the Southern United States and the top Mustang ace, ranking sixth among Air Force aces and seventh among American aces (courtesy Preddy Memorial Foundation @ http://www.preddy-foundation.org; collection of Sam Sox and Paul Grabb).

effort. The United States Marines, the United States Navy, and the United States Army Air Force all made use of the field for war purposes. The USAAF even lengthened the runways to enhance their use (Osborne 2007, 186).

The air force was able to employ the field as a refueling stop in its air ferry system. Troops going overseas used Lindley Field as an aerial debarkation facility. The air force trained bomber and fighter pilots on the field and also used Lindley as a basic training facility for new recruits.

In the 21st century, Lindley Field is now part of a large, modern, international airport, known as Piedmont Triad International Airport. Piedmont Triad, which serves Greensboro, Winston-Salem, and High Point, today shows no signs of its war efforts during World War II (Osborne 2007, 186).

The Importance of the Piedmont Region of North Carolina and Its Contributions to World War II: Forsyth County

The Miller Airport was three miles northwest of the center of Winston Salem in Forsyth County. The airfield was able to do its part to aid the war effort.

Miller Airport, Winston-Salem, North Carolina. In 1927, leaders of Winston-Salem learned that Charles Lindbergh and his *Spirit of St. Louis* were coming to their city. Wanting to have suitable facilities for him, the city planners began meeting immediately and identified a suitable site for an airport near what is now North Liberty Street in Winston-Salem. When Clint Miller donated $17,000 toward the facility, the Airport Corporation agreed on the name Miller Municipal Airport.

Richard "Dick" Reynolds, a son of R. J. Reynolds, had established a commuter airline and maintenance service in Rochester, New York. Dick and his sisters included Winston-Salem in their operation. Their investments in Miller Airport included electricity and new steel hangars.

After Reynolds Aviation dissolved, Lewis McGinnis and Camel City Flying Service assumed leadership for Miller Airport. Miller Airport distributed Piper and Stinson aircraft, continued to improve the airport structures and lighting, and even added a grandstand.

Smith Reynolds Airport. Eastern Airlines added Miller to its north-south route in 1940. After the Z. Smith Reynolds Foundation donated funds to modernize and expand the airport so that it could accommodate the requirements of a major commercial airline, the name of the airport became Smith Reynolds Airport on December 14, 1942. The name came from the younger brother (1911–1932) of Dick Reynolds and from the Smith Reynolds Terminal.

The Smith Reynolds Airport and Piedmont Aviation began concentrating on flight training and aviation support services in the 1940s. From 1942 to 1945, Smith Reynolds Airport served as a training base for pilots of the USAAF. Over 1,000 aviators received training there.

After the end of World War II (1947), Thomas Davis established in Winston-Salem a local airline: Piedmont Airlines. With only three DC-3 planes, the new airline served 22 airports with three DC-3 aircraft, known as Pacemakers.

Smith Reynolds Airport grew. It became the busiest airport in North Carolina in 1961, 1963, 1964, 1965, and 1969. With increased traffic to and from Charlotte, however, the last airline flight left Smith Reynolds Airport in January of 2000. It still houses a flight school (Piedmont Flight Training and Aviation Services), jet maintenance service, corporate jets, and chartering services (Digital Forsyth).

R. J. Reynolds Tobacco and German POWs. Although few remnants of World War II remain at the airport, the area did its part in the war effort. The foil division at R. J. Reynolds Tobacco Company made aluminum strips ("windows") that Allied planes dropped to jam the radar of the enemy. R. J. Reynolds remained open 24 hours a day to produce the billions of cigarettes for the service personnel; it increased production between 1940 and 1946 by 48 percent.

To help meet the demand for cigarettes for the military, the company requested the use of German prisoners of war in its plants. Some of these came from the prisons at Fort Bragg. Reynolds turned its storage shed #112 into a barracks. The United States released the POWs to return to Germany in 1946.

National Carbon Company. The National Carbon Company opened a new battery plant in the county. Allied Aviation produced weapons for the Allied Powers.

The United States Army Air Force and Its Office of Flying Safety. The United States Army Air Force moved its Office of Flying Safety to Winston-Salem in 1942. The office constructed barracks for some of its 600 personnel. It also built a hangar at the Smith Reynolds Airport and an operations building for the Office of Flying Safety.

The Contributions of the People at Home. Forsyth County sent 13,333 citizens to war. Others—including 34 women—volunteered to go also. Three hundred and one of those who left the county became casualties of war. Those remaining at home had to function without these local citizens and had to help in the war effort also.

Many of the workers in the North Carolina Piedmont worked in textiles; these factories retooled to meet the war needs. This was particularly true in Winston-Salem.

Those employed at Hanes Company, mostly locals, did what many of the manufacturing and textile companies in the state did: altered the products to help the war effort. The company made 38 million items of apparel for the armed forces.

North Carolinians worked in essential war industries and in industries necessary to keep the economy functioning. Those at home planted "victory gardens" and practiced the rationing of gasoline, food, and other items prescribed by the government (Tursi 1994, 229).

World War II Contributions of the Piedmont Region of North Carolina: Wake, Durham, Person, and Granville Counties

According to the 2010 census, Wake County is the second most populous county in North Carolina; Wake and adjoining Durham County include Raleigh, Chapel Hill, and Durham, among other cities and towns.

Both the Raleigh-Durham Airport and Camp Butner have long been important and were particularly so during World War II. Their history reveals much about their contributions and the area.

The Raleigh-Durham Airport. The Raleigh-Durham Airport is in the northwestern part of Wake County. The airport, which serves 9,000,000 passengers a year as of 2013, began in 1939 when the North Carolina General Assembly chartered the Raleigh-Durham Aeronautical Authority to construct an airport to replace the outgrown Raleigh Municipal Airport. Eastern Airlines president Captain Eddie Rickenbacker took out a full-page advertisement in 1940. He urged the counties of Wake and Durham and the cities of Durham and Raleigh to work together to build an airport. Raleigh and Durham heeded his advice and, after consultation with many others, work began on the construction of the airport; it would later become known as Raleigh-Durham Airport (RDU).

The Raleigh-Durham Army Air Field and the Raleigh-Durham Airport. In 1942 the United States government needed the airfield under construction in the Raleigh-Durham area. The military took over the construction of the airfield for use during World War II.

In January 1943 the field took the name Raleigh-Durham Army Air Field. It hosted barracks and three runways. The Raleigh-Durham Army Air Field became fully functional on May 1, 1943, and served as a training facility for the Army Air Corps until January 1, 1948. Four barracks were available for the Army Air Forces Air Technical Service Command personnel.

The United States government allowed Eastern Airlines to use the airfield. In 1943 Eastern began flights from the Raleigh-Durham Airport (RDU) to New York and to Miami. The four-hour flights to New York stopped in Richmond; Washington, D.C.; Baltimore; and Philadelphia. During the six-hour flights to Miami, there were stops at Charleston, Savannah, Jacksonville, Orlando, Vero Beach and West Palm.

In 1946 the federal government returned the 1,223 acres of land that it had acquired from RDU and used during World War II. RDU continues to function.

In 2000 the Airports Council International (ACI) ranked RDU as the second fastest-growing major airport in the United States. The ACI reported that passenger growth at RDU was second only to Washington-Dulles International Airport. As with any business, RDU continues to have good years and better years (Raleigh-Durham International Airport; Wikipedia, "Raleigh-Durham International Airport").

Camp Butner. During World War II, North Carolina trained more military personnel than any of the other 48 states. Fort Bragg, Camp Lejeune, and Cherry Point were the three largest permanent military installations in North Carolina.

The three largest *non*-permanent military installations in the state were Camp Mackall (Scotland County), Camp Davis (Onslow County), and Camp Butner (touching on Granville, Person, and Durham counties). Of these, only Camp Butner was in the Piedmont Region.

The establishment of the Camp Butner Reservation was primarily on land that the federal government purchased. Camp Butner included 40,000 acres (about 63 square miles) (North Carolina Department of Cultural Resources, 105).

The purpose of Camp Butner was primarily to train infantry divisions and various artillery and engineer units within the Fourth Services Command,

7. Sites in the Piedmont Region

Army Ground Forces. From 1942 through 1945, Camp Butner trained combat troops for deployment and for redeployment to both the European and Pacific theaters (The Town of Butner).

Camp Butner opened on August 4, 1942. At the dedication ceremonies, the camp received its name from Major General Henry Wolfe Butner (April 6, 1875–March 13, 1937), a Surry County native and commander of the First Artillery Brigade in World War I. North Carolina governor J. Melville Broughton participated in the dedication ceremonies.

Trainees participated in a variety of exercises on the gently rolling land that had once been agricultural acreage. The rehearsals of the men included river crossings, gas attacks, and camouflage preparation. Rifle ranges and artillery ranges provided them the practice they needed.

Camp Butner and Prisoners of War. Camp Butner served as a prisoner of war camp. Both German and Italian prisoners received housing at Butner. Their duties often included cooking in addition to other various and sundry duties (North Carolina Department of Natural Resources, "Camp Butner").

Robert D. Billinger, Jr., in his *Nazi POWs in the Tar Heel State*, discusses a problem at Camp Butner in 1945 when 200 German POWs refused to work after they allegedly had not received their pay on schedule. The caretakers, however, solved the problem by court-martialing the two leaders and by using tear gas grenades on the others (Luebken).

Butner After World War II. The War Department officially closed Camp Butner on January 31, 1947, and bulldozed some of the temporary quarters. The War Assets Department assumed responsibility for the acreage on April 26, 1947. Farmers who had the original ownership bought back over 20,000 acres. The North Carolina National Guard received about 5,000 acres; the NCNG assumed responsibility for maintaining the land for training purposes.

The State of North Carolina received 13,000 acres from the federal government. On November 3, 1947, the state assumed control of Camp Butner and assumed the responsibilities of the fire and police services for this acreage. These acres became the sites for a mental hospital, a correctional institution, state-owned farms, and a National Guard training facility.

In 1947 the state legislature designated that the governing body of the Town of Butner would be the State Board of Mental Health (now the Department of Health and Human Services). This board would "prepare, adopt and enforce ordinances and regulations for the development of both the State and privately owned property in the area."

The abandoned army hospital became the site for an inpatient facility to diagnose and treat those with psychiatric disorders, to restore them to health, and to return them to society. Named after the legislator who worked to advance mental health care in North Carolina, the John Umstead Hospital now serves 16 counties.

Some of the old barracks in the area became the Butler Training School. This school for those with mental health issues became (in 1948) "the Colony." A new era of mental health had begun in the state.

The governance of Butner has changed several times through the years. The municipality of Butner (incorporated in 2007) remains as a reminder of the role the area played in World War II and of its role in advancing mental health throughout the state and nation. Butner now has a town manager, a mayor elected for two years, and six council members elected for four years. The 2010 census listed the population of Butner as 7,591 (Town of Butner).

Chapter 8

Sites in the Western Coastal Plain

The Coastal Region of North Carolina extends from the Piedmont Region to the Atlantic Ocean. Not all the counties within the Coastal Region, therefore, touch the sea, and the characteristics of the counties vary significantly. To classify the areas within the Coastal Region more succinctly, the Coastal Region has two main subregions: the Western Coastal Plain and the Tidewater Region. The Western Coastal Plain extends from the eastern boundary of the Piedmont Region to the western boundary of the Tidewater subregion; the Tidewater extends westward from the sea "as far as the effects of the ocean tide are visible" (Lefler et al. 1959, 55).

In the Coastal Region of North Carolina alone there were more than 20 important military sites during World War II. An examination of the sites in the Western Coastal Plain of the Coastal Region is the main topic of this chapter. This consideration of each military site proceeds geographically from west to east.

World War II Contributions of the North Carolina Western Coastal Plain: Scotland County and the Laurinburg-Maxton Army Air Base (the Largest Glider Training Base in the World during World War II)

Scotland County is the county located in the most southwestern part of the coastal plain of the Coastal Region. The Laurinburg-Maxton Army Air Base was a military site located partially in Scotland County during World War II.

Some portions of the state of South Carolina border Scotland County on the south. Counties surrounding Scotland County are Richmond County on the west, Moore on the north, and Hoke and Robeson counties on the east.

Laurinburg-Maxton Army Air Base in the 1940s: Largest Glider Training Base in the World during World War II. In December 1941, Maxton (a community in Scotland County) learned that the federal government was interested in locating an air training school in the area. Laurinburg, Robeson County, Maxton, and Scotland County officials met to discuss the proposed army air base. Together, the four administrations obtained a total of 583 acres to lease to the federal government for a military reservation. Their hope was that the land would revert to the area for an airport after the war.

On April 20, 1942—a little over four months after the attack on Pearl Harbor—the government authorized the construction of Laurinburg-Maxton Army Air Base to begin on the acres secured by the four administrations. The federal Works Progress Administration provided much of the labor for the project. The initial cost of the construction of the Laurinburg-Maxton Army Air Base was more than $10,000,000. The base included more than 20 miles of paved roads (RobcoHistoryMus's Blog, "Photo of the Week: Army Santa"). The buildings were temporary constructions. Metal and restricted materials were used sparingly. The first unit trained at Laurinburg-Maxton Army Air Base in November of 1942.

General George Marshall and General Dwight D. Eisenhower visited the

Laurinburg-Maxton Army Air Base (photographs by U.S. Marine Corps, International News, and Graycraft Card Company, Danville, Virginia).

8. Sites in the Western Coastal Plain

North Carolina base on more than one occasion to observe the training. These visits meant parades and fanfare for the base and for the area.

Some of the units and the personnel who trained at Laurinburg-Maxton Army Air Base Units performed in important operations such as Operation Torch (North Africa) in November of 1942, the invasion of Italy (1943), and the invasion of Sicily (1943).

The United States Army Air Force used the airfield during World War II as a large training base for glider-towing aircraft, in particular. The airbase became the largest glider training base in the world and trained the glider pilots that were used during the D–Day Invasion.

On the night of June 5, 1944, American paratroopers of the 82nd and 101st Airborne Division parachuted from C-47 transport planes. Their landing zones were behind the Utah and Omaha beaches of Normandy, France. Following close behind these C-47s were Waco gliders, whose crews had often received training at Laurinburg-Maxton Army Air Base (Davis and Walker

Waco gliders could transport glider-borne infantry, artillery, and communications equipment. The Waco CG-4A could carry 13 men or 4 men and a jeep; the men often had received their training at Laurinburg-Maxton Army Air Base (National Museum of the U.S. Air Force).

2004b, 49). Waco gliders weighed two tons and had an 80-foot wingspan. The Ford Motor Company manufactured these gliders of wood, medal tubing and canvas; a tow rope connected these gliders to a C-47.

In 1944 the air base began training C-47 pilots in towing CG-4A Waco gliders, intended for the Normandy invasion; the base trained student officers in both ground fighting and advanced glider techniques. Before the Normandy invasion in June of 1944, glider pilot training class began at the base.

The base population dropped from 10,000 to 3,700 by September of 1945. By the end of the month, the population was only 914.

By the close of Laurinburg-Maxton Army Air Base in October 30, 1945, over 40 army and air force units had trained there. The Laurinburg-Maxton Airbase had been the largest Waco CG-4A glider pilot training base in the world.

Laurinburg-Maxton Army Air Base After World War II. After the closing of the Laurinburg-Maxton Army Air Base, the facility became a civil airfield (Laurinburg-Maxton Airport) and industrial park. It is the home of Charlotte Aircraft, a company that dismantles and scraps older aircraft. Airfield visitors can see 727s and DC-10s in the process of being taken apart and recycled.

Some of the buildings, Lee Mills Pond, and the large hangar from World War II still remain. The base chapel remains; it is now the Skyway Baptist Church (Wikipedia, "Laurinburg-Maxton Army Air Base").

World War II Contributions of the Western Coastal Plain of the North Carolina Coastal Region: Richmond County, Scotland County, Cumberland County, Hoke County, Harnett County, and Moore County; and Fort Bragg (U.S. Army), Pope Army Air Field (Spring Lake), Camp Hoffman (Later Camp Mackall), the Pine Needles Inn, and Knollwood Army Air Field

Associated with World War II Richmond County, Scotland County, Cumberland County, Hoke County, Harnett County, and Moore County are four World War II military sites. The best known of these sites is Fort Bragg.

Fort Bragg. Fort Bragg—originally Camp Bragg—dates from 1918. Its original purpose was to serve as an artillery training camp for soldiers during World War I.

8. Sites in the Western Coastal Plain

The name came from the Confederate commander General Braxton Bragg (1817–1876). Bragg—a North Carolina native and West Point graduate—had commanded the Army of Tennessee, achieved a significant victory at the Battle of Chickamauga (1863), served at the coastal defenses in Wilmington, and received appointment as Confederate president Jefferson Davis's adviser (History, "Braxton Bragg").

After Fort Bragg's use as an artillery training camp for World War I, the fort grew slowly. By the summer of 1940, Fort Bragg had a total of only 5,400 military personnel. After the passage of the Selective Service Act (September 19, 1940) and with the threat of war, the federal government constructed at Fort Bragg a reception center. There were 67,000 military personnel housed at the Fort Bragg by the end of the year (Fort Bragg).

In 1940 President Franklin Delano Roosevelt assigned Brigadier General William C. Lee—a North Carolinian—to develop airborne forces at Fort Benning, Georgia. The result was the first tactical parachute battalion. Brigadier General Lee recommended the creation of other airborne divisions; he advocated a size of more than 10,000 members and suggested the inclusion of support elements, artillery, and engineers.

In August 1942 Lee—a major general at the time—received command of the 101st Airborne Division, which moved to Fort Bragg in the fall of 1942. By the end of World War II, all five of the airborne divisions—the 82nd, 101st, 11th, 13th and 17th—and many independent units filled the Fort Bragg air with parachutes, troop transports and gliders. The 555th Parachute Infantry Battlion—the army's first black parachute unit—trained at Forg Bragg (Fort Bragg).

The Fort Bragg Reservation in 1942 was three times the size of the District of Columbia. From east to west, Fort Bragg at that time was 24 miles; the facility was 4 to 11 miles measuring north to south. It touched on several counties (Carolina News).

One of the outstanding generals who commanded Fort Bragg was Major General Omar Bradley. In 1942 General George S. Patton and his troops staged at Fort Bragg before their invasion of North Africa.

Fort Bragg had the first prisoner of war camp in the nation when it took in survivors of the German submarine *U-352*. Begun in 1942, the camp grew to hold 2,000 prisoners. These detainees primarily worked for the military.

Another important fact about Fort Bragg is that the 82nd Infantry Division reactivated at Fort Bragg. After the reorganization of the 82nd, it became the United States Army's first airborne division (Osborne 2007, 185).

By the middle of 1943, Fort Bragg had a population of more than

100,000. The site continued to receive new inductees by the thousands during the war years and trained tens of thousands of artillerymen.

In addition to airborne training, Fort Bragg trained the famous Second Armored Division: "Hell on Wheels"; this unit participated in the invasions of North Africa and Sicily. The Second Armored Division aided in the liberation of France, Belgium, and the Netherlands. "Hell on Wheels" was an important part of the invasion of Germany.

Fort Bragg has continued to serve long after World War II. The military site earned the name "Home of the Airborne" by 1951. It functioned as the Psychological Warfare Center (U.S. Army Special Operations Command), as headquarters for Special Forces soldiers, and as the combat basic training center for 200,000 young men during the years 1966–70. Fort Bragg—with its 140,618 acres—earned the reputation by 1989 as "one of the Army's premier power projection platforms." Fort Bragg still renders its services to its country (Military Bases).

Pope Air Force Base/Pope Army Air Field/Pope Army Airfield. Located at the north end of Fort Bragg near Fayetteville, North Carolina, Pope Army Air Field was originally Pope Air Force Base. The United States Department of War officially established the base in 1919. Pope Air Force Base, therefore, is one of the oldest air force installations in the nation (PCSAmerica.net).

About a century after its 1919 establishment, Pope Air Force Base—now Pope Army Airfield—still survives. Military One Source describes it as "one of the busiest bases in the military."

Pope Field took its name from First Lieutenant Harley Halbert Pope. Pope died on January 7, 1919, when the JN-4 Jenny that he and Sergeant Walter W. Fleming were flying crashed into the Cape Fear River. The site of the accident was near Fayetteville and Fort Bragg (PCSAmerica.net).

Harley Halbert Pope was born on May 26, 1879. He died on January 7, 1919, while he was still in this thirties. Pope's burial was on the military site that would come to bear his name. The air field still recognizes Pope's sacrifice by retaining his name (Find-a-Grave, "Harley Halbert Pope").

Pope Air Force Base/Army Air Field has had many different responsibilities through the years. Often a major duty of the base has been ensuring that the 82nd Airborne and the XVIII Airborne Corps (both based at nearby Fort Bragg) have the necessary air transportation. Pope has constantly provided close air support to the armed forces of the United States and has furnished airlift to American forces as needed; the United States Air Force Air Mobility Command, 43rd Airlift Wing, the 23rd Fighter Group, and the 18th Air Sup-

8. Sites in the Western Coastal Plain

Barracks at Pope Field in North Carolina (Carolina News, Fayetteville, North Carolina).

port Operations Group all call the base their home. In addition, Pope has been a leader in helping to develop U.S. tactics and air power.

The base has a population of about 57,000 military personnel and an additional 1,150 dependents. About 655 civilians work at Pope (About.com, "Installation Overview").

As a result of the actions of the 2005 Base Closure and Realignment Commission, Pope Field came under the army's control: a major event. The prediction is that "Pope will continue to put the *air* in *airborne* for Fort Bragg missions by providing airlift and close air support to American armed forces and to humanitarian missions flown all over the world." This military installation—almost one hundred years old—still has purpose (MilitaryBases.us).

Camp Hoffman (Later Camp Mackall). Three miles east of Hoffman, North Carolina, and forty miles east of Fort Bragg in North Carolina, was Camp Hoffman. Camp Hoffman had as its main purpose the support of Fort Bragg. Activated in 1940, Camp Hoffman (later Camp Mackall) would become the nation's second largest airborne training center. Camp Hoffman touched on both eastern Richmond County and northern Scotland County in North Carolina. Camp Hoffman was located south of the town of Southern Pines (Osborne 2007, 186).

Less than a year after the bombing of Pearl Harbor, the construction of what would be Camp Mackall began on November 7, 1942, on the Camp Hoffman grounds. World events would determine the new official name of the camp.

World War II and Camp Mackall were of particular interest to University of New Orleans historian Stephen E. Ambrose.

In his book *Band of Brothers: E Company, 506th Regiment, 101st Airborne from Normandy to Hitler's Eagle's Nest,* Ambrose describes in detail the construction at Camp Hoffman, which would become Camp Mackall. Ambrose calls Camp Mackall as "a marvel of wartime construction" (2002, 35). Ambrose describes the camp: "On November 7, 1942, it consisted of 62,000 acres of wilderness. Four months later it had 65 miles of paved roads, a 1,200-bed hospital, five movie theaters, six huge beer gardens, a complete all-weather airfield with three 5,000-foot runways, and 1,750 buildings. The barracks were heated; the cots had mattresses" (35).

Camp Hoffman became Camp Mackall by General Order Number 6 on February 8, 1943. Camp Mackall took its new name from an Ohio enlisted man: Private John Thomas (Tommy) Mackall (1920–1942) (Wikipedia, "Camp Mackall").

Private Mackall, who was with the 509th Parachute Infantry Regiment, was the first United States paratrooper to receive mortal wounds in combat

Division headquarters at Camp Mackall, North Carolina, circa 1940 (W. R. Thompson and Company, Publishers, Richmond, Virginia).

during World War II. His wounds came on the same day that construction began at Camp Hoffman.

French Vichy aircraft strafed the American aircraft landing near Oran, Algeria, during the Allied invasion of North Africa: Operation Torch. Private John T. Mackall—though mortally wounded—managed to crawl from the aircraft. He died in a British hospital from these wounds. Seven other paratroopers died in the incident. Other paratroopers suffered injury in the incident (Everything2).

Camp Mackall had other charges. At Camp Mackall, many enlistees received their primary training for the special forces of the United States Army. At the Resistance Training Laboratory, soldiers in the special operations forces learned to use resistance techniques that might be helpful in case of capture (Osborne 2007, 186).

The celebrated 11th Airborne Division prepared at Camp Mackall for its famous Knollwood Maneuver. There is more about the training and the service of the 11th Airborne in the section on Knollwood Airport/Knollwood Army Auxiliary Airfield in this volume.

Camp Mackall had within its confines the Colonel James "Nick" Rowe Training Compound. This obstacle course has the reputation of being one of the most difficult to navigate in the United States Army. The course bears the nickname the "Nasty Nick" in honor of Rowe (Wikipedia, "Camp Mackall").

In addition to "Nasty Nick," within the confines of the camp were facilities for about 500 prisoners of war. These prisoners worked at the camp and in the fields. Secretly, the POWs received instruction in the fundamentals of democracy while they were at Camp Mackall.

The deactivation of Camp Mackall as a training center came in 1948. The camp became a retreat for army personnel. Although most of the buildings from the World War II era have not survived, some of them remain and indicate where the facility was (Osborne 2007, 186).

World War II Contributions of the Sandhills Area of the Western Coastal Plain of the North Carolina Coastal Region: Mid Pines Inn and Golf Club, the Pine Needles Inn (and Glenn Miller), Knollwood Airport and the Knollwood Army Air Field, the Knollwood Maneuver, and the Moore County Airport

The Sandhills area divides the Piedmont Region from the coastal plain area. The Sandhills provide evidence of a former time when the ocean was higher than the land or the land was lower than the coastline. This region of North Carolina provided the setting of some important military sites during World War II (Wikipedia, "Sandhills [Carolina]").

By the late 1800s the Sandhills region of North Carolina had become a popular visiting place for travelers. In 1895 James Walker Tufts—the grandson of a developer in the Sandhills area of North Carolina—purchased 6,000 acres for $1.25 per acre; Tufts had made his money from soda fountains. Tufts's intention was to construct hotels and golf complexes for tourists and local residents (Pinehurst).

Mid Pines Inn and Golf Club. During World War II the military engaged facilities in the Coastal Region of North Carolina area—and elsewhere in the state and nation—in the war effort. One of these resorts was the Mid Pines Inn and Golf Club.

The Mid Pines facility was a result of the Tufts family's interest in golf for the Sandhills area. The Tufts family had already been successful with Pine Needles Inn and Golf Course; they turned their sights on Knollwood, an area

Opened in 1921, the Mid Pines Inn and Golf Club was the vision of the Tufts family. The United States Army and Air Corps used the facility during World War II. After postwar renovations, the Mid Pines Inn and Golf Club reopened; the resort is still popular today. This postcard shows the 18th hole and the club (Dexter Press, Inc., West Nyack, New York).

between Pinehurst and Southern Pines, to accommodate the overflow from Pine Needles Inn. The Tufts commissioned Donald Ross to design and build a new golf course. Their adjacent Mid Pines Inn opened in 1921 (Where2Golf).

The United States Army and the United States Air Corps used the Mid Pines Inn to house military police. Some of the necessary changes made by the military to the structures involved putting furniture into storage. The decorative plaster walls with their gold trim received coats of army tan paint and sustained holes punched through the walls for room-to-room communication. The golf course was left unattended and soon was overgrown.

After the end of World War II, Frank and Maisie Cosgrove purchased the Mid Pines; they immediately began restoring and continuing the development of Mid Pines. To preserve the tender grass on the course, the groundskeepers had to cut the wild golf course grass "bit by bit to preserve the tender grass below. It took nearly a decade to restore the course to its glory and charm." The Mid Pines Inn and the Golf Club continue to be popular for tourists and locals alike (AJGA).

Pine Needles Inn (and Glenn Miller). The Pine Needles Inn between Pinehurst and Southern Pines, North Carolina, opened in 1928. An article on the history of the Pine Needles Inn describes the facility envisioned by the Tufts family as "a glorious Jacobean Tudor landmark and regional jewel." During the Great Depression, the Pine Needles Inn had to close (1931) for financial reasons. The inn reopened in 1935 as a resort for the public. The service of the Pine Needles Inn to the military officially began in 1943; the inn at that time began housing the U.S. Army's Technical Training Command (St. Joseph of the Pines).

In 1942 Major General Walter R. Weaver of the U.S. Army earned the charge of the Technical Training Command. Major General Weaver decided to use the nation's hotels—particularly its resort facilities—to house his training schools and his troops. When the experimental plan met with criticism both from civilians and from the military, he insisted that "the best hotel room is none too good for the American soldier" ("Hist. AAFTTC" and its Predecessors, 1 January 1939–7 July 1943, II, 278–279, as cited by Craven, W. F. and I. L. Cate. *The Army Air Forces in World War II: VI: Men and Planes*, pages 153–154).

The Corps of Engineers—at Major General Walter R. Weaver's request—began to secure other hotels, apartment houses, and facilities for the military in the Sandhills area of North Carolina and across the nation. Major General Weaver established his own command in the resort community between Pine-

The Pine Needles Inn, between Pinehurst and Southern Pines, North Carolina. The many roles of the facility (est. 1928) have included military site, hospital, and inn (Macks' 5, 10, & 25¢ Stores, Sanford, North Carolina; Genuine Curteich-Chicago "C. T. Art-Colortone" Post Card).

hurst and Southern Pines. The Pine Needles Inn was designated as a military facility.

Among the troops serving their country and residing in the Southern Pines and the Pinehurst area was a notable musician: Glenn Miller, captain in the Army Specialist Troops.

Captain Glenn Miller received housing in 1943 at the Pine Needles Inn and was charged with organizing the Army Air Force bands in order to raise the morale of the troops (St. Joseph of the Pines).

Americans and the British audiences—in particular—received Glenn Miller's music well. Steve B. Davis in his article "Glenn Miller: Another Mysterious Disappearance" asserts that Miller's "music was the anthem of the 1940s."

Alton Glenn Miller was born on March 1, 1904, in Clarinda, Iowa. He studied the trombone and began arranging music with a new sound. At first he played with the Dorsey Brothers and with Ray Noble in Britain. He started his own orchestra and became a successful entertainer, recording artist, arranger, trombonist, and movie actor.

Between 1939 and 1942 Glenn Miller and his orchestra were on the top ten chart 70 times. Miller was earning $20,000 a week in 1942 when he applied for a commission to the United States Navy; Bing Crosby served as a recommendation. This application did not work out as planned.

Glenn Miller in his late '30s finally received acceptance to the United States Army. His assignment was to the Army Air Forces (AAF), where he organized an Army Air Forces Band: the Glenn Miller Army Air Force Band.

Captain Miller and the AAF Band were very successful. Between Miller's 1942 enlistment and his 1944 disappearance (missing in action), he and the AAF band gave over 800 performances, 300 of which were personal appearances and the other 500 of which were broadcasts that millions listened to and acclaimed. Captain Glenn Miller also hosted a weekly radio show.

The plane in which he was flying disappeared over the English Channel on December 15, 1944. The mystery of its disappearance and that of its crew and passengers has never been solved.

Many Americans—and North Carolinians, in particular—remember that Glenn Miller was a resident at the Pine Needles Inn for a while. Even today music connoisseurs recognize his orchestra's signature resonance: combining the clarinet and the saxophone for the melody and using other saxophones for a complementary harmonic line. Listeners still identify and enjoy his renditions of "In the Mood," "A String of Pearls," "Little Brown Jug," "Rhapsody in Blue," "Chattanooga Choo Choo," and "Moonlight Serenade."

Captain Glenn Miller's patriotism is exemplary. Glenn Miller's estate continues to support recreations of the Glenn Miller Orchestra, which still entrance civilian and military audiences. The film *The Glenn Miller Story* (1953), biographies, history books, and even a stamp from the United States Postal Service ensure remembrance of Glenn Miller and his contributions (The Official Site of Glenn Miller).

The Pine Needles Inn and its contributions continue. The Diocese of Raleigh purchased the Pine Needles Inn in 1948. A few months later (July 1, 1948), the facility reopened as a 75-bed, acute care facility, St. Joseph of the Pines Hospital, and served the area until 1966. The Sisters of Providence of Holyoke, Massachusetts, assumed management of the North Carolina facility in 1966; they extended their service to home care in 1968 and later to a nursing home under their guidance and support. What was St. Joseph of the Pines is now an important part of a retirement community (St. Joseph of the Pines).

Knollwood Airport/Knollwood Army Auxiliary Airfield. The Knollwood Airport began when the Tufts family—which had established both Mid Pines and the Pine Needles Inn—opened a dirt runway in 1929 and named it Knollwood Airport. This airport with a unique and interesting history figured prominently into World War II and—after some changes—still exists today.

The Knollwood Airport remained part of the Knollwood Development Company from 1929 until 1935. In that year Moore County acquired the airport from the Knollwood Development Company.

The United States Army Air Corps leased the airport in Moore County from 1942 to 1945. The Air Corps designated the facility as the Knollwood Army Auxiliary Airfield, used the airfield as a communications training base, and incorporated it into the historic Knollwood Maneuver (Moore County Airport).

The Knollwood Maneuver. The use of large-scale airborne formations was the initiative of the German military in the Battle of France (1940) and in the Invasion of Crete (1941). The operations were deemed a success, despite heavy German casualties.

The Allies decided to experiment with airborne divisions on their own. The end result was two British and five American airborne units, plus many smaller groups.

One of the most famous of these American divisions was the 11th Airborne Division, trained at North Carolina's Camp Mackall and activated on February 25, 1943. Major General Joseph M. Swing was in command at the time.

The 11th Airborne Division consisted of the 511th Parachute Infantry Regiment, the 187th Glider Infantry Regiment, and the 188th Glider Infantry Regiment. The number of men in the division was only 8,321—about half of a typical American World War II infantry division. Their training was to be intense because the group was to be an elite division.

There was much discussion among high-ranking officers such as General George Marshall, Lieutenant General Leslie J. McNair, Major General Joseph M. Swing, and General Dwight David Eisenhower as to the usefulness and feasibility of such large-scale maneuvers. General Dwight David Eisenhower expressed reservations about the use of the airborne units during Operation Husky in Sicily:

> I do not believe in the airborne division. I believe that airborne troops should be reorganized in self-contained units, comprising infantry, artillery, and special services, all about the strength of a regimental combat team. To employ at any time and place a whole division would require a dropping over such an extended area that I seriously doubt that a division commander could regain control and operate the scattered forces as one unit [11th Airborne Division].

8. Sites in the Western Coastal Plain

In September of 1943 General George Marshall—who supported large-scale tactics and the 11th Airborne—convinced General Dwight David Eisenhower to set up a review board to evaluate a large-scale maneuver. North Carolina would figure prominently in the experiment.

Lt. Gen. McNair recognized the rigorousness of the airborne training for prospective airborne troops—especially since the problems with Operation Husky. Those attempting to make the cut and to become airborne had endured strict preparation, especially at Camp Mackall (North Carolina).

Prospective paratroopers completed lengthy forced marches. Some grueling exercises involved two towers on the Camp Mackall grounds. Prospective airborne troops jumped from the 250-foot (76-meter) tower and from the 34-foot (10-meter) tower in order to simulate landing by parachute. Those in training practiced jumps from transport aircraft also; if someone paused in an aircraft doorway before jumping, the result was automatic failure.

The failure rate for those in training for the airborne was high. Still, applicants were plentiful because of the prestige and the pay rate, which was higher than that for regular troops in training for the infantry.

Major General Joseph M. Swing was in charge of preparing the exercise involving a division of airborne forces: the air corps, parachutes, gliders, and the artillery. The division that would participate in the experiment was the 11th Airborne, trained in North Carolina. The review board for the maneuver carried Major General Swing's name: the Swing Board (11th Airborne Division).

The objective of the December 7, 1943, Knollwood Maneuver was for the 11th Airborne Division to serve as the attacking force and to capture Knollwood Army Auxiliary Airfield. This experimental maneuver would hereafter bear the name the Knollwood Maneuver.

The defending forces at Knollwood would consist of a composite combat team from the 17th Airborne Division and a battalion from the 541st Parachute Infantry Regiment; their charge was to defend the Knollwood Army Auxiliary Airfield, to protect the surrounding area, and to repel the airborne assault. Lieutenant General Leslie J. McNair and the Swing Board would observe the entire operation. The United States War Department—and ultimately General Eisenhower—received the observations and the reports of the experimental maneuver. These observations and reports would help to decide the success of the mission (11th Airborne Division).

The Knollwood Maneuver occurred on the night of December 7, 1943. It was the result of the delivery of 200 C-47 Dakota transport aircraft and 234 Waco CG-4A gliders to the troops of the 11th Airborne Division

("Angels") at 13 separate locations. Eighty-five percent of the troops reached their intended targets.

To accomplish the event, the two hundred C-47's would form four separate groups. Two groups would drop paratroopers. Two groups would drop towing gliders. Each of the four groups would depart from a different Carolina airfield. Between them, the four groups deployed 4,800 airborne troops in the first surge.

Before dawn on December 8, 1943, these airborne troops had accomplished their mission: seizing from the defending troops the Knollwood Army Auxiliary Airfield. The 11th Airborne Division had also successfully secured the area where the rest of the division planned to land.

In addition, the 11th Airborne Division was able to accomplish a coordinated ground attack against a reinforced infantry regiment. The Angels also successfully achieved several aerial resupply missions and evacuated some casualties with transport aircraft.

The Swing Board and Lieutenant General Leslie J. McNair—the overall commander of the United States Army ground forces—gauged the Knollwood Maneuver to be successful. General Dwight David Eisenhower allowed the divisional-sized airborne force to remain (Wikipedia, "11th Airborne Division [United States]").

In 1945—after World War II—the Knollwood Army Auxiliary Airfield became the Pinehurst–Southern Pines Airport. The North Carolina airport, which is five miles northeast of Pinehurst and three miles north of Southern Pines, currently bears the name Moore County Airport (Moore County Airport).

The Knollwood Airport/Knollwood Army Auxiliary Airfield changed names again in 1945 after World War II. The airport became the Pinehurst–Southern Pines Airport in that year. Piedmont Airlines provided service from 1945 until the late 1960s.

The Moore County Airport. The year 1980 brought another name change. The facility became the Moore County Airport, which remains the official title today.

Moore County leased the fixed base operations (FBO) from 1945 until January 13, 1992. Air Moore, Inc./Pinehurst Jet Center was one of the latest FBOs.

In October of 1991 Moore County Airport scheduled airline service with Charlotte Commuter Air (CCAir). This regional airline headquartered in Charlotte, North Carolina, operated as USAir Express and provided commercial air service to and from Charlotte, North Carolina, for more than a decade.

In January 1993, Moore County purchased from Pinehurst Jet Center the 16 years remaining on the FBO lease and all business assets. The county now owned the airport, the land, the buildings, and the assets of the FBO business. North Carolina Senate Bill 942, enacted by the North Carolina General Assembly on July 20, 1993, gave the Moore County Airport Authority the right to operate and maintain the Moore County Airport facilities.

During the late 1990s and the early 21st century, the growth of Moore County Airport was significant. The origin and destination traffic in 1998 peaked at 50,000 passengers.

Passenger traffic at Moore County Airport began to decrease after 9/11 (September 11, 2001). CCAir found it necessary to cease service to the Moore County Airport (April 15, 2002) (Moore County Airport).

One can still find the Moore County Airport where it was during World War II: five miles northeast of Pinehurst and three miles north of Southern Pines, North Carolina. The Commemorative Air Force has a World War II airplane based at the airport for visitors. Interested apprentices can arrange for flying lessons at the airport; one can charter a flight also. Vestiges of the service of the area designated as *Knollwood* to the World War II effort are still evident (Pilot.com).

World War II Contributions of the Western Coastal Plain of the North Carolina Coastal Region: Wayne County and Seymour Johnson Field/Air Force Base

Goldsboro, North Carolina, is the largest city in Wayne County. As such, the city hosted an airstrip in the early 1940s. The airstrip carried the name Seymour Johnson Field.

Seymour Johnson Field/Air Force Base Before World War II. Seymour Johnson Field received its name from Navy Lieutenant Seymour A. Johnson (1904–1941), a Goldsboro native. Before World War II began, Lieutenant Johnson died in an airplane crash (March 5, 1941) near Norbeck, Maryland.

Seymour Johnson was the son of Dr. John N. and Lilly Johnson of Goldsboro. A 1920 graduate of Goldsboro High School, Johnson attended the University of North Carolina at Chapel Hill for three years, entered the United States Naval Academy at Annapolis, Maryland, and earned his commission as an ensign after graduation from the naval academy.

Seymour Johnson earned his pilot wings from Pensacola, Florida, in 1929. He served as a pilot aboard battleships and aircraft carriers.

Lieutenant Johnson had volunteered in 1937 to serve as a test pilot. In 1938 he received assignment to the Anacostia Naval Air Station. He was still serving as a test pilot during his final mission in 1941.

Seymour Johnson Field/Air Force Base During World War II. Lieutenant Johnson was testing a Grumman F4F-3 fighter plane on March 5, 1941, when he reported from 43,000 feet that he was low on oxygen. This lack of oxygen was the apparent cause of his death. Lieutenant Seymour Johnson's final resting place is in the Arlington National Cemetery in Washington, D.C.

At the time of his death, Lieutenant Johnson had clocked more than 4,000 hours in various naval and Grumman aircraft. He was to have received promotion in June 1941 to commander.

The war department asserted in August of 1940 that the airport located two miles southeast of Goldsboro was essential to the national defense. A full year before the attack on Pearl Harbor, the budget of the department allocated $168,811 for the construction of a U.S. Army Air Corps technical training school. A local push began to name the field for Lieutenant Seymour Johnson.

The official activation of the Goldsboro field as Headquarters, Technical School, Army Air Forces Technical Training Command, came on June 12, 1942. The announcement of the official name of the facility did not come until later.

On October 30, 1942, congressional representative Graham H. Barden informed the *Goldsboro News-Argus*, "The Army Air Forces Technical Training School in Goldsboro had been named Seymour Johnson Field." It is significant that the base carries the name of Seymour Johnson; "Seymour Johnson is the only Air Force base named in honor of a naval officer" (Seymour Johnson Air Force Base, "Fact Sheet").

In June of 1943, the base received a second charge: to prepare officers and enlisted men for overseas duty. The unit earned a new designation: Provisional Overseas Replacement Training Center.

In September 1943, Seymour Johnson Field received a third assignment: to provide required basic military training for the cadets who were training to become technical officers in the United States Army Air Corps. The 75th Training Wing would conduct the program through its Aviation Cadet Pre-Training School.

In October of 1943 the 326th Fighter Group arrived; in January of 1944 the group began the preparation of replacement pilots for the P-47 Thunder-

8. Sites in the Western Coastal Plain   95

This postcard of the Seymour Johnson Field in North Carolina contains official photographs from the United States Army and Marine Corps (Graycraft Card Company, Danville, Virginia).

bolt aircraft. Seymour Johnson Field received in April of 1944 a new primary mission: the basic training of P-47 pilots (Seymour Johnson Air Force Base, "Fact Sheet").

Seymour Johnson Field/Air Force Base After World War II. Even at the end of the war in Europe (World War II), Seymour Johnson Field/Air Force Base continued to serve the nation and the world. A new function for Seymour Johnson was that of a central assembly station to process and train troops receiving reassignment in the continental United States and the Pacific theater of operations.

By September of 1945, the role of central assembly station was no longer a mission of Seymour Johnson Field. The new mission became an Army–Air Force Separation Center. Its deactivation came in May of 1946.

The United States Corps of Engineers arrived in late 1952, demolished some old buildings, and began constructing new buildings. Goldsboro mayor Scott B. Berkeley, Sr., and local community leaders began campaigning for the reopening of the installation. Their campaign was successful.

The reactivation of Seymour Johnson Air Force Base as a tactical air command base came on April 1, 1956. The 83rd Fighter-Day Wing received assignment to the base as the primary unit three months later. On December 8, 1957, the 4th Fighter Wing replaced the 83rd.

Seymour Johnson Air Force Base ("History") reports, "Since reopening, the base has been home to B-52 bombers, KC-10 and KC-135 tankers from Strategic Air Command and F-4 and F-16 fighters from the Michigan Air National Guard."

On February 7, 1977, Goldsboro annexed the Seymour Johnson Air Force Base. This annexation would prove to benefit both.

In 1991 the construction of a federal prison on the grounds of what was a part of the Seymour Johnson Field was complete. The inmates supplemented the work force and helped to maintain the base grounds (Seymour Johnson Air Force Base, "History").

Seymour Johnson Field/Air Force Base served the country well during World War II and afterward. The base was able to accommodate 27,000 troops at its strength during World War II.

Seymour Johnson Air Force Base trained more than 250,000 troops during World War II. Some of these were the first bombers to fly over Germany (This Day in North Carolina History).

The air force closed Seymour Johnson Air Force Base at the end of World War II. Two veterans—Goldsboro mayor Scott Berkeley (a World War I pilot) and John D. Lewis (a World War II pilot)—were particularly concerned. The two decided to work to bring the base back to Goldsboro.

Their efforts were successful. On April 1, 1956, the base re-opened; Seymour Johnson was now a part of the Tactical Air Command (Seymour Johnson Air Force Base, "History").

The 83rd Fighter-Day Wing moved to the base in July of 1956. The 4th Tactical Fighter Wing replaced the 83rd Fighter-Day Wing on the base a year later. The 4th Tactical Fighter Wing had destroyed 1,016 enemy aircraft; this was more than any other 8th Air Force unit had to its credit. The 4th produced 38 aces. Seymour Johnson Air Force Base has been the site for the training and preparation of other air force units also (Seymour Johnson Air Force Base, "History").

Seymour Johnson Field/Air Force Base in the 21st Century. The new century brought changes to Seymour Johnson Field/Air Force Base. Turner Watson, writer for the *Goldsboro News-Argus*, reported on December 16, 2005, a significant announcement from Rodney Tabron (spokesperson for the federal prison camp at Seymour Johnson). Tabron stated that by the first week in April of 2006 the camp would be vacant. The inmates would be in other facilities, and the staff would have found other positions within the system (*Goldsboro News-Argus*).

Maxwell Builders reported on some of the physical changes to what had been the federal prison at Seymour Johnson Air Base. One of the most significant of these changes involved the work in 2010 to turn the camp into the home of the 567th Redhorse Squadron. Another important renovation was the updating and enlargement of the facilities for the 4th Training Squadron (Maxwell Builders).

On the last Thursday of each month public tours of the base are available to tourists. Interested visitors, however, must secure reservations three weeks in advance through the Goldsboro Travel and Tourism Department at 308 North William Street.

The City of Goldsboro exalts itself and the base on its downtown Web site. The site notes: "The city of Goldsboro is the proud home of Seymour Johnson Air Force Base, home of the 4th Fighter Wing. Seymour Johnson received the Commander in Chief's Installation Excellence Award—Air Force for 2001, the highest award given to a military base" (Downtown Goldsboro Development Corporation).

The base has the largest inventory of F-15Es in the world. On display at the base are both F-15E Strike Eagle fighter jets and KC-135 Stratotankers (North Carolina Department of Commerce).

To attest to the continued importance of the Seymour Johnson Air Force Base and particularly one of the units of the North Carolina base, the Doolittle Award recognized the 4th Fighter Wing. This prestigious award came in 2011 (Air Force Historical Foundation).

The base continues to serve the community. It offers—among other services—access to radiology, physical therapy, and even an anticoagulation clinic. To indicate the congenial relationship between the base and the city of Goldsboro, a model of air force pilot wings rests prominently above the city hall in Goldsboro (U.S. Department of Veterans Affairs, "Goldsboro").

World War II Contributions of the Western Coastal Plain of the North Carolina Coastal Region: Pitt County and Its Contributions to World War II: Greenville Airport, an Outlying Field of the Cherry Point Marine Air Station

Pitt County and the Pitt-Greenville Airport have a long history. The name Pitt dates from 1760; the importance of the county and the airport persist.

The Establishment of Pitt County, North Carolina. Pitt County is a county in North Carolina with an area of 655 square miles. Its land in the North Carolina Coastal Region is ideal for agriculture. Although Pitt County is in the Coastal Region, the county and its county seat are 90 miles from the closest beach: Atlantic Beach, North Carolina (Pitt County Government).

Pitt County indicates that the United States Census reports the total population of the county to be 172,554. The population density of Pitt County is about 258 people per square mile. The largest city in the Pitt County is Greenville, with a population of 86,017 (Pitt County Government).

The area that is now Pitt County was originally a part of Beaufort County, a large county in North Carolina. In 1760, Beaufort County split into five counties—one of which was Pitt County.

Pitt County is in the Western Coastal Plain—as opposed to the Tidewater Subregion—of the Coastal Region. The counties adjacent to Pitt County (2013) include Martin County, Beaufort County, Craven County, Lenoir County, Greene County, Wilson County, and Edgecombe County. Pitt County currently operates under a county-manager type of government (Pitt County Government).

Pitt County—like Pittsburgh, Pennsylvania, and several other places in the United States and Canada—took its name from the English statesman William Pitt (1708–1778), Earl of Chatham. William Pitt was born in London, England, and studied at Oxford University.

Pitt served as British secretary of state in the late 1750s. Though Pitt never came to America, his advocacy of freedom brought him popularity in North Carolina and the new country (Shmoop).

Congress established the Works Progress Administration (WPA) in April of 1935. The program—rather than distributing a "dole"—paid for work rendered. Some of the construction work of the WPA included the building of baseball fields, schools, public buildings, and the Greenville Airport in North Carolina (Davis 2003, 131).

The Establishment of the Greenville Airport. In 1940 the WPA built the Greenville Airport in North Carolina on land that the city of Greenville and Pitt County owned jointly. Through April 30, 1942, a program for training civil pilots operated from the airport. On May 1, 1942, the United States Navy leased the field; the new function of the airport was to serve as an outlying field for the Marine Corps Air Station at Cherry Point.

According to the Civil Aeronautics Administration, the Greenville Airport remained underutilized in the early 1940s. On November 30, 1942, however, the Civil Aeronautics Administration, which was responsible for air traffic control, safety programs, and airway development, announced an upgrade to the underutilized field.

After the upgrade, the first flying squadrons from the Marine Corps reported to the field. The first two squadrons to arrive were the VMSB-343 and the VMSB-344. They arrived in January of 1944 (Living New Deal).

Marine Scout Bombing Squadron 343 received activation at Marine Corps Auxiliary Landing Field Atlantic, North Carolina, on August 1, 1943. Its transfer to Marine Corps Outlying Field Greenville came on December 1943; VMSB-343 trained there until July 15, 1944, before assignment to overseas duty. The squadron left from Marine Corps Air Station Miramar on August 31, 1944, for Marine Corps Air Station Ewa, Hawaii.

The VMSB 343 made the 1,100-mile flight to Midway Atoll on October 27; it conducted patrols as part of the Hawaiian Sea Frontier. From April 1945 until the end of the war, the squadron operated off Sand Island. The squadron had seen limited combat action because of its assignment: flying anti-submarine patrols from Midway Atoll. The squadron did take part in the occupation of Northern China after the war; it received decommissioning on June 10, 1946 (Wikipedia, "User:Looper5920/Sandbox").

The Greenville Airport is still in operation. It does, however, carry a different name since it reverted back to the city and county. It is—in 2013—the Pitt-Greenville Airport.

The Pitt-Greenville Airport in the 21st Century. The former Greenville Airport is outside the city of Greenville, North Carolina. The airport covers 872 acres and serves the area around Pitt County and Greenville, North Carolina (Wikipedia, "Pitt-Greenville Airport").

Mainly used for general aviation and charters, the Pitt-Greenville Airport (PGV Airport) has three runways; it had 123,700 passengers in 2012. The PGV Airport has one commercial airline: U.S. Airways Express; U.S. Airways Express offers daily flights to Charlotte, North Carolina (iFly.com).

Chapter 9

The Southern Tidewater Subregion of the Coastal Region

An examination of the World War II military sites in the Western Coastal Plain of the North Carolina Coastal Region was the main topic of Chapter Eight. The Western Coastal Plain—a part of the Coastal Region—extends from the eastern boundary of the Piedmont Region to the western boundary of the Tidewater Subregion.

The Tidewater Subregion extends from the eastern boundary of the Western Coastal Plain as far east as the Atlantic Ocean. The physical boundary of the Tidewater Subregion is as far west "as the effects of the ocean tide are visible" (Lefler and Newsome 1959, 55).

Chapter 9 explores the vital military sites in the Southern Tidewater Subregion of the Coastal Region of North Carolina. The Tidewater Subregion provided more than 20 important military sites during World War II. This consideration of each military site in the Tidewater Subregion progresses geographically from south to north. Brunswick County, Fort Caswell, Southport, and the Southport Naval Station are southernmost and are first for examination.

World War II Contributions of the Southern Tidewater Subregion of the North Carolina Coastal Region: Fort Caswell (Brunswick County)

The congressional authorization for the construction of a fort on Oak Island dates from 1825. Part of the original fort remains today on the site.

The Early History of Fort Caswell. The purpose of the Brunswick County fortification on the eastern tip of Oak Island at that time was for defense; the locale around Oak Island, Bald Head Island (then Smith Island), and Southport (then Smithville) was susceptible to attack—especially from pirates who took refuge in the area.

9. The Southern Tidewater Subregion of the Coastal Region

In 1825 Fort Caswell covered 2,800 acres at the eastern tip of Oak Island; it is at the mouth of the Cape Fear River. To the north of Fort Caswell is the Elizabeth River; to the south is the Atlantic Ocean (Oak Island Accommodations).

The stone and earthworks fort was ten years (1826–1836) in the making. It long had the reputation of being one of the strongest forts in the world and one of only three masonry forts in North Carolina. Most of the main fort still stands today (*Southport Times*).

The original shape of the fort was pentagonal. Building materials included earthen mounds, brick, and masonry. A citadel was conspicuous on the premises (Oak Island Accommodations).

In 1833 the fort—even before its completion—took its name from Richard Caswell (1729–1789), the first and the fifth North Carolina governor (1776–1780; 1785–1787).

Military Uses of Fort Caswell. Fort Caswell served the nation and the world during many conflicts. It was in use by the military during the Civil War, the Spanish-American War (April 21, 1898–December 10, 1898), and World War I (1914–1918). During the Haitian War (1915–1934), the Caswell facilities housed troops as needed and personnel employed in the local area (*Southport Times*).

Heavy damage to Fort Caswell occurred in January of 1865. When the Fort Caswell soldiers had to abandon the facility, they themselves ignited the powder magazine that contained all the remaining gun powder. This action caused much destruction to the fort, the earth mound fortifications, and the citadel.

With federal appropriations in April 1896, some repair work on Fort Caswell began. The completion of the repairs, however, dates from 1916.

Fort Caswell served as the Cape Fear Coastal Defense Headquarters; three companies of coast artillery corps defended it. Fort Caswell, then, remained one of the most important east coast military posts (Oak Island Accommodations).

The United States government reacquired Fort Caswell in 1941, at the beginning of World War II; Fort Caswell had been in military disuse. Fort Caswell had two important tasks during the conflict. It served as an army base for housing and training troops. With the danger of German U-boats off the Carolina coast, Fort Caswell also had the important duty of serving as a lookout post.

Fort Caswell After World War II. After the end of World War II (1946), the federal government declared that Fort Caswell was war surplus and designated for disposal. The Baptist State Convention of North Carolina in 1949 purchased the 250 acres from the federal government for $86,000.

The Fort Caswell facility included 77 buildings. Located at the mouth of the Cape Fear River, the Elizabeth River to the north, and the Atlantic Ocean to the south, Fort Caswell seemed a perfect area—to the Baptist Convention—for peace and relaxation. The North Carolina Convention rented the facilities for a religious retreat and convention center. It is still available for this use. Tourists cannot, however, enter the private property (*Southport Times*).

The property briefly had another use for a short period of time during the 1990s. Fort Caswell housed troops and some personnel employed near its facilities during the Persian Gulf War (August 2, 1990–November 2, 1995). One hundred sixty-five workers who worked at a nearby ocean terminal and loaded ships going to the Persian Gulf occupied some of the housing. After the war, Fort Caswell again housed troops and personnel as they unloaded ships (Oak Island Accommodations).

World War II Contributions of the Southern Tidewater Subregion of the North Carolina Coastal Region: Brunswick County, Southport, and the Southport Naval Station

The Southport Naval Station (in Brunswick County) was one of the southernmost World War II military sites in the Tidewater Subregion of North Carolina's Coastal Region. Southport Naval Station was slightly north of the southernmost Tidewater military site: Fort Caswell.

Strategic Location of Brunswick County and Southport. Brunswick County is a North Carolina county near the mouth of the Cape Fear River. The county is part of the Wilmington Metropolitan Statistical, which had a population of 2,351, according to the 2000 census.

As early as the early 1940s, the military recognized both the strategic location of the town of Southport and its possibilities for contributing to national security. The United States Navy designated Southport as a Naval Section Base in 1941 (Wikipedia, "Southport, North Carolina").

9. The Southern Tidewater Subregion of the Coastal Region

Ferries in the Southport Area. Ferries have long been vital to visitors to and residents of Eastern North Carolina. In the mid–1920s, Captain J. B. "Toby" Tillett instituted convoy service across the Oregon Inlet. Barges and tugboats were his transport vessels.

Currently, the Ferry Division of the North Carolina Department of Transportation (DOT) uses 7 routes, 21 ferryboats, and 400 employees. A full-service shipyard, a dredge, tugboats, barges, and support vessels are vital to the division.

The figures indicate the importance of the Ferry Division of the North Carolina DOT. Ferries convey more than 1.1 million vehicles and more than 2.5 million passengers across five North Carolina bodies of water each year. These five bodies of water are the Currituck Sound, the Pamlico Sound, the Cape Fear River, the Neuse River, and the Pamlico River (NCDOT).

The Neuse River is the widest river in the United States by the time it reaches the Pamlico Sound. Even among North Carolinians this fact is not common knowledge.

Southport Naval Station. At the Southport Naval Station, assignees had certain responsibilities during World War II. The Southport Station was responsible for conducting ship repairs—as necessary—for the United States Navy, coordinating sailing schedules, and defending the coastal area—especially against submarine attack. By the end of the war, however, the Southport Naval Station was no longer an active military installation in North Carolina (North Carolina Museum of History, "NC at Home and Battle").

The Sinking of the SS John D. Gill (WR-4), the Vessel Sunk Closest to Southport. Built in 1941, the SS *John D. Gill* (WR-4) was an 11,641-ton steam tanker. The *Gill* was capable of transporting 142,000 barrels of oil in a single load; its route was between the Texas oil fields and the east coast of the United States. Its cargo of crude oil was precious, and the mission of Captain Allen D. Tucker was vital to the war effort.

On March 12, 1942, Captain Tucker was taking the SS *John D. Gill* to the Atlantic Refinery Company's Philadelphia plant. This was the second trip of the *Gill* and Captain Tucker through Torpedo Alley, which was off the east coast of the United States.

The German *U-158*, which would become the fifth most successful U-boat in history, had sunk a ship just two days before and had already sunk a total of four. The *U-158*, which was captained by Erwin Rostin, was sailing undetected near the SS *John D. Gill*.

At 10:10 p.m. a torpedo from the *U-158* struck the no. 7 tank on the starboard side of the *Gill*. With its high gasoline content, the Texas crude oil spewed from the gapping hole. When a carbide flare self-ignited, the sea became a vat of burning crude oil. The men struggled to escape the sinking SS *John D. Gill* but found themselves in burning oil.

Though severely burned himself, Quartermaster Edward F. Chaney, Jr., launched a life raft. By swimming underneath it, he was able to push it beyond the burning oil for his comrades; he called out to the others and was able to pull some of his severely injured shipmates to the raft.

A United States Coast Guard cutter (the USGC-186) stationed at Southport picked up some of the survivors at 7:05 a.m. Out of the 49 men aboard the SS *John D. Gill*, only 26 would survive. The SS *John D. Gill* sank 24 miles off the coast of North Carolina at 9:00 a.m.

Edwin F. Cheney, Jr., Able Seaman on the SS* John D. Gill*, and the Recipient of the Merchant Marine Distinguished Service Medal. For his heroic actions on March 12, 1942, Edwin F. Cheney, Jr., Able Seaman on the SS *John D. Gill*, received the Merchant Marine Distinguished Service Medal for his valor. President Roosevelt awarded this medal to Cheney. Cheney's award was the first earned Merchant Marine Distinguished Service Medal in World War II. The citation reads:

> For heroism above and beyond the call of duty during enemy attack when he released and launched a life-raft from a sinking and burning ship and maneuvered it through a pool of burning oil to clear water by swimming under water, coming up only to breathe. Although he had incurred severe burns about the face and arms in this action, he then guided four of his shipmates to the raft, and swam to and rescued two others who were injured and unable to help themselves. His extraordinary courage and disregard of his own safety in thus rescuing his shipmates will be an enduring inspiration to seamen of the United States Merchant Marine everywhere [Tilley].

***Dosher Memorial Hospital in Southport and the Men on the SS* John D. Gill.** Josephine Hickman, a volunteer Red Cross nurse at Dosher Memorial Hospital, spoke of the survivors from the SS *John D. Gill*: "We didn't think even half of them hardly could live they were so burned, almost to a crisp, and covered with oil. Some of them were burned so bad that ... the bandages were all over their heads. Only their mouths were open. You just fed them in between the bandages" (World War II U.S. Navy Armed Guard).

Only five trained nurses were on the staff when the men arrived at Dosher; most of those caretakers on duty were Red Cross volunteers. The staff worked for 20 straight hours to care for the men.

Joseph S. Laughlin was 15 years old at the time. His father was manager of the hospital. Joseph remembered carrying the dead. "They were burned so bad their flesh would come off in your hands," he indicated in an interview (World War II U.S. Navy Armed Guard).

Catalino Tingzon. The young mess boy Catalino Tingzon died in the attack on the SS *John D. Gill.* When Southport residents were unable to contact Tingzon's relatives in the Philippines, the town buried him in the Northwood Cemetery (World War II U.S. Navy Armed Guard).

On March 12, 1994, the Southport Historical Society donated and dedicated a memorial marker to Catalino Tingzon and to those on the SS *John D. Gill,* one of more than 170 ships sunk off the eastern coast of the United States. The ancient granite stone sits in a concrete base in Waterfront Park; the back of the stone faces the Cape Fear River.

The sides of the granite are roughly cut; both the back and the front faces of the marker are smooth and inscribed. The inscription reads:

> Dedicated to the memory of Catalino Tingzon interred in Northwood Cemetery and all Merchant Marine Seamen and U.S. Navy Armed Guard on the tanker SS *John D. Gill* torpedoed and sunk off Cape Fear by the German submarine *U-158* [on] March 12, 1942. [T]he citizens of Southport cared for the survivors and mourned for those who lost their lives. Erected March 12, 1994[,] by the Southport Historical Society [Documenting the American South].

Larry Maisel of the museum at Fort Johnston spoke about the warfare off the coast at Southport, North Carolina: "Few people, not from here, realize that Southport had a ringside seat to the U-boat war. In 1942, seeing burning ships from the waterfront was common. *U-158,* which sank the tanker *John D. Gill* off our coast in 1942 was the best known. There were numerous ships sunk by torpedoes, but the *Gill* was the closest to Southport. It's the one about which the monument on the waterfront (donated by the Historical Society a few years ago) was erected" (Maisel 2013).

On June 30, 1942, the *U-158*—the German submarine that sank the SS *John D. Gill*—was itself sunk west of Bermuda. The *U-158* had no survivors (World War II U.S. Navy Armed Guard).

Dr. Margaret D. Craighill. Born in Southport, North Carolina, in 1898, Dr. Margaret D. Craighill became the first woman physician to become a commissioned officer in the United States Army. She had all the credentials for the appointment.

Craighill had graduated Phi Beta Kappa from the University of Wisconsin (1921); in 1922 she had earned the MS degree. After serving briefly as a physiologist in the chemical warfare department at the United States Army's Edgewood Arsenal in Maryland, Craighill enrolled in the Johns Hopkins University School of Medicine. After completing her studies in medicine in 1924, she served in postgraduate positions in gynecology, surgery, and pathology at both Yale Medical School and the Johns Hopkins Hospital.

Craighill maintained (1928–1937) an obstetrics and gynecology practice in Greenwich, Connecticut, while serving at Greenwich Hospital as an assistant surgeon and attending gynecologist. Simultaneously, Craighill maintained a position as private assistant to Dr. J. A. McCreery, a general surgeon at New York's Bellevue Hospital.

After beginning an association with the Woman's Medical College of Pennsylvania in Philadelphia (1940), she earned the appointment to acting dean. Craighill sought to enhance the medical curriculum and to improve faculty-student relationships, the teaching hospital, and the curriculum. Craighill, however, was willing to forgo these responsibilities to pursue active military service after the beginning of World War II.

The Sparkman-Johnson Bill was the one that would permit women in the army and navy Medical Corps. On April 16, 1943, President Franklin Delano Roosevelt—commander in chief of the armed forces—signed the Sparkman-Johnson Bill into law.

Craighill received her commission one month later; she was the first woman doctor to receive one. Craighill's assignment included serving as a liaison with the Women's Army Corps (WACS). "In the course of her duties she traveled 56,000 miles, visiting war zones in England, France, Italy, the African Gold Coast, Egypt, Iran, India, China, New Guinea, and the Philippines. Craighill challenged the persistent notion that American women were unsuited to a military role" (U.S. National Library of Medicine).

One of the difficult parts of the new position was ensuring the confidentiality of the medical records of a service woman. A woman's medical reports typically went to the unit commander, who was usually male.

Major Craighill noted: "Privacy in regard to medical conditions is deplorably lacking in Army hospitals, as was pointed out in War Department Circular 310: *Maintenance of Ethical Standards by Non-Professional Personnel.* The practice of passing the records through numerous hands ... quickly makes a diagnosis common knowledge and a topic of conversation. This is particularly embarrassing to women ... and leads to hesitation about seeking medical advice" (U.S. Army Medical Department).

9. The Southern Tidewater Subregion of the Coastal Region

Craighill served admirably. In recognition of her exemplary wartime service, Craighill received promotion to the rank of lieutenant colonel and earned the Legion of Merit Award.

When the war ended in 1945, Craighill became a consultant on women veterans' medical care, the first position of its kind within the Veterans Administration.

After her April 8, 1946, discharge from the United States Army after World War II, Craighill returned to the Women's Medical College in Philadelphia. In September of the same year, she went to Topeka, Kansas, to begin filling a surgical position at the Winter Veterans Hospital.

Margaret D. Craighill, 1946 (National Library of Medicine).

Craighill earned a new title and new responsibilities. She became the chief consultant for medical care of women veterans. With nine other chiefs of branch sections around the states, Craighill was responsible for overseeing the medical care of women veterans.

In 1946 Margaret Craighill tapped into her benefits under the GI Bill. She was enrolled in the first class of the Menninger Foundation School of Psychiatry in Topeka, Kansas, and was able to extend her medical education even further (Wikipedia, "Margaret D. Craighill").

Later, she re-established her private practice in Connecticut, and was named chief psychiatrist in residence at the Connecticut College for Women in New London. Craighill died in 1977 at the age of 78 in Southbury, Connecticut (U.S. National Library of Medicine).

World War II Contributions of the Southern Tidewater Subregion of the North Carolina Coastal Region: Fort Fisher and Kure Beach (New Hanover County)

Fort Fisher in North Carolina was in the Southern Tidewater area of the Coastal Region. Located at the tip of Pleasure Island and between the Cape Fear River on the west and the Atlantic Ocean on the east, Fort Fisher was especially important in the Civil War and in World War II.

Fishing Pier, Kures Beach, N. C.

This postcard shows Kure Beach and the fishing pier near Fort Fisher. The August 4, 1945, message from a husband and wife to a couple in Charlotte reads: "The perverbial [sic] 'Having a good time. Wish you were here.' It's wonderful about the news. No more war during my lifetime." Although the war in Asia and in Europe had not ended and no peace treaties had been signed, the writer of the postcard seemed to anticipate a coming peace (E. C. Moore and Company, Wilmington, North Carolina).

Fort Fisher, Kure Beach, the Kure Beach Pier, and the Fort Fisher State Recreation Area. The location of Fort Fisher to Kure's Beach was a strategic one. The name Kure's Beach later became Kure Beach, mainly during World War II and in the postwar era. To avoid confusion, this document uses henceforth the current name of Kure Beach.

The proximity of Fort Fisher to Kure Beach and to the coastline made patrolling the coastal area easier for the military. This accessibility was particularly important during World War II, when U-boats posed a constant threat.

A dominant feature in the picture on the postcard showing Kure Beach (called "Kures Beach" on the card) is the fishing pier. Kure Beach Pier (built in 1923) is the oldest fishing pier on the Atlantic Coast. It is only 15 miles south of Wilmington.

Many World War II service members—especially those at Fort Fisher— were able to visit the beach and the pier for recreation when they were off duty: "Many of the post's trainees were from interior regions of the United States, and had never before seen a beach—let alone tried to live near one.

9. The Southern Tidewater Subregion of the Coastal Region 109

The adjustment was difficult, and more than a few soldiers balked at the notion of dining on fried clams and oysters. To acclimate the men to their new environment, the post offered swimming lessons, advice on how to avoid sunburn, and beach safety instructions" (North Carolina Historic Sites).

Built originally by L. C. Kure on property that he bought from the Town of Kure Beach at the turn of the century, the pier fulfilled Kure's dream of providing entertainment for local residents. The cottages, pavilions, bars, and bathhouses he tried all failed, but his pier idea succeeded.

In 1923 L. C. Kure built the 120' × 22' pier on pine pilings. Within a year, however, the pier was no longer there—perhaps partly because of sea worms or marine borers.

In 1924, L. C. Kure rebuilt the pier; its new dimensions were 240' × 32'. For the pilings, he poured reinforced concrete, a new process at the time. While L. C. Kure still owned the pier, these pilings withstood six hurricanes—the worst of which was the Great Atlantic Hurricane of 1944 during World War II.

L. C. Kure sold the pier to his son-in-law Bill Robertson in 1952. Hurricanes—two in 1954, two in 1955, one in 1958 and another in 1960—continued to plague the coast and the coastal pier construction. In fact, Hurricane Hazel (October 15, 1954) destroyed Robertson's entire Kure Beach Pier. Surprisingly, construction crews found that some of the 1924 pilings L. C. Kure had placed were still intact.

There were no hurricanes on Kure Beach from 1962 to 1984. Mike Robertson purchased the pier from his father Bill Robertson in September of 1984 after Hurricane Diana destroyed about half the length of the pier. Robertson rebuilt the pier to 711 feet from the high tide line.

In 1996 Hurricane Bertha destroyed the pier. Mike Robertson rebuilt the pier again—and continues to keep the pier in repair.

Fort Fisher military personnel are not generally present today to enjoy the pier, but it is still there. Pier owner Mike Robertson invites one and all to visit the pier—now standing at an elevation of 26 feet above sea level. He reminds visitors that hurricanes give those at the beach "the most stress and press," but "364 days a year this is the best place in the country to live, raise kids, and enjoy God's second biggest pond" (Robertson).

Today the Fort Fisher State Recreation Area—near the original Fort Fisher—is a North Carolina State Park for residents of and visitors to New Hanover County, North Carolina. This recreation area and the Fort Fisher Museum help to preserve and disseminate the history of the area; their location is about two miles south of Kure Beach on the ocean. Visitors today can take the Fort Fisher Ferry from Southport and cross the Cape Fear River; the 35-minute cruise is "the best $5 scenic cruise you've ever seen" (Pleasure Island).

Initial Preparations at Fort Fisher for World War II. Just as the Civil War impacted Fort Fisher, World War II also would affect the area. The New Hanover County war efforts—including enhancing defense, building ships, improving the chemical and petroleum businesses—expanded in the early 1940s. Some of the initial construction work at or near Fort Fisher included concrete coastal reinforcements.

The population of New Hanover County soon exploded—especially around the Fort Fisher and the Wilmington areas—with the military preparations. Military personnel arrived soon, and the traffic increased proportionately (Wikipedia, "Fort Fisher State Recreation Area").

Fort Fisher Specifications in World War II. During World War II, the Fort Fisher site was 50 miles from Camp Davis, which was northeast of Wilmington and in the Holly Ridge area. Fort Fisher, however, served well as a remote firing range for Camp Davis. Fort Fisher personnel were able to patrol the coastline—particularly along Kure Beach—and watch for U-boats.

Fort Fisher was soon well-equipped and self-contained. Bunkers protected the necessary supplies and ammunition, even at the cost of destroying in their construction a four-gun bastion from the Civil War. The specifications for Fort Fisher included "48 frame buildings, 316 tent frames, showers and latrines, mess halls, warehouses, radio and meteorological stations, a post exchange, photo lab, recreation hall, outdoor theater, guardhouse, infirmary, and an administration building. In addition to these facilities, the site featured a 10,000-gallon water storage tank, a motor pool, a large parade ground, and three steel observation towers along the beach.... New firing installations ... included ... batteries of 40-millimeter automatic cannons and 50-caliber machine guns" (North Carolina Historic Sites).

By 1944, when the anti-aircraft training at Fort Fisher had ended, the facility had added a cafeteria that seated 80, a hospital with 350 beds, a dental facility, and an area covering several hundred acres. The Army Service Forces (ASF), operating through the Fourth Service Command, maintained Fort Fisher. Stationed at Fisher were the needed personnel and equipment (North Carolina Historic Sites).

When World War II was at its peak, Fort Fisher had automatic cannons, machine guns and anti-aircraft training facilities. One of the remaining bunkers is still available for view behind the North Carolina Aquarium at Fort

9. The Southern Tidewater Subregion of the Coastal Region 111

Fisher. The NC Military History Museum at Fort Fisher houses military artifacts, including some from World War II (Kure Beach).

The Early Airstrip at Fort Fisher. In addition to the other improvements at Fort Fisher, observers noted the creation of a large runway. This construction "destroyed a sizable portion of the once-formidable 'land front' of the 80-year-old bastion. In these unstable times, national defense took precedence over historic preservation. Nevertheless, most of the new trainees were aware of the area's significance, and Camp Davis's post literature highlighted Fisher's historic past (North Carolina Historic Sites).

The building near Fort Fisher of a grass landing strip was an important part of the work; this landing area enabled the resupplying of aircraft patrolling the coast. Today the Fort Fisher Visitor Center occupies the middle of the original landing area; the now-paved parking lot for the Visitor Center was originally the north end of the grass landing strip (Wikipedia, "Fort Fisher State Recreation Area").

Training at Fort Fisher. The first World War II military training at Fort Fisher began in October of 1941. Enlisted personnel received versatility training, studied anti-tank warfare, and practiced offensive techniques against armored vehicles of modern warfare. Fort Fisher was an essential area for anti-aircraft trainees; with this increased emphasis on anti-aircraft training, the fort found it necessary to relinquish its balloon barrage school to a post in Tennessee.

Anti-aircraft gunners assigned to Fort Fisher received most of their instruction at an isolated anti-mechanized target range (constructed in the summer of 1942) on Federal Point: "It was 'a forlorn spit of sand and scrub growth pinched between the Atlantic Ocean and the Cape Fear River,' asserted a member of the 558th AAA Battalion, 'a quagmire of sand, sand, and more sand. It was strictly a no-nonsense place designed to put grit and fire in the bowels and brains of its trainees'" (North Carolina Historic Sites).

The training schedule that Fort Fisher imposed on its trainees was rigid: six days a week. During the daylight hours one could see from the ground target sleeves on long cables being towed by planes over coastal North Carolina. At night one could observe firing aided by searchlights and could see the tracers arching the dark sky.

Cpl. Theodore "Ted" Litwin of the 445th AAA Battalion reported that by the time the Fort Fisher range closed (1944) "at least 43 different anti-aircraft battalions, coast artillery regiments, and engineer, signal corps, ordnance, and air warning units had trained [there]" (North Carolina Historic Sites).

The discipline, the mosquitoes, and the sand of Fort Fisher remained unchanged since the time the fort was in use during the Civil War era.

World War II Contributions of the Southern Tidewater Subregion of the North Carolina Coastal Region: Ethyl-Dow Corporation, Kure Beach, and the German Attack on the North Carolina Coast (New Hanover County)

In June of 1930 the Ethyl-Dow Corporation sent several of its employees to the East Coast of the United States to determine a suitable location for a new Dow Chemical Plant. The purpose of the new seaside facility would be to extract bromine from seawater.

The Selection of Kure Beach for the Dow and Ethyl Gasoline Plant. Kure Beach seemed to be the ideal site for the business. This North Carolina site provided an area that was not congested, that was somewhat private, and—of course—that had plenty of saltwater. By 1933 the plant was complete, and Kure Beach hosted the Dow and Ethyl Gasoline Company on the Cape Fear Peninsula.

The Purpose of the Ethyl-Dow Plant on Kure Beach. The new Ethyl-Dow Plant could remove ethylene dibromine from the bromine extracted from the seawater. Ethylene dibromine (EDB), a derivative of bromine, was a necessary ingredient to achieve the 100-octane gasoline necessary for proper combustion in the engines of planes. EDB helped to keep both airplane and vehicle engines running smoothly.

Dow projected in 1933 that it could produce 6 million pounds of EDB each year and that this production would be adequate for several years to come. Two years later the North Carolina plant capacity had already reached 20 million pounds. By 1938 the Kure Beach location was supplying 30 million pounds of EDB per year (Trespass Against Us).

The Kure Beach location of the Ethyl-Dow Corporation was important. The plant was the only one on the East Coast that extracted bromine and ethylene dibromine (EDB) from seawater for aviation fuel (North Carolina Historic Sites).

During the early days of World War II, lead was a gasoline additive for enhancing the performance of petrol—especially aviation fuel. Leaded gas, however, had negative effects on engines; the lead often shortened engine life by blocking the flow of the fuel and clogging the engine. The ethylene dibromine helped to disperse the lead from the engine through the tailpipe.

The Kure Beach Ethyl-Dow Plant became the first company in the world to use a chemical reaction to draw an element (bromine) from compounds contained in seawater. The plant operated between 1933 and 1946.

Before the closure of the Kure plant in 1946, 1,500 people had found employment at the Kure Beach location. Other companies throughout the world sought—often unsuccessfully—to replicate its bromine-extraction process (New Hanover County).

The German Attack on the Ethyl-Dow Plant on Kure Beach. Osborne (2007) reports that on July 25, 1943, a German U-boat fired five shots at the Ethyl-Dow Plant on Kure Beach. All five shots, however, were inaccurate and landed in the Cape Fear River.

Osborne acknowledges, however, that other accounts set the date of the attack as July 15, not July 25. He writes: "It is also told that the German submarine was sunk the next day by U.S. aircraft. Postwar German documents, however, fail to record this attack, and there are no records of a German submarines [sic] having been sunk on July 26, 1943 (or July 16, 1943) along the U.S. east coast" (182).

According to another source (North Carolina Historic Sites), "at least 3 shots" were fired "on July 15, 1943. Carlton Sprague, a platoon commander in C Battery, 558th AAA Battalion, remembered that while his unit was stationed at Fort Fisher, a German submarine surfaced under cover of darkness and lobbed five shells at the Ethyl-Dow chemical plant.... All of the enemy shells overshot their mark and plunged into the Cape Fear River. Apparently, a news blackout followed, and over the years the story has drifted into legend."

Ralph Terrell Horton, Sr., was an employee of Ethyl-Dow at the time of the 1943 attack by the German submarine. Later the chair of the New Hanover County Commissioners, Horton spoke often with his family about the attack on the plant during his employment there.

After World War II, Horton established the Horton Iron and Metal Company. The company functioned as a scrap iron and metal recycling company. Horton remembered his company cutting up 61 of the Liberty Ships in line for disposal after the war.

Horton Iron and Metal Company is still in existence. The manager today is Ralph Terrell "Terry" Horton, Jr. Terry is the son of the original owner and remembers his father talking about the war and about employment at the Ethyl-Dow Company (Horton, interview by the author, November 27, 2013).

United States Coast Guard (Mounted) Beach Patrol. Beginning in September of 1942, the United States Coast Guard received authorization to use horses for beach patrol. The horses came from the United States Army; the uniforms for the Mounted Beach Patrol came from the Coast Guard; the equipment and riding gear were from the Army Remount. By 1943 the Coast Guard had 3,222 assigned animals (U.S. Coast Guard, "U.S. Coast Guard Beach Patrol").

William "Billy" H. Sutton: Enlistee in the U.S. Coast Guard (Mounted) Beach Patrol. On June 22, 1943, William "Billy" H. Sutton of Wilmington enlisted in the Coast Guard one day before his eighteenth birthday, which was on June 23, 1943. His assignment was to the U.S. Coast Guard (Mounted) Beach Patrol. Before his discharge in 1945, Billy Sutton recalls serving as tower watchman during the daytime and riding horseback with a partner at night.

Sutton remembers joining a diverse group of men in the Mounted Beach Patrol of the Coast Guard. He spent much of his time at Gause Landing on Ocean Isle, which had a building for housing, a small recreation hall, and a stable.

With his prior experience with horses, Sutton was perfect for the Beach Patrol assignment. He served alongside jockeys, horse trainers, and the former rodeo rider Royce Cates, who cared for the horses; Sutton recalls that the horses were still in excellent condition after the war and that the Army Remount sold the horses at public auction in a park in Wilmington.

Much of Sutton's basic training was at Hilton Head: "Fearful of what each day and night might bring, he and others rode up and down long, isolated stretches of

This photograph shows eighteen-year-old William "Billy" H. Sutton in uniform. Sutton remembers well his night patrols on Kure Beach. His responsibility was to search for "saboteurs, surveyors, and submarines" (courtesy William H. Sutton).

beach—keenly aware of Wilmington's vulnerability with its shipyard, Ethyl Dow plant and Bluethenthal Field—looking for German submarines and saboteurs. Meanwhile, supplies and wreckage washed ashore, fishermen picked up survivors and Billy and others saw the glow from burning ships offshore (UNC-TV).

Sutton credits radar for removing the necessity for the night patrols and tower watches. The system—although new at the time—was able to detect a periscope 10 miles away.

After his discharge, Sutton was able to use his GI benefits to advantage. He is a graduate of the University of North Carolina with a major in commerce (Sutton, interview by author, November 12, 2013).

The Ethyl-Dow Company on Kure Beach Today. The closure of the Ethyl-Dow plant on Kure Beach was primarily a result of the introduction of gasoline without lead. Bromine production became less profitable after its need diminished with the advent of unleaded gas (New Hanover County).

Some remains of the Ethyl-Dow chemical plant at Kure Beach are still evident. The ruins, however, are within the "buffer zone" that the United States Army owns; this area is off-limits to the public (Wikimapia, "Ruins of the Ethyl-Dow Chemical Plant"). Osborne (2007, 182) reminds those interested in viewing the former Kure Beach site of the Ethyl-Dow Corporation that the grounds are not readily available for visitors. After the closure of the Ethyl-Dow Corporation, the area became a part of the buffer zone for a post-war facility: Sunny Point Military Ocean Terminal.

World War II Contributions of the Southern Tidewater Subregion of the North Carolina Coastal Region: Wilmington

The Tidewater Region of North Carolina provided more than 20 important military sites during World War II. Both New Hanover County—the second smallest county in North Carolina—and Wilmington are in the Southern Tidewater Subregion of the North Carolina Coastal Region; New Hanover County and Wilmington are north of Brunswick County and Southport.

New Hanover County covers only 199 square miles. Although it is small in size, New Hanover County made great contributions to World War II and the war effort. Wilmington—the main city of the county—did its part also.

Wilmington and the North Carolina Shipbuilding Company in World War II. The city of Wilmington occupies most of the 199 square miles of New Hanover County. The city has undergone many changes during the 20th century.

The city housed a flourishing shipbuilding industry during World War I. Cotton exports from the Wilmington area thrived during the war period.

The city suffered during the Great Depression. A rebirth of the World War I shipbuilding industry accompanied World War II. The construction of the "brand-new" North Carolina Shipbuilding Company for World War II dated from 1941. The plant operated between 1941 and 1946 and "built 243 Liberty and C-2 hulls ... for [the] Navy and Maritime Commission" (Stick and Fontenoy, 1032). The North Carolina Shipbuilding Company was the largest employer in the state during World War II. In late 1943 the industry was at its height; it employed 23,000 workers: 20 percent black and 20 percent women.

New Hanover County had a total population of about 43,000 early in the war. At its peak during late 1943, the population was about 100,000 (Wilbur Jones Compositions, LLC).

Wilmington, however, did even more than establish, develop, and support the essential, thriving shipbuilding industry for World War II. In fact, in 2011 Representative Mike McIntyre authored and presented to the United States House of Representatives legislation (HR 2717) to develop through the Department of Veterans Affairs a way to designate each year a city as an American World War II City. The considered cities would, according to the presented legislation, present evidence that each had both supported the war effort and tried to preserve that history (Wilbur Jones Compositions, LLC).

Wilmington had many attributes for naming it as the American World War II City. In addition to sponsoring the North Carolina Shipbuilding Company during the Second World War, the city had in its vicinity many defense industries. One of these prominent industries was Block's Shirt Factory, which produced over one million shirts for the American armed forces.

***Wilmington and the USS* North Carolina.** The USS *North Carolina* is not a ship constructed at the North Carolina Shipbuilding Company in Wilmington, but it is moored in Wilmington, North Carolina. The battleship was important to World War II and remains important to the state.

The USS *North Carolina* was the first battleship constructed in sixteen years; the laying of its keel was on October 1937. Its commissioning dates from April 9, 1941, when it became the first of ten fast battleships to join the Amer-

9. The Southern Tidewater Subregion of the Coastal Region

ican fleet in World War II. The USS *North Carolina* and the USS *Washington* (BB-56) comprised the *North Carolina* Class.

At the time of its commissioning on April 9, 1941, the *North Carolina* had the reputation of being "the world's greatest sea weapon." The *North Carolina* had in 3 turrets 9 16-inch, 45-caliber guns; in 10 twin mounts, she had 20 5-inch, 38-caliber guns. Her crew in wartime could consist of 144 commissioned officers and 2,195 enlisted men—both those in the United States Navy and as many as 100 Marines.

The record of the *North Carolina* during World War II was impeccable. She earned 15 battle stars and participated in every major Pacific naval offensive. When the fast battleship *North Carolina* protected the carrier *Enterprise* in August of 1942, the *North Carolina* established the primary role of fast battleships as protectors of aircraft carriers. The *North Carolina* steamed 300,000 miles, destroyed 24 enemy aircraft, sank an enemy troopship, and completed 9 shore bombardments; she even endured the hit by a Japanese torpedo on September 15, 1942. Despite the 6 radio announcements that the *North Carolina* had sunk, she survived World War II with only 67 men wounded and 10 killed in action.

After the decommissioning of the USS *North Carolina* on June 27, 1947, she remained on inactive reserve in Bayonne, New Jersey, for 14 years. In 1958 North Carolina citizens began the successful Save Our Ship (SOS) campaign to save the battleship from the torches and to bring her to North Carolina. The battleship arrived in Wilmington on October 2, 1961. At a dedication ceremony on April 29, 1962, the USS *North Carolina* became the North Carolina memorial to World War II veterans and to the 10,000 who died in service (Battleship *North Carolina*).

Wilmington, the United States Armed Forces, and the United Service Organization Club in Wilmington. Wilmington housed or was in close proximity to all five of the United States Armed Forces: The Bluethenthal Army Air Force Field/Base was in Wilmington. The United States Army was nearby at Camp Davis and Fort Fisher. Anti-submarine warfare (ASW) patrols operated along the Cape Fear River and at Southport. Camp Lejeune of the United States Marine Corps was at Jacksonville; the Air Station operated from New River. Coast Guard bases operated from Wilmington, Southport, and Wrightsville Beach (Wilbur Jones Compositions).

In 1941 the Army Corps of Engineers constructed the Wilmington USO Club (now the Community Arts Center) to serve those in the armed services. The facility is still standing at Second and Orange streets.

U. S. O. Club, Wilmington, N. C.

The Wilmington USO sponsored dances, plays, music programs, art exhibits, socials, and even radio broadcasts. When the Wilmington USO ended full-time operations in 1946, the city purchased the building for daily programs for children and young adults. A 2008 renovation restored the facility to its 1941 appearance (E. C. Moore Company, Wilmington, NC).

The center, currently named the Hannah Block Historic USO Building, accommodates a World War II–era museum. The Hannah Block Building offers arts programs for the community and surrounding counties (City of Wilmington, North Carolina).

Wilmington and Its Three Camps for Prisoners of War. The Wilmington area housed three POW camps from February 1944 to April 1946. The first camp was the one at Shipyard Boulevard and Carolina Beach Road. The camp later moved to Robert Strange Park at Eighth and Ann streets. Bluethenthal Field housed 550 Germans captured (1943) from Afrika Korps in 1943. These prisoners worked on the farms and in the industries. The prisoners attempted no breakouts and caused little difficulty (Wilbur Jones Compositions, LLC).

North Carolina, New Hanover County, and Wilmington Residents: Their Military Service. Thousands of Wilmington-area women and men participated in the armed services along with other North Carolinians. The service details of the New Hanover servicemen included "a Tuskegee Airman, a P-51

Mustang ace; submarine skipper; Navy frogmen and special operations; Marine and Army infantry; Army artillery; physicians and nurses; crewmen on destroyers/carriers/amphibious ships" (Wilbur Jones Compositions, LLC).

More than two hundred men with connections to New Hanover County did not return home after their military service; they earned the Purple Heart. Three of these died at Pearl Harbor.

Two graduates of New Hanover High School earned the Medal of Honor. Charles Murray and William Halyburton—both graduates of New Hanover High School—each received the Medal of Honor; William Halyburton received his award posthumously. Jones indicates that New Hanover High may be the only high school in the nation with more than one Medal of Honor winner.

Two navy pilots from New Hanover County earned the Navy Cross; one of the two, in fact, earned a total of three Navy Crosses. One air force pilot from New Hanover County earned the Distinguished Service Cross for Midway; a New Hanover County man in the United States Army received (posthumously) the Distinguished Service Cross for his actions at Normandy. Residents served well during World War II and earned numerous commendations: Silver Stars, Bronze Stars, Distinguished Flying Crosses, Purple Hearts, and Air Medals (Wilbur Jones Compositions, LLC).

Emphasizing these outstanding accomplishments, however, is not meant to take away from the many others who participated. All who served sacrificed for their country and for the war effort. Those left behind also gave their best.

World War II Contributions of the Southern Tidewater Subregion of the North Carolina Coastal Region: Wilmington and Bluethenthal Air Field

The first airport specifically designed to serve the area around Wilmington began in 1927. The airfield carried the name Bluethenthal Field. The name came from Arthur "Bluey" Bluethenthal, a North Carolina native.

Arthur Bluethenthal. Arthur Bluethenthal was born in Wilmington on November 1, 1891. A student at Princeton, he served as football center from 1910 to 1912. In 1911 and again in 1912, "Bluey" was an All-American. The 186-pound, 5'9' player helped to lead the Tigers to an 8-0-2 season in 1911; the Tigers gave up only 15 points.

After his graduation from Princeton, Bluethenthal accepted the offer to serve as a Princeton line coach. He served next as line coach at the University of North Carolina. Bluethenthal was able to work part time at the coaching jobs while also working as a tobacco broker and for his father's New York dry goods company.

Bluethenthal enlisted in the American Field Service (ambulance) in May 1916. He served with the French 129th Infantry Division at the Battle of Verdun. For his conspicuous bravery in the battle, France awarded him the *Croix de Guerre* with Star (1997 International Jewish Sports Hall of Fame).

Bluethenthal received several transfer duties before joining the French Foreign Legion in the summer of 1917; he received his requested assignment to flight training. His March 1918 assignment was to what the French called the Lafayette Flying Corps: the group of Americans in the French service as pilots.

Sergeant Bluethenthal reported to the Escadrille 227. He was the squadron's only American at the time (1997 International Jewish Sports Hall of Fame).

Bluethenthal was on an artillery observation mission on June 5, 1918, less than three months after entering Escadrille 227. Enemy fire hit the bomber that the 27-year-old was piloting. His location was Maignelay, France, which is about 50 miles north of Paris. The plane crashed, and Arthur Bluethenthal died.

Arthur Bluethenthal was the first North Carolinian to be killed in World War I. After the end of the war, his body was brought home (1921). Bluethenthal lies in Oakdale Cemetery in Wilmington. France posthumously awarded Bluethenthal a second *Croix de Guerre* with Palm and the *Medaille Militaire* (Wikipedia, "Arthur Bluethenthal").

In June of 1918 Captain Hugh Alwyn Inness-Brown published a tribute to Arthur Bluethenthal in the *Paris Herald*. A portion of the memorial reads:

> In the death of Arthur Bluethenthal, killed in an aerial battle some days ago, France and America lost one of their staunchest patriots. To come to death alone, high in the air, with no friend to tell the story of the struggle and to be buried in a lonely spot near the front, unofficially, with little publicity, would have been the fate that Bluethenthal would have desired, could he have chosen. At all times, he shunned being considered a hero [Wikipedia, "Arthur Bluethenthal"].

Bluethenthal Field. In Bluethenthal's honor, his hometown of Wilmington, North Carolina, named its air field Bluethenthal Field. This field, named for the first Wilmingtonian killed in World War I, dates from 1927. Its location was three miles northeast of downtown Wilmington.

In 1940 officials and politicians worked to upgrade and improve Bluethenthal Field. These improvements would prove important in the days to come.

9. The Southern Tidewater Subregion of the Coastal Region

The tarmac paving of Bluethenthal Field, 1940. At the right of the group of unidentified men facing the camera is Addison Hewett, Sr., a New Hanover County commissioner (courtesy Mark Flatman and Ted Hewett, who is the grandson of Addison Hewett, Sr.).

Wilmington Army Air Field. The day after the bombing of Pearl Harbor—December 8, 1941—the United States Army Air Force (USAAF) moved into Bluethenthal Field. The USAAF remained there for the entire duration of World War II. The Third Air Force used the field for antisubmarine patrols.

To ensure that the air field could accommodate the operation of the military aircraft, the USAAF received permission from the government to expand the airfield. The USAAF named the field Wilmington Army Air Field. The construction of three 7,000-foot runways enabled the USAAF to carry out its charge: to defend the area, to carry out air patrols (especially along the coast), to conduct antisubmarine patrols, and to train P-40 and P-47 fighter pilots.

Fort Davis Army Air Field. Planes carrying targets for the anti-aircraft gunners who were training at Fort Davis left from the airfield. The portion of the Wilmington Army Air Field that dispatched these planes and targets received the name Fort Davis Army Air Field. The Fort Davis Army Air Field is not to be confused with Fort Davis, located at Holly Ridge, North Carolina (Osborne 2007, 181).

New Hanover County Airport/New Hanover County International Airport. After the end of World War II, the federal government deeded Wilmington Army Air Field to New Hanover County at no cost. In the 1950s the name of the Wilmington Army Air Field became the New Hanover County Airport. In 1988 the name of the public airport became New Hanover County International Airport.

Wilmington International Airport. The owner in 2013 of the airport continues to be New Hanover County; the Wilmington Airport Authority assists the director in the management of the facility. The name of the public airport is now Wilmington International Airport. The name change came on December 17, 1997, from the New Hanover County Airport Authority.

Technically, the location of the Wilmington International Airport is not in Wilmington itself but in unincorporated Wrightsboro, which is a part of New Hanover County. Wilmington International Airport is halfway between Miami and New York City; this location made it an accessible, desirable entry point to the country. The airport housed over 130 private aircraft in 2011. The terminal has 8 gates; there are 2 runways. New Hanover County owns Wilmington International Airport. Wilmington Airport Authority leases the airport for $1 per year; the lease will not expire until 2019.

There is still some evidence of the runways from the 1940s. The decommissioned runways are no longer in use. One of them ends at the VA Hospital on the campus of the airport. Part of another runway is "grown over" (Ware).

Prisoner of War Camps in Wilmington and at Wilmington Army Air Field (1944–1946). Wilmington was the site of three prisoner-of-war (POW) camps from February 1944 to April 1946. At one time, 550 German prisoners occupied the camps.

The first camp was at the corner of Shipyard Boulevard and Carolina Beach Road. When this location became too small, the camp was relocated to the downtown area; the facility was at Ann Street, which is between 8th and 10th avenues.

The third site was at Bluethenthal Field/Wilmington Army Airfield. These prisoner worked in the mess hall for the officers and kept the grounds of what is now Wilmington International Airport (Wikipedia, "Wilmington, North Carolina").

Wilmington International Airport and the Space Shuttle Program. Interestingly, Wilmington International Airport was one of four airports located along the East Coast that met the requirements to aid in the Space Shuttle Program. The airport received the designation as an emergency abort landing site. Wilmington's 8,007-foot runway surpassed the 7,500-foot requirement for the minimum runway required for emergency space shuttle landings (Wikipedia, "List of Space Shuttle Landing Sites").

World War II Contributions of the Southern Tidewater Subregion of the North Carolina Coastal Region: Onslow County and Camp Lejeune

Camp Lejeune is carved from 200 miles of wilderness. Located in Onslow County near Jacksonville, North Carolina, Camp Lejeune is on both sides of the New River; portions of the camp are along the Atlantic Coast.

The construction of Camp Lejeune was in response to the rising international tensions during the 1930s; even with the uncertainty of the situation, the United States began the shift from peacetime status to a state of military readiness. Major General Thomas Holcomb, Marine Corps commandant, ordered Major John C. McQueen in the summer of 1940 to "select a pilot ... get a plane ... and find us a training center" (Marines, "Origins of Base Camp Lejeune").

Captain Verne McCaul and Major John C. McQueen surveyed by air the land from Corpus Christi, Texas, to Norfolk, Virginia. When they saw an inlet and 14 miles of undeveloped beach bisected by the New River, they knew they had found an ideal place for the United States Marine Corps camp. Initially, the installation had the designation New River. Later the camp received the name Camp Lejeune after Lieutenant General John Archer Lejeune (Marines, "Origins").

Lieutenant General John Archer Lejeune (1867–1942). Born in Louisiana, John Archer Lejeune attended Louisiana State University. When the family could not afford his uniforms, his mother dyed his father's Confederate uniforms for John to wear.

Lejeune earned an appointment to the naval academy at Annapolis. He graduated from Annapolis in 1888, and in 1890 he received a commission as second lieutenant. As a captain, Lejeune participated in the Spanish-American War while serving on the USS *Cincinnati* (C7).

Lejeune graduated from the United States Army War College (1910). He helped to quell uprisings in Panama (1903) and—as a lieutenant colonel—in Cuba (1911). After his command of the 2nd Advanced Base Regiment in Vera Cruz, Mexico (1914), he received promotion to brigadier general; at Quantico, Virginia, he became the first commander of the Marine barracks there.

During World War I, he led a brigade of the 32nd Division at Brest, France; participated in the Soissons Offensive; was in charge of the 4th Marine Brigade; and earned promotion to major general. As commander of the 2nd Division of the American Expeditionary Force, he became the first officer of the United States Marine Corps to command an army division in combat. After the 1918 armistice when he triumphantly led his unit into Germany, he earned the Legion of Honor and the *Croix de Guerre* from the people and the government of France. Other recognitions included the Army Distinguished Service Medal (presented by General John J. Pershing) and (for his service in World War I) the Navy Distinguished Service Medal.

Major General Lejeune was once again commander of the Marine barracks at Quantico. He received the honor of being named the 13th commander of the United States Marine Corps. Lejeune served as commander until his retirement in 1929. Until 1939, he served as superintendent of the Virginia Military Institute until he had to retire because of poor health. While retired, he became the first Marine to ever hold the rank of lieutenant general. His burial in 1942 was in Arlington Cemetery.

Marine Barracks, New River, North Carolina, became Camp Lejeune near the end of 1942. This name change of one of the largest Marine training facilities in the world was to honor Camp Lejeune and to remember Lieutenant General John Archer Lejeune: "the greatest Leatherneck" (USS *Kidd*).

Establishment of Camp Lejeune. From the coastal wilderness of two hundred square miles emerged the modern base. With storm clouds of war looming, the construction of the facility was a hurried process.

Despite the rush for completion of the camp, the east side of Camp Lejeune included modern offices and up-to-date technical schools. The barracks at Camp Lejeune were not all the typical wooden constructions of most camps; many of the tents and huts soon gave way to bricks.

The permanent area of Camp Lejeune had a $7,500,000 naval hospital in 1944. The camp featured "commodious homes for married officers, comfortable quarters for unmarried officers, 10 theaters, five service clubs for enlisted personnel, a golf course, a boat house, and a wide variety of recreational facilities" (Genuine Curteich-Chicago, "C.T. Art Colortone Creation").

9. The Southern Tidewater Subregion of the Coastal Region　　125

When President Roosevelt signed Executive Order 8802, discrimination in defense programs was not allowed after 1941. African American troops arrived for training in the Montford Point area of Camp Lejeune. Women received training at Camp Lejeune in all areas of the military—except combat. Hundreds of dogs received preparation for war at Camp Lejeune (Marines, "Origins").

Tent Camp No. 1, or Camp Geiger. In 1941, not all the areas of Camp Lejeune consisted of permanent, brick structures. Marines of the First Division reported to a crowded tent camp on the west side of Camp Lejeune.

The No. 1 Tent Camp contained primarily 20-foot-square tents; these tents were in a grid-like street pattern. This first tent camp consisted mostly of six-man canvas tents.

The First Division did not remain long in the tents, however. The unit soon shipped out to the Pacific Theater of World War II.

Tent Camp No. 2. Tent Camp No. 2, though not geographically connected with Camp Lejeune, is considered a part of Camp Lejeune. Tent Camp No. 2 offered huts made of compressed cellulose (Homosote). These 14-person accommodations, however, were not superior to tents. Corrugated steel Quonset huts would replace the Homosote huts (Marines, "Tour Historic MCBCL").

Camp Lejeune was superior to many other training facilities. The billing for Camp Lejeune in 1945 was the most "complete Marine Training Base ever built" (Marines, "Origins").

By the end of the war, corrugated steel Quonset huts replaced most of the tents, but the battered Homosote huts remained until the early 1950s and the removal of all the huts. With new concrete block barracks, the tent camp was rededicated in 1953 and renamed in honor of General Roy S. Geiger (Marines, "Tour").

United States Marine Corps General Roy Stanley Geiger (January 25, 1885–January 23, 1947) served during World War II. He became the first Marine to lead an army: the 10th United State Army. Geiger served as marine aviator and as a commander of the I Amphibious Corps and the III Amphibious Corps (Wikipedia, "Roy Geiger").

Since the 1970s, Camp Geiger has had numerous rebuilding efforts to meet the modern-day needs of the Corps' School of Infantry-East (Marines, "Tour").

Today, Camp Geiger is a United States Marine Corps base and is just off

U.S. Route 17 in an area called the Greater Sandy Run Area. Marines recruited through the Eastern Recruiting Region usually call Camp Geiger home. Camp Geiger houses the United States Marine Corps School of Infantry East. Camp Geiger and the Marine Corps Air Station New River share the same main gate (Wikipedia, "Camp Geiger").

Camp Lejeune Today. After World War II Camp Lejeune continued to grow. It functioned well as a training center and a support center for other units and especially the Fleet Marine Force (FMF). Its population (military and non-military) by the early 1990s had reached 110,000. The 152,000 acres held more than 7,650 structures (Marines, "Origins").

World War II Contributions of the Southern Tidewater Subregion of the North Carolina Coastal Region: Onslow County and Montford Point

In 1939 the United States declared its first peacetime draft. This action increased the expenditures for defense and often provided economic opportunities for those participating in the military. African Americans, however, did not always have the assurance of being able to benefit economically from the peacetime draft; neither could they enter all branches of service. In the 1930s, for instance, African Americans could not enlist in the United States Marine Corps (USMC); the USMC was the only branch of the Armed Services that excluded them.

Civil Rights Organizations at Work in 1941. The National Association for the Advancement of Colored People (NAACP), the Brotherhood of Sleeping Car Porters, the Urban League, and other civil rights organizations were concerned with the treatment of African Americans. These organizations threatened a march on the streets of Washington, D.C., on July 1, 1941, unless the federal government provided treatment that was more equitable for this minority group.

President Roosevelt, however, had some concerns about meeting these demands. Part of his reluctance to approve the requests of these various civil rights groups was political. He recognized that the South might withdraw its support for his domestic programs and for his foreign agendas (McLaurin 2007, 1–5).

9. The Southern Tidewater Subregion of the Coastal Region

Executive Order 8802, June 25, 1941. On June 25, 1941, President Roosevelt signed Executive Order 8802. To appease Southerners, however, the order did not ban racial segregation by the government or by firms contracting with the government. The order did, however, forbid governmental agencies or firms with governmental contracts from discriminating "in the employment of workers in defense industries of Government because of race, creed, color, or national origin." A new commission—the Fair Employment Practices Commission—would enforce the order (McLaurin 2007, 5).

Construction of the Segregated Montford Point in 1942. Although African Americans could enlist in the United States Marine Corps as a result of Executive Order 8802, these new enlistees received training assignment (1942–1949) to a segregated facility: Montford Point. The construction of Montford Point near Jacksonville and at Camp Lejeune began in April of 1942.

African American "boots" (new recruits) in drill training at Montford Point in March of 1943. When the United States Marine Corps began enlisting African Americans on June 1, 1942, it broke a 167-year-old tradition. Montford Point was a section of Camp Lejeune, the 200-square-mile Marine base at New River (Roger Smith, Office of War Information, Library of Congress, LC-USW3- 023008-D).

The North Carolina Marine Camp in the Coastal Region of the state was on a peninsula that jutted into the New River. Access to the river provided opportunities for additional types of training. Montford Point opened in August of 1942.

The 19,168 African Americans who trained at the Montford Point Camp endured the same demanding training as all other recruits for the Marine Corps. These African Americans prepared at Montford Point were as capable and deserving of the title Marine as all other Marines (McLaurin 2007, 5–8).

Reversal of Segregation in the Military (1948) and the Deactivation of Montford Point (1949). On July 26, 1948, President Truman issued Executive Order 9981, which established equality of treatment and of opportunity in the armed services of the United States. Executive Order 9981 reversed segregation in the military (Harry S Truman Library and Museum).

The deactivation of Montford Point Marine Camp dates from September of 1949. This action ended seven years of segregation at the Montford Point Marine Camp.

Camp Johnson. On April 19, 1974, Montford Point Camp received a new name: Camp Johnson. The new designation honored Sergeant Major Gilbert H. "Hashmark" Johnson (1905–1972). Sergeant Major Johnson was one of the first African Americans to enlist in the United States Marine Corps. This Montford Point drill instructor was a veteran of both World War II and the Korean War. Camp Johnson remains (as of 2013) the only Marine Corps installation to carry the name of an African American. Visitors can study exhibits on the United States Marine Corps at the Montford Point Museum at Camp Johnson in Jacksonville, North Carolina (National Montford Point Marine Association, Inc.).

Jacksonville, North Carolina, is adjacent to the North Carolina Southern Outer Banks. The city is home also to the Marine Corps Air Station New River and the United States Marine Corps' Marine Corps Base Camp Lejeune (Wikipedia, "Jacksonville, North Carolina").

The Montford Point Marines and the Congressional Gold Medal. In 2011, the Montford Point Marines received the highest civilian honor of the nation: the Congressional Gold Medal. The House of Representatives unanimously voted this award to the Montford Point Marines (Marines, "The Montford Point Marines").

World War II Contributions of the Southern Tidewater Subregion of the North Carolina Coastal Region: Camp Davis (Onslow County)

The location of Camp Davis was 50 miles north of Wilmington in the Southern Tidewater Subregion of the Coastal Region. This important site in Onslow County was only 5 miles from the Atlantic Ocean. The nearest town was Holly Ridge, population 28.

Selecting the Site for Camp Davis. The selecting of the site for what would eventually be Camp Davis began in 1939—more than two years before the attack on Pearl Harbor. The historian Clifford Tyndall notes that this survey of the coast of North Carolina by Colonel George Gillette indicated the feasibility of the development of the coastal area and the necessity of protecting the coast from enemy attack. The title of Gillette's resulting map was "The Un-Guarded Coastline." Gillette came to consider this one of the most important maps he ever made.

The United States Department of Defense studied Gillette's map. In November of 1940 the Department of the Navy chose Onslow County to host a Marine warfare amphibious training center: Camp Lejeune. The army chose Holly Ridge for its installation: Camp Davis (Tyndall 2006, 1–3).

The War Department in December of 1940 announced that it would construct an installation near Holly Ridge, North Carolina; this declaration resulted in an influx of men seeking employment. More than 22,000 would find employment when Camp Davis reached its peak. The derivation of the name Camp Davis was from Major General Richmond P. Davis (StoppingPoints.com, "Camp Davis").

Major General Richmond P. Davis. Major General Richmond P. Davis (1866–1937) was born in Statesville, North Carolina. In 1887 he graduated from the United States Military Academy. After serving during World War I as the commander of the 151st Field Artillery Brigade in France, he received the appointment to the position of chief of artillery for the 9th Corps of the Army. After earning the promotion to general (1927), he held the position of commander of the Coast Artillery Training Center in Fort Monroe, Virginia. His last position was commander of the 4th Corps Area, Atlanta, Georgia (Tyndall 2006, 1–3).

The Facilities of Camp Davis. Construction of Camp Davis began in 1940. A total of 32 miles of streets, an airfield, and 978 buildings distinguished

An instructor at Camp Davis, North Carolina, demonstrating the 50-caliber anti-aircraft machine gun (W. R. Thompson and Company Publishers, Richmond, Virginia).

Camp Davis, which was a segregated facility. Although the first soldiers did not arrive until April of 1941, by 1943 Holly Ridge had a population of 110,000. Both black and white men trained at the segregated Camp Davis (StoppingPoints.com, "Camp Davis").

Training at Camp Davis. Camp Davis was a premier training facility for battalions learning to launch high-altitude barrage balloons and for units practicing anti-aircraft activities. With the advent of World War II in 1941, all the barrage balloon units at Camp Davis dispatched to such critical areas as the West Coast of the United States and Panama Canal (Osborne 2007, 186–87).

The waterfront location of the southern edge of Camp Davis provided an excellent location for a firing range for the anti-aircraft (AA) gunners. Two other firing ranges—at Sears Point near New River and northwest at Maple Hill, North Carolina—were ideal for training personnel in anti-aircraft artillery. Much of the AA-training areas were swampy; mosquitoes and rattlesnakes were plentiful. Trainees sometimes called the camp "Swamp Davis."

Camp Davis as a Prisoner of War Camp. After the construction of a stockade in the Maple Hill area in 1943, five hundred German prisoners received housing assignments there. These prisoners were willing to work at tasks that did not help the American war effort; they were examples of good conduct.

On the government lands, the prisoners repaired roads and dug drainage ditches. Some of the prisoners even received assignments to help local residents with cutting pulp wood and with farming. The rule was no abuse of the prisoners in any form (Tyndall 2006, 35–36).

Camp Davis (1944–1946). Camp Davis closed in October of 1944, and AA-training moved elsewhere. In 1945, however, the camp opened again as an AAF convalescent hospital and redistribution center. The United States Marine Corps used parts of Camp Davis as both a center for training and a redistribution center; then Camp Davis closed again. One can still see some remains of Camp Davis, Osborne states, on the northwest side of United States Highway 17 in Holly Ridge.

The United States Navy and the Missile Testing Site. In late 1946 the United States Navy acquired the firing range on Topsail Beach and used it for testing its ramjet-powered missiles: "The Flying Stovepipe." Eight towers measuring 35 feet housed both photography and tracking equipment; one of them still stands at an ocean fishing pier. Four of the towers have become parts of homes (Osborne 2007, 186–87).

To conduct these highly secretive experiments using ramjet-powered missiles, the United States Navy had moved 500 individuals onto the base in 1946 and converted Sears Landing into the United States Naval Ordnance Testing Facility. The goal was to develop jet-powered missiles that could destroy a moving target 20 miles away.

To perform these tests, the navy partnered with the Applied Physics Laboratory of Johns Hopkins University and with a civilian contractor: the Kellex Corporation. Other constructions included a pontoon bridge, a launching platform, and a shelter that was bombproof.

Launching these heavy missiles was a classified program some called "Operation Bumblebee"; the name came from the "seemingly impossible aerodynamic challenges ... [resembling] those of a bumblebee in flight." The 18 months of Operation Bumblebee resulted in more than 200 launched rockets and "provided an impetus to the development of jet aircraft engine technology and insights into rocketry incorporated later in the space program. In 1948 the Navy closed up shop at Topsail Island and shifted operations to White Sands, New Mexico, and Cape Canaveral, Florida, to take advantage of better weather conditions" (StoppingPoints.com, "Missile Tests").

Even more evidence of these experiments remains. The Jolly Roger Inn on Topsail Beach has used a launching platform for its patio; the owner of the inn says this launch pad is still visible. The assembly building is now a museum that highlights the local history and particularly the rocket experiments. The Holly Ridge area and Topsail Beach advertise that they welcome visitors to the area.

World War II Contributions of the North Carolina Southern Coastal Region: Morehead City (Carteret County)

Morehead City was a relatively new town in the state of North Carolina at the time of its 1860 establishment. When compared with the two oldest North Carolina towns, the formation of Morehead City came more than a century and a half later. The oldest North Carolina city—Bath—dates from 1705; the second oldest North Carolina city—New Bern—dates from 1710.

Location of Morehead City. Morehead City is in Carteret County, North Carolina. This port city lies about 130 miles southeast of the North Carolina state capital of Raleigh.

Morehead City is 40 miles east of Jacksonville, which had a prominent role during World War II. Jacksonville served both Camp Lejeune and Montford Point during World War II (CityTownInfo.com, "Morehead City, North Carolina").

The Port of Morehead City has been and remains a port of embarkation and debarkation for the Second Division of the U.S. Marine Corps at Camp Lejeune. Global Security reports that Camp Lejeune military troops often travel North Carolina Highway 24 from Swansboro to Morehead City, or from Morehead City to Swansboro.

Morehead City as an Accessible, Early Port City. The land that is now Morehead City became an acquisition of Shepard Point Land Company in the 1850s. The name Morehead City came from John Motley Morehead, who was the 29th governor of North Carolina and who was also a member of the Shepard Point Land Company; this company purchased 600 acres for a new endeavor in the vicinity of Morehead City.

A primary objective of the Shepard Point Land Company was to use advantageously the deep, natural channel of the Topsail Inlet (now the Beaufort Inlet) advantageously. This deep inlet was hoped to provide improved access to Morehead City and the newly purchased land, to the Intra-Coastal

9. The Southern Tidewater Subregion of the Coastal Region   133

Waterway, to the Newport River, and to the North Carolina town of Beaufort, the third oldest town (1709) in the state.

The Shepard Point Land Company planned also to improve and deepen the port near Morehead City. Such an improved port would lessen the pressure on the Wilmington Port; furthermore, a deepened, improved port at Morehead City would allow points within the state to ship products—such as timber and naval stores (lumber, turpentine, pitch, etc.)—to other places.

The North Carolina Railroad was chartered in 1849 and completed in 1856. It ran from Goldsboro (about 50 miles from Morehead City) through Raleigh, Greensboro, and finishing in Charlotte, a total distance of 223 miles. Governor John Motley Morehead and other progressive leaders had encouraged the development of the railway company.

The Atlantic and North Carolina Railroad that ran between New Bern and Goldsboro was complete by April 29, 1858, and was operating fully by July 1858. This railway system allowed increased accessibility from western, northern, and southern inland points to the Morehead City Port (Wikipedia, "Morehead City"). A North Carolina Highway historical marker indicates the eastern terminus of the railroad that the State built (1851–1856) from Goldsboro to Charlotte (North Carolina Department of Cultural Resources, "North Carolina Railroad").

The federal troops took over Morehead City and the surrounding area during the Civil War. Economic and population growth was static for a while.

During the 1880s, however, the construction of the Atlantic Hotel (1880–1933) in Morehead City and the improved accessibility to the Morehead City region resulted in renewed interest in the area. The railroad promoted the area with its Atlantic Hotel as the "Summer Capital by the Sea." With the train depot, the beaches, and the positive reputation of the hotel with its ballroom, visitors became more frequent in Morehead City (North Carolina Department of Cultural Resources, "North Carolina Railroad").

The vital railway system continues to add to the economy of Morehead City and the adjoining area. The Norfolk Southern still runs on the tracks in the middle of Arendell Street in downtown Morehead City. The Atlantic and East Carolina and the Southern Railway have used the tracks on Arendell for more than a century.

Morehead City in World War II. In 1941, the United States Navy purchased 58 acres within the former Camp Glenn, which was in use during World War I. The area that would become the Morehead Naval Section Base was on this acreage.

This Camp Glenn photograph (DLC/PP-1916:45168) was the work of the Wootten-Moulton Firm and dates from 1916 (restrictions on publication; Library of Congress, PAN U.S. MILITARY).

The construction of the Morehead Naval Section Base on the former Camp Glenn location dates from November of 1941. The United States Navy spent more than $1 million on building and repairing ammunition and explosives magazines, barracks, a pier with extensions to accommodate patrol ships and other vessels, an administrative building, a mess hall, a medical structure, and other necessary shops and maintenance facilities. The Morehead City Naval Section Base was important as a naval repair station (North Carolina Department of Cultural Resources, "North Carolina Shipbuilding Company").

Morehead City was an important part of the coastal patrol for locating German submarines until the summer of 1942. Naval patrol craft and Coast Guard cutters operated out of Morehead City. With the decrease in German U-boats off the North Carolina coast, Morehead City had fewer responsibilities in guarding the shore line and the coastal waters.

Morehead City and Its Post–World War II Responsibilities. In 1944, the North Carolina Department of Conservation and Development bought a segment of the property for its marine-research facilities. The Institute of Marine Sciences, the North Carolina Division of Marine Fisheries, and the Ferry Division of the North Carolina Department of Transportation continue to operate from this Morehead City location (Morehead City, North Carolina).

CHAPTER 10

The Central Tidewater Subregion of the Coastal Region

An examination of the World War II military sites in the Southern Tidewater Subregion of the North Carolina Coastal Region was the main topic of Chapter Nine. This chapter focuses on the Central Tidewater Subregion, its military sites, and its contributions to World War II.

First, this chapter will examine World War II sites in or near New Bern. This section will consider also the Barbour Boat Works, Camp Battle, Cherry Point, and Havelock—all in the vicinity of New Bern.

World War II Contributions of the Central Tidewater Subregion of the North Carolina Coastal Region: New Bern (Craven County)

New Bern boasts a rich history, as the second oldest city in North Carolina. It dates back to 1710. The location of Tryon Palace, New Bern is a favorite location for tourists.

New Bern serves as the county seat of Craven County. The city is 87 miles northeast of Wilmington and 112 miles east of Raleigh, the capital of the state of North Carolina. The location of New Bern is at the convergence of the Neuse and the Trent rivers. This was an essential location to protect during World War II (Wikipedia, "New Bern").

World War II Contributions of the Central Tidewater Subregion of the North Carolina Coastal Region: Barbour Boat Works

Herbert W. Barbour founded Barbour Boat Works in New Bern in 1933. Located on the Trent River, Barbour Boat Works was at the foot of Metcalf

This undated photograph shows two men working on the hull of a ship at Barbour Boat Works, Inc., in New Bern, North Carolina (courtesy Digital Collections, Naval and Maritime History Collection, Barbour Records, J. Y. Joyner Library, East Carolina University, http://digital.lib.ecu.edu/11213, Identifier/Call Number: 758.0.0.297).

Street. The establishment of this industry in New Bern during the Great Depression was a welcome event. The boat yard operated in this location for more than half a century (Shipbuilding History, "Barbour Boatworks, New Bern, NC"). One of the first vessels from Barbour Boat Works dates from 1934. This fishing vessel, named *Pocket Change*, is still active.

Barbour Boat Works in the 1940s. Barbour Boat Works contributed to the war effort during World War II. Many of its rendered services were to the United States Navy. In 1942 Barbour launched from its Trent River location the first modern naval mine sweeper.

Between 1942 and 1944, the Barbour Boat Works produced at least 14 vessels to aid the war effort. The types of vessels that Barbour produced for the United States Navy included rescue ships, minesweepers, and net layers (Shipbuilding History).

One of the many impressive ships from Barbour Boat Works was the wooden-hulled, net-laying USS *Abele* (AN-58) of the Ailanthus class. The

Abele had one 3"/50-caliber gun and three 20-mm guns. An examination of her career will give a hint as to her contributions, the contributions of the other vessels from New Bern, and the contributions of Barbour Boat Works. The laying down of the *Abele* was January 8, 1943, at New Bern; her launching was August 19, 1943. The commissioning of the 168'6" vessel was June 2, 1944.

The ports *Abele* used sound like a geographical atlas of World War II. She made stops and served at Guantanamo Bay, Cuba, the Panama Canal Zone, Manzanillo, Mexico, San Diego, Pearl Harbor, and Iwo Jima (where the *Abele* laid torpedo nets). She spent time in the Leyte Gulf area, survived attacks by Japanese suicide boats and aircraft, downed one enemy aircraft and helped in the downing of another, assisted in the laying of five miles of anti-torpedo nets across the harbor entrance of Okinawa, and recovered the anti-torpedo net at Tinian after the war. *Abele* returned to the United States in November. She had won a battle star for her service.

Her decommissioning came on March 1, 1946. The United States Navy removed the vessel from its roster on March 28, 1946, and transferred the *Abele* for disposal to the Maritime Commission on May 7, 1947 (Wikipedia, "USS *Abele* [AN-58]").

The Barbour Boat Works closed in either the 1980s, the 1990s or 2001, depending on the source (S&ME Engineering Integrity; Shipbuilding History; East Carolina University Digital Collections).

The Site of the Barbour Boat Works in the 21st Century. Whatever its date of closure, however, Barbour Boat Works left behind a rich naval history. Unfortunately it also left behind "asbestos containing materials, PCB transformers, and contaminated soil, groundwater and river sediments. The site was positioned to join the State Superfund list. The hope was to restore this land as part of the adjacent Tryon Palace Historic Site and North Carolina History Center, thus providing public attractions designed to enhance enjoyment of the New Bern waterfront for all. S&ME's environmental assessment and remediation allowed this *hope* to become *reality*" (S&ME Engineering Integrity).

Today, the site of the former Barbour Boat Works is now the location of the North Carolina History Center. The nearby Tryon Palace opened the North Carolina History Center in October of 2010. The 60,000-square-foot center is on 6 acres; the steel and glass frontage faces the river.

The new building contains the Pepsi Family Center and the Regional History Museum, with information on maritime events. There is a museum store, classroom space, a performance hall, and—on the waterfront—a café. The center and the area welcome visitors (Wikipedia, "Tryon Palace").

World War II Contributions of the Central Tidewater Subregion of the North Carolina Coastal Region: Camp Battle

North Carolina—like the rest of the nation—suffered during the Great Depression. The stock market plunged. Industries failed. Unemployment rose. Salaries fell. The land suffered from drought and floods.

Establishment of the Civilian Conservation Corps. President Roosevelt recognized and addressed the problems of the Great Depression at his third press conference (March 15, 1933). One of his solutions was the establishment of the Civilian Conservation Corps (CCC) (Davis 2003, 3, 38). Roosevelt said, "The idea is to put people to work in the national forests and on other Government and State properties on work which would not otherwise be done; in other words, work that does not conflict with existing so-called public works" (Roosevelt 1938, 68–70).

On April 5, 1933, by Executive Order Number 6101, President Roosevelt started the CCC. The act brought about the largest and most rapid mobilization of men in history. Within three months 300,000 men had enrolled and had settled in the 1,468 camps (Roosevelt 1938, 107, 110).

The New Bern CCC Camp. One of the newly established CCC camps was just northwest of New Bern. These CCC workers served the New Bern area and helped to stabilize the erosion on the Outer Banks when called to do so.

Camp Battle as an Army Base. In December of 1941 the CCC camp in the New Bern area began a different operation. It became a base for the United States Army units that were protecting bridges over the Neuse and Trent rivers. In 1942 the 111th Infantry—a Pennsylvania National Guard unit—received orders to report to Camp Battle at New Bern (NCpedia).

Camp Battle as a Prisoner of War Camp. After serving as a CCC camp and as an army base, Camp Battle had a new responsibility in 1944. Camp Battle began in 1944 to house German prisoners of war.

More than 600 prisoners of war received internment at Camp Battle. The camp—named for Confederate Major General Cullen A. Battle—had

10. The Central Tidewater Subregion of the Coastal Region

The Neuse River Bridge (left, background) and the Trent River Bridge (right) are two well-known landmarks in the New Bern area. The region around the two rivers was an important area for the army units at the CCC Camp—later Camp Battle—to protect (Aerial Photography Services, 2511 South Tryon Street, Charlotte, NC 28203).

only one fatality on file for the German prisoners. The record indicates that a "mentally unsound" German soldier had tried to escape; searchers found his body in a nearby swamp (Forgotten NC).

Prisoner of war camps were not rare in the United States nor in the state of North Carolina. More than 10,000 German prisoners were interned in 18 North Carolina camps during World War II. Across the United States, more than 600 camps held 378,000 prisoners (Luebken).

Billinger indicates that the prisoners and camps were numerous. Surprisingly, however, most people were unaware of the existence of the camps. Except for the guards, the camp workers, the police and FBI agents, most people were oblivious to the presence of the prisoners (Billinger).

Visitors who go to the Glenburnie Park area northwest of New Bern to view Camp Battle will find no remnants of the camp itself. A historical marker, however, indicates the location where Camp Battle once stood; the marker is almost at the corner of Highway 43 South and Glenburnie Road (New Bern North Carolina Real Estate).

World War II Contributions of the Central Tidewater Subregion of the North Carolina Coastal Region: Cherry Point (United States Marine Corps Air Station in Craven County)

During World War II more troops received training in the state of North Carolina than in any other state in the nation. The three largest World War II military installations in North Carolina during this critical period were Fort Bragg, Camp Lejeune, and Cherry Point (North Carolina Department of Cultural Resources, "Camp Butner").

The Establishment of Cherry Point. The United States Marine Corps had searched in the summer of 1940 for an appropriate location for an air station on the East Coast of the United States. The searchers selected a site on the south side of the Neuse River in Craven County, North Carolina (North Carolina Department of Cultural Resources, "Cherry Point").

A post office had once served the Blades Lumber Company and its people in the area where the south side of the Neuse River and the east side of Hancock Creek met in a point. The post office closed in 1935, but the area with its cherry trees maintained the name Cherry Point.

On July 9, 1941, Congress appropriated the funds for securing and clearing 8,000 acres of swamp land, farmland, and timberland near Cherry Point and for the necessary construction and development of this area near New Bern. On August 6, 1941, the clearing, drainage, and malaria control for the site commenced.

The airfield officially received the name Cunningham Field, Cherry Point on September 4, 1941. The name was in honor of Lt. Col. Alfred A. Cunningham, the first Marine officer to become an aviator.

Cunningham Field received a re-designation on December 1, 1941. The new name was Headquarters Squadron, U.S. Marine Corps Air Station, Cherry Point. Although the name Cunningham Field was no longer in use, a boulevard on the base preserved the aviator pioneer's name (Marines, "Marine Corps Air Station Cherry Point").

Soon the Cherry Point area would support 20,000 people. The first aircraft—a J2F Grumman amphibious biplane—landed at the Marine Corps air station on March 18, 1942. The pilot of this amphibious biplane was Lieutenant Colonel Thomas J. Cushman, the first commanding officer of Cherry Point. The first Marines began their arrival in August 1942; this was one year after the clearing of the land began.

10. The Central Tidewater Subregion of the Coastal Region

This is a view of the administration building at the Marine Corps Air Station in Cherry Point, North Carolina (Zaytoun News Agency, New Bern, North Carolina: Genuine Curteich-Chicago "C. T. Art Colortone" Post Card).

Cherry Point and World War II. Beginning in World War II and since, Cherry Point has functioned as the administrative unit for the commanding general of the air station and his staff. Cherry Point has maintained and operated facilities and provided "services and material to support forces of the Navy and other activities and units, as designated by the Chief of Naval Operations" (Marines, "Marine Corps Air Station Cherry Point, Cherry Point, NC").

Marine Air Corps Station Cherry Point grew rapidly to become the largest Marine airfield in the world. During World War II, Cherry Point was the home of the Third and Ninth Marine Aircraft wings.

Cherry Point After World War II. Cherry Point has been the home of the Second Marine Aircraft Wing since 1946. Its troops have participated in World War II and every major military engagement since that war. Cherry Point troops have served during the Cuban Missile Crisis and in the Dominican Republic, Vietnam, Lebanon, Grenada, Panama, Desert Storm, and the Iraq War (North Carolina Department of Cultural Resources, "Cherry Point").

The Headquarters Squadron received the Meritorious Unit Commendation for its service from July 1985 to October 31, 1986. Its support administratively, operationally, and logistically, both for the Marine Corps Air Station

Cherry Point and for all Second Marine Aircraft Wing tenant commands, was the meritorious achievement (Marines, "Marine Corps Air Station Cherry Point").

Cherry Point remains both one of the world's largest Marine Corps air stations and one of the best all-weather jet bases in the world. From its original size of 8,000 acres, Cherry Point has increased to more than 13,000 acres; in addition Cherry Point has some 16,000 additional support acres. Because of its lengthy runway, Cherry Point can serve as an emergency-landing site for space shuttle launches from Cape Canaveral, Florida (My Base Guide).

Marine Transport Squadron 1 operates from Cherry Point. The squadron uses its military transportation for search and rescue missions for the local community, for Marine aviators, and for medical evacuations as necessary.

In addition to its service impact on the area, the economic impact of Cherry Point in 2012 was $2.2 billion. The community recognizes the importance of the Cherry Point Air Station and seeks to preserve and protect the establishment (Wilson).

One Cherry Point Outlying Service: Marine Corps Auxiliary Air Facility in Atlantic, North Carolina. The United States Marine Corps established some outlying services during World War II. One of these facilities was the Marine Corps Auxiliary Air Facility in Atlantic, North Carolina (Clancy, "US Naval Activities" World War II by State).

Atlantic, North Carolina, is an unincorporated town in Carteret County, North Carolina. Atlantic is 31 miles from Beaufort, 44 miles from Cherry Point, and 34 miles from Morehead City, North Carolina (Wikipedia, "Marine Corps Air Station Cherry Point"; Mapquest).

In 1942 the United States Navy purchased 1,470 acres of land in Atlantic, North Carolina. Construction of a satellite airfield for the Marine Corps air station in Cherry Point began that same year; in 1943 further work began on a third runway for the Atlantic facility. The three asphalt runways would eventually measure 3,500 feet.

The commissioning of Atlantic as Marine Corps Auxiliary Airfield came in 1943; the 1943 complement of aircraft numbered 35 SBDs (Scout Bombers Douglas/Dauntless) and one amphibious Grumman 15 (J2F). The airfield had a hangar with a 78' × 20' door; the United States Marine Corps operated the hangar, but the owner was the United States government. By 1945 the Atlantic facility had barracks for 815 troops, workshop structures, and other buildings. The total cost had been $1.26 million.

Marine dive bombing squadrons, an Air Warning Squadron (AWS-16), and the flying squadron VMSB-934 with its new Curtiss SB2C Helldivers received assignment to Atlantic. By 1945, however, aviation activity began to decline.

John Voss reported the closure of the Atlantic Outlying Field came sometime between 1956 and 1965. He noted that the Norfolk Sectional Chart indicated "OLF Atlantic (Navy) (Closed)" (Freeman 2013).

The Atlantic Field—though closed—has served the North Carolina National Guard and the Marine Corps as needed. As late as September 20, 2013, one hundred North Carolina National Guard Soldiers of the 1–130th Attack Reconnaissance Battalion and the United States Marine Corps Special Operations Command conducted training exercises at Atlantic Field (Jordan 2013).

World War II Contributions of the Central Tidewater Subregion of the North Carolina Coastal Region: Havelock, North Carolina (Craven County)

On its "Welcome to the City of Havelock" Web page, the City of Havelock admits to priding itself on being the home of the United States Marine Corps Air Station Cherry Point, the Second Marine Aircraft Wing, and the Fleet Readiness Center-East.

Important Facts About Havelock, North Carolina. Havelock, in Craven County, is "in Eastern North Carolina, midway between historic New Bern and the beautiful beaches of the Crystal Coast." The population of the North Carolina city in 2013 was 22,500. One image on the page shows the entrance sign to the city; the sign welcomes visitors to both Havelock and Marine Corps Air Station Cherry Point (City of Havelock).

The driving distance from Havelock to New Bern is 18 miles, and from Havelock to Marine Corps Air Station Cherry Point is 7 miles (Mapquest).

Historical Facts About Havelock, North Carolina. In the 1850s the Atlantic and North Carolina railroads built a depot on Miller Avenue in what is now Havelock. The railroads gave the depot the name Havelock Station.

The name came from Sir Henry Havelock, a British officer. His 1857 service during the mutiny in India was distinguished; eight cities in the world received their names from him (Wikipedia, "Havelock, North Carolina").

Just prior to World War II, the government appropriated funds for the establishment of United States Marine Corps Air Station Cherry Point in the

Havelock Station area of North Carolina. The official creation of the town of Havelock, however, dates from 1959—not 1940.

The main highway of Havelock is currently U.S. Highway 70. This west-east highway runs through the center of Havelock. In 2015 a scheduled bypass for U.S. Highway 70 is to begin.

Fontana Boulevard (North Carolina No. 101) is another important road in the area. Two entrances to the United States Marine Corps Air Station Cherry Point lead from 101 (CityTownInfo.com).

Reminders of the Past. Visitors to Havelock—the home of the United States Marine Corps Air Station Cherry Point—have numerous educational and natural sites to visit near town.

Those tourists who like nature have many opportunities for leisure activities. Havelock is located within the Croatan National Forest. The beaches of the Atlantic are easily accessible. The location of Havelock is along the Neuse River.

The Aviation Museum in Havelock helps to preserve the history of the Marine Corps and aviation in the eastern section of North. There is an emphasis on World War II and its aircraft. The museum has exhibits, programs, and collected artifacts. Several planes are on exhibit about the grounds. Inside the building are displays and planes, including an F4B-3 biplane and a model of an AV-8B Harrier.

Havelock has a 9/11 Memorial Plaza which was dedicated on September 11, 2011, ten years after the attack on the Twin Towers. On display is an artifact from the World Trade Center site that New York provided to Havelock. Important pieces—artifacts, bricks, and other remains from sites affected by 9/11—are a part of the memorial.

A circular wall that doubles as a bench surrounds the 9/11 Memorial Plaza. On the wall are the names of the attacked sites and the time of each attack. Visitors can sit on the bench and pause, reflect, and honor the memory of those lost. The memorial is open around the clock; lights make the site inviting even at night. The location of the memorial between Highway 70 and the police and fire department provides a safe environment (New Bern).

Chapter 11

The Three Capes of North Carolina

Along the coast of North Carolina is a chain of sandy barrier islands, or banks. The island chains enclose shallow water bodies, or sounds. Points or projections of land that protrude into bodies of water are capes. North Carolina has three main capes. From south to north, the three great North Carolina capes on the eastern coastline are Cape Fear, Cape Lookout, and Cape Hatteras.

The Capes of the North Carolina Coastal Region and Their World War II Contributions: Cape Fear (Harnett County)

Cape Fear is a promontory point jutting into the Atlantic Ocean from Bald Head Island. Its name may have come from the fear that Sir Richard Grenville's crew experienced in 1585 when exploring the area. It is the most southerly of the three North Carolina capes.

Cape Fear is the location of many World War II sites. These sites include the North Carolina Shipbuilding Company, the Barbour Boat Works, Bluethenthal Field, Wilmington Army Airfield, Fort Davis, Fort Caswell, and Fort Fisher. For more information on these important locations consult the index.

The Capes of the North Carolina Coastal Region and Their World War II Contributions: Cape Lookout (Carteret County)

As a part of Carteret County, Cape Lookout is the central cape of the three main capes of North Carolina. The geographic location of Cape Lookout enhanced its ability to aid in the war efforts. Cape Lookout and its contributions to World War II are the main subjects of this section.

Cape Lookout and Its Features. Each of the three main North Carolina capes extends underwater. The result of these extensions has been linear formations, or shoals; these shoals may consist of sand, silt, and/or gravel. These shoals off the coast of North Carolina can be dangerous to seagoing vessels that can easily run aground.

The Lookout Shoals stretch for 21 miles. Lighthouses and lights on Cape Lookout have sometimes helped to guide ships in these treacherous coastal waters (University of North Carolina at Chapel Hill).

The waters of the Outer Banks near Cape Lookout were difficult to navigate. If a vessel was sailing south, it needed to avoid the northbound waters of the Gulf Stream by staying close to the land; if a vessel was sailing north, it needed to stay in the Gulf Stream in order to avoid the southbound Labrador Current. Where the cool Labrador Current mixed with the Gulf Stream, an intense fog often resulted.

In colonial days especially, pirates launched attacks against seagoing vessels from the protected coast near Cape Lookout. The same convoluted coast offered some security for the robbers returning to hide with their plunder. This area off Cape Lookout earned the nickname *Horrible Headland*.

Cape Lookout and Its Lighthouses. The United States Congress realized the need for some lighthouses on the eastern seaboard. The completion of the first Cape Lookout Lighthouse dates from 1812. This first lighthouse was a 96-foot tower of brick. An octagonal wooden covering of cedar shingles encircled the tower; red and white painted stripes decorated the covering.

The lighthouse was a failure. Its light was only visible 11 miles in good weather—not the 18 miles intended for poor weather. Mariners complained that it was more dangerous to seek the light of Cape Lookout than to navigate the shoals.

In 1857 Congress set aside $45,000 for a new lighthouse for Cape Lookout. The 163-foot-tall Cape Lookout Lighthouse, lit in 1859, became a model for other lighthouses. The new lighthouse used the Fresnel lens from the old structure; the fixed white light was visible for 19 miles—even in salt spray winds—from the new height (LighthouseFriends.com).

After the Civil War, the lighthouse underwent major repairs: "Cape Lookout was painted with large, diagonal checkers that appear as alternating black and white diamonds. Following the traditional daymark aids to navigation, the black diamonds are orientated north and south toward the shallow waters of the shoals and around the headlands, while the white diamonds are

11. The Three Capes of North Carolina

orientated east and west facing the deeper waters of Raleigh's Bay to the east and Onslow Bay to the west" (LighthouseFriends.com).

A lightship off the coast provided visual help for mariners (1904–1933); the use of a lightship resumed during World War II. The light from Cape Lookout became flashing (not fixed) with "a three-mantle oil-vapor lamp with occulting screens." With German submarines off the shore, "brown outs" helped to avoid assisting the enemy (LighthouseFriends.com).

Cape Lookout and World War II. Between World War I and World War II, the station at Cape Lookout functioned primarily as a life-saving station. This remained true even after the bombing of Pearl Harbor and throughout 1942.

Meanwhile—as in World War I—"wolf packs" of German submarines prowled the waters off the coast of eastern North Carolina in World War II. Their threat was even stronger than it had been earlier. Chapter Three discusses the Coast Guard Cutter *Dione,* the German U-boats, and "Torpedo Junction" off the eastern coast of North Carolina. Before the "Atlantic Turkey Shoot" was over (January–April 1942), German submarines had sunk more than 80 American ships off America's eastern shores.

The United States Navy by the end of 1942 began to respond in kind to the German attacks on the Atlantic coast. The deployment of anti-submarine vessels, the instigation of brownouts at night, and aircraft patrols became the rule. Still, hundreds of sailors died off the Atlantic Coast before the end of World War II.

During World War II, Cape Lookout became an important military site, a place to be defended, and sometimes a sanctuary and anchorage for ships—including merchant ships attacked by U-boats. Three gun mounts and several barracks at the tip of Cape Lookout helped support the army coastal defense post. A coast guard station on the cape helped in the protection and defense of the cape.

The shape of Cape Lookout is similar to that of a fish hook. The water inside the "hook" bears the name "Lookout Bight"; this water at times served as an anchorage and haven for ships. An anti-submarine net and a mine field helped to protect Lookout Bight and the vessels there from the enemy.

Cape Lookout After World War II. After World War II, the War Department transferred its lease of Cape Lookout back to the navy for coast guard use (Osborne 2007, 183).

On May 18, 1982, the Fort Macon Station assumed the rescue duties of

Cape Lookout Coast Guard Station. Cape Lookout took the new name Cape Lookout Light Station.

Another change occurred on July 14, 2003. The United States Coast Guard transferred the Cape Lookout Light Station to the National Park Service in a ceremony. Visitors had permission to climb the historic tower. Several other events allowed guests to visit the light station.

An inspection of the Cape Lookout tower in January of 2008 indicated that there were safety issues. The closure of the tower kept climbers and visitors from the area until further repairs.

On July 15, 2010, after the repairs were complete and the inspections were passed, the lighthouse re-opened to visitors. The lighthouse, which dates from 1859, continues to serve the area and the state (National Park Service, "Cape Lookout").

The Capes of the North Carolina Coastal Region and Their World War II Contributions: Fort Macon

Fort Macon, the United States Army masonry fort used in the Civil War and the Spanish-American War, answered the call to service again during World War II.

The Establishment of Forts in the Beaufort Area. The construction of forts in the Beaufort area was in response to the raids by pirates and enemy warships during the colonial period and the 18th and 19th centuries. North Carolina leaders attempted the construction of Fort Dobbs (1756), but the fort remained incomplete. In 1808–1809 and during the War of 1812, Fort Hampton guarded the area; after the abandonment of the fort, the structure fell victim to soil erosion and the hurricane of 1825.

The Construction and Early Use of Fort Macon (1826–1934). In 1826, the United States Army Corps of Engineers began construction of the 26 vaulted rooms of Fort Macon; the purpose of the 5-sided fort was to provide the needed coastal defense for Beaufort Inlet and Beaufort Harbor. The masonry walls were 4.5 feet thick. The garrisoning of Fort Macon dates from 1834.

North Carolina seized Fort Macon from Union forces at the beginning of the Civil War. The Union seized the fort again. Fort Macon served as a federal prison 1867–1876. During the Spanish-American War it was again garrisoned. After Fort Macon closed in 1903, North Carolina purchased it as a

11. The Three Capes of North Carolina

Fort Macon adjoins Atlantic Beach, North Carolina, which is near Morehead City. Fort Macon is one of America's best preserved forts. Located at Beaufort Inlet, it has gun emplacements, arches, and a moat (Aerial Photography Services, Inc., 2511 South Tryon Street, Charlotte, North Carolina).

state park in 1923 for $1. The Civilian Conservation Corps restored Fort Macon in 1934–1935 (North Carolina State Parks).

Fort Macon and World War II. When the United States entered World War II, the United States Army leased Fort Macon from the State of North Carolina. The occupation of Fort Macon began immediately (December 1941) and endured until November 1944; the United States Army returned Fort Macon to North Carolina on October 1, 1946 (North Carolina State Parks).

Because of the important harbor location of Fort Macon near Beaufort, Cape Lookout, and Morehead City, troop occupation of the fortification was essential. On December 17, 1941, United States Army officers from the Third Coast Artillery District, Fort Monroe, Virginia, contacted state officials in Raleigh, North Carolina, to stress the need for garrisoning Fort Macon for security.

The century-old Fort Macon closed as a state park in December 1941. The federal government re-opened it as a brick fort devoted again to coastal defense. The War Department contracted on January 1, 1942, to return Fort Macon (in fully functional condition) to the North Carolina State Division of Parks in six months; the lease was renewable.

On December 21, 1941, the administrative headquarters battery and two gun batteries began to move into Fort Macon and the coast guard station. With each battery consisting of about 180 men, the Fort Macon facilities soon housed from 500 to 600 troops.

Battery A positioned its guns two miles west of Atlantic Beach on the sand dunes. Battery B placed four 6.1-inch guns on the sand dunes on the ocean side of the area as part of the harbor defenses of Beaufort Inlet. Sand bags fortified the position, and camouflage nets helped to hide the weapons. The battalion located the ammunition magazines behind the guns on the dunes; 30-calibre machine guns provided protection. The men situated two searchlights (60 inches in diameter) on wooden platforms and established two 60-foot towers supported by wires to provide target sightings.

In the summer of 1942, two 6-inch fixed-mount navy guns on two concrete pads (30 feet in diameter) and a concrete observation bunker replaced the four guns placed by Battalion B. From the beach, remains of the bunker are still visible.

Battery A positioned its guns two miles west of Atlantic Beach on the sand dunes. The harbor protection system became more sophisticated with time; there is still evidence today of the former protection system.

The United States Army removed weapons, barracks, searchlights, and other equipment before returning Fort Macon to the state. The United States government paid $11,450 for damages to North Carolina and left behind pumps, a concrete dock at the coast guard station, a sewage system, and other items. Fort Macon reverted to the State of North Carolina in October of 1946 (Branch).

The Capes of the North Carolina Coastal Region and Their World War II Contributions: The Sinking of the U-352 off the North Carolina Coast

After the United States declared war against Germany on December 11, 1941, German Admiral Karl Dönitz immediately began planning the details of *Paukenschlag*. As noted in Chapter Three, *Paukenschlag* was the German codename for Operation Drumbeat, or Timpani Beat. The intent of the operation was to use German long-range submarines to strike the American coastal waters (Chen).

***Characteristics of the* U-352.** One of the first German submarines to reach the coast of the United States under Operation Drumbeat was the *U-352*. Flensburger Schiffsbau was the builder of the 218-foot, VII-C submarine. The C-type vessel was larger than previous B-type submarines. Germany built 660 C-type submarines; this C-type was the one Germany most frequently launched during World War II.

The *U-352* had a launch date of May 1, 1941; its commissioning was on August 28, 1941. The *U-352* had a surface speed of 17.7 knots and a submerged speed of 7.6 knots. In the forward torpedo compartment this particular U-boat housed 8 torpedoes; it carried 4 additional torpedoes in the forward tubes, one in the aft torpedo tube, and an additional one in the aft torpedo compartment. The *U-352* could staff 4 officers and 56 enlisted men (BFDC).

The* U-352 *in April and May of 1942. Kapitänleutnant Hellmut Rathke commanded the *U-352*. As a result of the confrontation off the Atlantic coast of North Carolina, 13–17 Germans died; 33 survived the battle and became the first German prisoners of war in the United States (BFDC; Discover Diving; U.S. Coast Guard, "*U-352*").

The *U-352* had only three patrols before its demise. On January 15, 1942, the *U-352* left Kiel, Germany, for Bergen, Norway; its arrival was January 19, 1942. The second patrol was from January 20, 1942, through February 26, 1942; the *U-352* joined seven other boats to form a "wolfpack" for patrolling the Iceland, Scotland, and Faroes areas.

On April 7, 1942, the *U-352* left St. Nazaire, France, for the last leg of its journey toward the Atlantic coast of North Carolina. After its refueling by the *U-459* in late April, the *U-352* encountered the SS *Freden*, a Swedish ship. On May 5 and May 6 the *U-352* attempted to sink the *Freden* by firing four torpedoes at it. None of the shots hit the *Freden*; all four were misses or detonation failures.

The *Freden* continued to New York. The *U-352* resumed its path towards North Carolina.

On May 9, 1942, the *U-352* fired two torpedoes at a vessel off the North Carolina coast; both torpedoes missed their marks. The ship it fired upon was a United States Coast Guard Cutter: the *Icarus*, commanded by Lieutenant Maurice D. Jester.

The cutter replied with five depth charges that blew off the deck gun and damaged the conning tower and internal parts of the *U-352*. The next two charges from the *Icarus* brought the *U-352* to the water surface.

Kapitänleutnant Rathke ordered the crew to abandon ship. All the while the *Icarus* was continuing to attack with 3-inch guns and machine guns. The *Icarus* brought the survivors from the *U-352* as prisoners of war to the Charleston Naval Yard, in South Carolina (BFDC).

***The* U-352 *Today*.** Today the *U-352*, "the first U-boat to be sunk by the United States Coast Guard in World War II," lies on its starboard side at a 45-degree angle; it rests in 115 feet of water about 26 miles southeast of Beaufort Inlet. Divers can arrange to explore the *U-352* (Discovery Diving). The *U-352* is the wrecked vessel that most divers first come to North Carolina to explore (BFDC).

It was 1975 before the re-location of the *U-352*. George Purifoy found the vessel over a mile from the site that the United States Navy had identified. Purifoy found the deck gun in 1978, and Dave Bluett was able to recover the propeller, which weighed 1,500 pounds (Discovery Diving).

The sinking of the *U-352* by the less well-equipped *Icarus* was a notable event. The fact that the *U-352* was the first submarine sunk by a United States Coast Guard Cutter in World War II was even more notable. The taking of the first German prisoners of war off Cape Lookout was another significant happening. Lieutenant Maurice D. Jester (1889–1957) received the Navy Cross for his actions. North Carolina and Cape Lookout were making their names known with their contributions during World War II (U.S. Coast Guard, "*U-352*").

The Capes of the North Carolina Coastal Region and Their World War II Contributions: Cape Hatteras (Dare County and Hyde County)

Cape Hatteras is the point on the Atlantic coast of North America that extends farthest to the southeast. Of the three headlands—Cape Hatteras, Cape Lookout, and Cape Fear—protruding into the North Carolina coastal water, Cape Hatteras is the largest (Wikipedia, "Cape [geography]").

Cape Hatteras and the Graveyard of the Atlantic. Because so many ships have wrecked off the coast of Cape Hatteras, the area has earned the name Graveyard of the Atlantic. One cause of these many wrecks has been the ships' attempting to use the ocean currents to increase their speed, underestimating the depth of the water, and running aground on the linear formations (shoals) of sand, silt, and/or gravel, especially off Cape Hatteras. Turbulent waters and frequent storms were causes of still other accidents (Wikipedia, "Cape Hatteras").

11. The Three Capes of North Carolina

Cape Hatteras, Patrols, and World War II Wrecks. With increased traffic off the coast of Cape Hatteras, the inherent hazards to ships in the Hatteras waters, and the dangers of German U-boat attacks especially in the early 1940s, the number of wrecks off the North Carolina coast increased. Especially in 1942, the East Coast of the United States saw a tremendous amount of activity; the most turbulent region on this East Coast was near the Outer Banks: Torpedo Alley or Torpedo Junction.

In 1942 alone, 81 ships sank off the North Carolina coast. Of these vessels, 29 sank off the coast of Cape Hatteras; this Graveyard of the Atlantic in 1942 added 8 tankers, 16 cargo ships, the *U-701*, 1 freighters, 1 tug, 1 passenger ship, and an anti-sub (Sunken Ships of the Outer Banks).

During the early months of World War II, patrols on horseback, in aircraft, from houses, and in vessels at sea were important near Cape Hatteras. Residents along the coast of North Carolina were accustomed to watching for U-boats, shipwrecks, survivors, and debris. These coastal residents did not serve as paid patrol members, but the populace realized the importance of observing and reporting what they saw.

As lights at sea from ships—friendly and enemy—became more numerous in 1942, some of the coastal residents recall using blackout curtains or shades, turning off lights, and taping the tops of their headlights at night to give no information about location to enemy ships. It was, however, August of 1942—after most of the attacks had ended—before the United States government ordered blackouts (Duffus).

Cape Hatteras Lighthouse. The purpose of the Cape Hatteras Lighthouse was primarily to protect the Atlantic Coast side of Cape Hatteras. Its light could warn ships of dangers, and the caretaker could observe the waters for emergency situations.

The construction of the first lighthouse at Cape Hatteras began in 1799. The lighting was not complete until October of 1803. The 90-foot sandstone structure had a whale oil lamp.

However, the poorly constructed lighthouse was too short to be effective; its light was often too weak to warn mariners. The sandstone blended in with the sandy dunes, and mariners did not readily see it. In 1853 the Lighthouse Board decided to add 60 feet to the structure, fit it with a Fresnel Lens that used both refraction and reflection, and paint it red and white.

By the 1860s, the lighthouse was badly in need of repairs. Instead of performing repairs on an old lighthouse, the Lighthouse Board allocated funds to build a new structure. The tallest brick lighthouse in America—the Cape

Hatteras Lighthouse—was complete and lit by a kerosene lens on December 1, 1870; in 1934 the light became powered by electricity.

In 1873 the Lighthouse Board assigned the Cape Hatteras Lighthouse its daymark pattern: black and white stripes that wrapped about the lighthouse from top to bottom; this pattern allowed for easy recognition of the 198.49 foot structure. The Cape Hatteras Lighthouse also received a distinctive light pattern (nightmark).

The Lighthouse Board decommissioned the Cape Hatteras Board between 1935 and 1950; a skeletal tower housed the light. The National Park Service received the Cape Hatteras Lighthouse in 1937.

The black-and-white structure, however, remained a visual guide to daytime travelers on land and sea. It was important especially in 1942 to vessels off the coast during the daytime. An erected tower provided a needed beacon at night; in 1950 the coast guard returned the beacon to the lighthouse when erosion lessened in the area.

Because of beach erosion, the Lighthouse Board allocated funds in 1999 for moving the lighthouse. The station is again 1,500 feet from the ocean; the 2,900-foot move placed it near its original distance from the sea.

The United States Coast Guard continues to operate and maintain the light. The National Park Service maintains the lighthouse and the facilities (National Park Service, "Cape Hatteras Light Station").

The Beach Jumpers. Ocracoke Island, which is off the North Carolina coast and near Cape Hatteras, was the site of an obscure—yet vital—program for the war effort of the United States. This enigmatic project of the United States Navy was the Beach Jumpers. The location of much of the training for these Beach Jumpers was in the dunes near Cape Hatteras.

The Beach Jumpers Project dates back to 1943, which was even before the construction of the naval station. Training for amphibious operations and preparation for tactical cover and deception units were components of the program.

The facility at Loop Shack Hill and the Beach Jumpers read signals from a magnetic cable running from Ocracoke to Buxton (near Cape Hatteras); the cable produced pulses when underwater vessels (that might be German submarines) were in the area. With this equipment, the Beach Jumpers were able to discover and track clandestine German submarine activity off the eastern coast of North Carolina. The U.S. Navy area, the naval station near Cape Hatteras, and the training grounds for the highly secretive Beach Jumpers were off limits to visitors.

11. The Three Capes of North Carolina

Visitors to the Cape Hatteras area will find that the Ocracoke Preservation Museum hosts an exhibit on the Beach Jumpers. Photographs are a key element in the display.

At the 2009 reunion of the U.S. Navy Beach Jumper Association, the members installed a granite marker on Ocracoke to commemorate their top secret operation. The granite appears at the original site: Loop Shack Hill (OcracokeGuide.com, "Ocracoke Attractions").

Douglas Fairbanks, Jr., and the Beach Jumpers. Douglas Fairbanks, Jr., was a well-known actor who appeared in more than 100 movies and television shows during his lifetime. He gave up his film career for a time, however, to serve his country.

Fairbanks (1909–2000) worked with Adlai Stevenson to lobby for entry into World War II. Because of his views on war, Fairbanks received death threats from those who disagreed with him.

Fairbanks obtained a commission in the naval reserve in June of 1941. He trained with the Royal Navy on an officer exchange program; his studies included work both at the HMS *Tormentor* Advanced Training and Amphibious Operations Base and at the Commando Training School in Ancharry Castle, Scotland. He brought his knowledge of naval deception, its skills, and its philosophy with him to the United States.

Because of Fairbanks's training, he suggested to Admiral Kent Hewitt the use of a special unit to deploy forces in North Africa and in the Mediterranean especially. The two men were able to convince Washington of the advisability of such units. The Beach Jumpers Project started in 1943.

Fairbanks did not have the rank to command the project, but he received another appointment. Working with the British, Fairbanks was to plan, oversee, and organize plans. Stealth and deception helped ensure "great success at Sicily, Salerno, Southern France, and the Philippines during World War II.... [Fairbanks] retired from the reserve as a captain in 1954. He wrote an enormously entertaining book about his wartime experience, 'A Hell of a War'" (Patrick).

Few people knew of the military work of Navy Captain Douglas Fairbanks, Jr., or of the Beach Jumpers Project he planned and executed in North Carolina and elsewhere for the war effort. He explained his service in this way: "I can only describe it with words that are considered rather corny these days: conviction, conscience, doing what I thought was right, the hell with the results" (Patrick).

Lieutenant Commander Douglas Fairbanks, Jr., received recognition for his military service from other countries and from the United States. Douglas earned the Legion of Merit Award with Bronze V (for valor), the Italian War cross for Military Valor, the French *Légion d'honneur* and the *Croix de Guerre* with Palm, and the British Distinguished Service Cross. He earned the Silver Star among other medals from the United States (Wikipedia, "Douglas Fairbanks, Jr.").

The amphibious training base at Ocracoke received men during 1943 and 1944. The trainees would become part of Units 6, 7, 8 and 9. Trainees conducted practice invasions; they used firecrackers, smudge pots for smoke, tinfoil-covered balloons, and tape recorders with loud speakers to imitate battle. The Beach Jumpers remained active until 1946; the organization resumed activity again in 1951–1972.

Beginning in 2009, the granite national historic marker on Loop Shack Hill honored the Beach Jumpers who served from 1943 to 1972. Vera Douglas, the third wife of the late Douglas Fairbanks, was in attendance. Several Beach Jumpers who had trained at Ocracoke were in attendance (U.S. Navy Beach Jumpers Association).

The Naval Station at Ocracoke. The navy base at Ocracoke received its commission on October 9, 1942. It became an amphibious training base on January 16, 1944, and a combat information center in 1945. The United States Naval Station at Ocracoke closed in 1946 (OcracokeIsland.com).

Accessibility to Ocracoke Island was possible only by a state operated ferry or private boat or plane. Among the duties of those serving there were refueling five boats that patrolled the Outer Banks, providing boats, and giving technical support to Allied convoys. The station was able to accommodate 400 enlisted men in the barracks and feed 1,500 people in its dining hall before its 1946 closure (U.S. Navy Beach Jumpers Association).

British Cemetery on Ocracoke Island. In May of 1942 a German submarine torpedoed the HMS *Bedfordshire*; the encounter was some 40 miles south of Ocracoke Island. Winston Churchill, prime minister of the United Kingdom from 1940 to 1945, had approved the loan of 24 antisubmarine vessels to the United States; the 170-foot *Bedfordshire* was one of those.

On board the HMS *Bedfordshire* were 4 officers and 33 crewmen. The United States Coast Guard searched for the crew after the attack, but their mission was unsuccessful. All 37 British soldiers drowned. The only bodies recovered were the 4 that washed ashore and that the Coast Guard recovered 3 days later (OcracokeGuide.com).

British Graveyard on Ocracoke Island. Photo by Wesley Strong

The British Cemetery on Ocracoke Island. Concrete crosses mark where four members of the British Navy and the HMS *Bedfordshire* lie. A lease agreement between the British government and the State of North Carolina helps to maintain the cemetery (Aerial Photography Services, 2300 Dunavant Street, Charlotte, North Carolina).

Only two of the bodies were identifiable: Thomas Cunningham and Stanley R. Craig. A cemetery on Ocracoke Island received all four of the bodies. Two of the gravesites bear the marking "unknown." The other two graves mark where Thomas Cunningham and Stanley R. Craig rest (Ocracoke-NC).

A plaque memorializes the four members of the Royal Navy. On the marker are the words of Robert Brooke: "If I should die think only this of me that there's some forever corner of a foreign field that is forever England" (Ocracoke-NC).

Each year a formal memorial on the Friday nearest to the May 11 anniversary recognizes the deaths of the British soldiers aboard the HMS *Bedfordshire*. During the ceremony, current members of the military place a wreath on each grave. Other parts of the ceremony include an oration, the reading of names, the playing of "Taps," and a 21-gun salute (Outer Banks).

Chapter 12

The Northern Tidewater Subregion: Nags Head, Manteo, Edenton, Elizabeth City, Weeksville, Vultee

In the Northern Tidewater Subregion of the North Carolina Coastal Region, the three main sites of military activity were the Manteo/Nags Head area (the most southern of the three), the Edenton area with its air station, and Elizabeth City (the most northern of the military sites in the coastal/tidewater region). This chapter first considers the Nags Head area.

The Northern Tidewater Subregion of the North Carolina Coastal Region and Its Vital World War II Efforts and Contributions: Nags Head

Nags Head (sometimes spelled "Nag's Head") is a part of Dare County. Nags Head had valuable contributions to make to the war effort; its history dates back to the 1700s.

The Nags Head Legend. One legend about how the Nags Head area received its name is that pirates in the area would lead a nag with a lantern about its neck through the sand dunes at night. Captains at sea would see the light on the nag's neck and mistake it for the light from a ship riding in a safe harbor; the bobbing light would lure the vessels at sea into the shoals, where they would run aground and wreck. The thieves could then take their bounty.

For many years there were few lights from homes and businesses to guide travelers on land or on sea in the Nags Head area on Bodie Island. The area is not populous even today.

A Lighthouse for the Nags Head Area. In 1837 on orders of the federal government, Lieutenant Napoleon L. Coste of the revenue cutter *Campbell* examined the eastern coastline of North Carolina. Lieutenant Coste was to determine lighthouse sites that might supplement the one at Cape Hatteras.

Coste reported that ships headed southward had difficulty navigating the waters near Bodie Island. A beacon near or on Bodie Island could help them travel through the dangerous area. Congress listened and appropriated money the same year. Because of difficulties in obtaining the land, however, construction of the lighthouse on Pea Island (near Bodie Island) did not begin until 1847. Other problems followed.

An unsupported brick foundation caused problems to the 54-foot structure less than two years after its completion. Efforts to repair the construction problems failed.

By 1859 a second lighthouse was in use on Pea Island near Bodie Island. Because of a fear that the Union troops would use the lighthouse during the Civil War, retreating Confederates blew up the lighthouse themselves.

After a period of darkness on the Bodie Island coast, the third Bodie Island lighthouse was complete by 1872. The third lighthouse was not on Pea Island as the first two had been, however. This third structure was on a 15-acre site that the government had purchased for $150 on Bodie Island itself.

The Bodie Island Lighthouse utilized some of the workers and equipment from the 1870 Cape Hatteras Lighthouse. By 1872 the Bodie Island Lighthouse was able to display its nightmark (the light from the Fresnel lens) and its horizontal stripes.

The later addition of a lightning rod to the tower helped to provide proper grounding during electrical storms. Screening for the lantern helped guard against geese crashing into the lens.

Nags Head is the closest city to the Bodie Island Lighthouse. The area around the lighthouse was not populous. The lightkeeper was often without family because Bodie Island was largely undeveloped. Manteo had the closest school in the 1870s, but Manteo was on Roanoke Island and was accessible only by boat in the early days; later, school buses could reach Manteo and schools in Nags Head were available.

In 1932 the Bodie Island Lighthouse was electrified. This was true throughout World War II and made the watch for German submarines easier for the Americans (National Park Service, "Bodie Island Light Station").

The* U-85 *and the* USS Roper *Meet off the Outer Banks. The first German submarine that the United States forces sank during World War II was the *U-85*. The date of this occurrence was April 14, 1942. The action was 15 miles off the Outer Banks of North Carolina's coast, near both Nags Head and Manteo. (Note: The first U-boat sinking by the United States Coast Guard did not occur until May 9, 1942. A description of that encounter is a part of the section on Cape Hatteras.)

Lieutenant Commander Hamilton Howe was in charge of the *Roper*, which fired the depth charges to the *U-85*. The United States servicemen recovered 29 bodies. The Hampton (Virginia) Cemetery contains the bodies. The waters off the coast of the Outer Banks continue to hold the *U-85*; divers still visit its remains, discovered in the 1970s by Jim Bunch.

Amy Lifson, in her article "Into the Deep" (2012), noted that the sinking of the *U-85* "marked the beginning of the end of Germany's unopposed assault on ships along the Mid-Atlantic coast."

The Bodie Island Lighthouse Today. The Bodie Island Lighthouse is still in use. The electrification of the lighthouse in 1932 enabled the watch for German submarines to be more accurate; this electrification has eliminated the need for full-time lighthouse keepers today.

In 1953—after World War II—the National Park Service received the property of the Bodie Island Lighthouse (with the exception of the tower itself). The lighthouse still serves as a navigational aid and is open to the public for tours. The former lightkeepers' duplex currently serves as a visitor center for the Cape Hatteras National Seashore and as an office for the Park Ranger (National Park Service, "Bodie Island Light Station").

The Northern Tidewater Subregion of the North Carolina Coastal Region and Its Vital World War II Efforts and Contributions: The Dare County Airport (Manteo) and the U.S. Navy Auxiliary Air Station

The Dare County Airport and the U.S. Navy Auxiliary Air Station. The Dare County Airport, located on the Outer Banks, had an activation date of September 1, 1943. This 340-acre facility is about one mile northwest of the center of the center of business district of Manteo. The airport has two runways in 2013; a small museum traces the history of aviation on the outer banks for visitors.

A public airport was not available in Dare County before the 1940s; at that time, only a small private airport was available to meet most of the flight needs of the area. The community began its push for a public airport for the area. By the time of the bombing of Pearl Harbor, the construction of a public airport with two runways was in progress for Manteo and Dare County.

When the attack on Pearl Harbor occurred, the United States Navy was planning the construction of a naval auxiliary air station on Cape Hatteras. After the attack, however, the navy decided to concentrate on the airport already being constructed on Roanoke Island at Manteo (Dare County).

The U.S. Navy Auxiliary Air Station. The commissioning of the navy auxiliary air station in Manteo came on March 3, 1943, after the completion of its construction. The Civil Air Patrol and the United States Navy would both use the airport. Squadrons of aircraft including the F4U Corsairs, the F6F Hellcats, the PBY Catalinas, and the SB2C Helldivers trained there (County of Dare, North Carolina).

The United States Coast Guard and the United States Navy were able to use the navy auxiliary air station as Coastal Patrol Base 16 (CBP16). From this station, anti-submarine patrols conducted surveillance missions from July 1942 to August 1943. Using private aircraft, North Carolina volunteers of the Civil Air Patrol flew patrols from CBP16 over the ocean to look for those in distress, for enemy ships, and for enemy U-boats (RoanokeIsland.net, "Attractions").

Reversion to Caretaker Status. The airfield, with Coastal Patrol Base 16, reverted to caretaker status on December 15, 1945. Dare County requested control of the airfield; it received this control in 1947. The Dare County Airport Authority took control in 1983 (RoanokeIsland.net, "Recreation").

The Northern Tidewater Subregion of the North Carolina Coastal Region and Its Vital World War II Efforts and Contributions: Edenton

Located on the Inner Banks of North Carolina, Edenton is the county seat of Chowan County. The United States Census for 2010 gives the population of Edenton as 5,004. Although Edenton was small in its number of residents during World War II, it had some definite contributions to make to the war effort (Census Viewer).

Marine Corps Air Station Edenton. The United States Navy constructed Marine Corps Air Station Edenton during World War II. The Marine Operational Training Group 81 (MOTG-81) received assignment to Edenton.

Subordinate squadrons to MOTG-81 received assignment to Marine

Corps Air Station Edenton also. The MOTG-81 trained pilots and both air and ground crews; the medium bomber PBJ-1 was the aircraft used predominantly for training. The PBJ-1 was a modification by the United States Marine Corps and the United States Navy of the B-25 Mitchell bomber (Wikipedia, "Marine Operational Training Group 81").

Naval Auxiliary Air Station Edenton. After the end of World War II, Marine Corps Air Station Edenton received a new designation: Naval Auxiliary Air Station Edenton. Marine Air Base Squadron 14 (MABS-14) administered the facility throughout the Korean War and during the early years of the Cold War.

During that period, the facility served both the United States Marine Corps fighter squadrons (usually flying the F9F-2 Panther, Grumman's first jet fighter) and the United States Marine Corps attack squadrons (usually flying the AD-4B and AD-5 Skyraider). Another change in Naval Auxiliary Air Station Edenton would come in the 1960s.

The Decommissioning of Naval Auxiliary Air Station Edenton. The year 1960 marks the year of the decommissioning of Naval Auxiliary Air Station Edenton. The local government obtained the station to use as a civilian airport.

Northeastern Regional Airport Today. Northeastern Regional Airport in 2013 is a public-use airport in Chowan County. The town of Edenton owns the airport, which is about 3.5 miles from the center of Edenton. The airport has gone through several changes during its lifespan (Wikipedia, "Northeastern Regional Airport").

After the departure of the military the air traffic control tower remained, but it never reopened. This means that the private airport is a UNICOM (Universal Communications) station. The facility has air-to-ground communication by a private agency.

One runway was still operational at the decommissioning in 1960. The dimensions of the useable runway were 8,000 feet by 200 feet.

By 2013 the runway dimensions had decreased to 6,000 feet by 100 feet because of the displacement of the approach ends. Although there is no precise lighting on approach, a Category I Instrument Landing System is available (Wikipedia, "Northeastern Regional Airport").

The Northern Tidewater Subregion of the North Carolina Coastal Region and Its Vital World War II Efforts and Contributions: Elizabeth City

Elizabeth City is in the Coastal Plain of North Carolina. Interestingly, this city of 18,478 (2012) is in both Camden County and Pasquotank County (U.S. Census Bureau, "Elizabeth City").

Pasquotank County and Elizabeth City. Pasquotank County is one of the narrow, long counties of North Carolina in the category that teacher-writer Shields calls the "finger counties." He includes Currituck, Camden, Perquimans, Chowan, and Pasquotank counties in the finger county category. Elizabeth City is the county seat of Pasquotank County.

Shields notes that the word *Pasquotank* is from the Algonquian Indian word *pasketanki*, meaning "where the current of the stream divides or forks." Certainly Elizabeth City, Camden County, and Pasquotank County are all river and water-related. In fact, Elizabeth City is "at the narrows," or where the Pasquotank River becomes less wide.

Shields observes that Pasquotank County is at a fork in the stream. He explains that this stream can take travelers where they need to go. Even better, he remarks, the stream may take them where they want to go (Shields 2000).

Located near the mouth of the Pasquotank River, Elizabeth City has earned the title "Gateway to the Outer Banks." The town/city dates from 1793 when Adam and Elizabeth Tooley donated and sold land for the town of Redding, which later became the town of Elizabeth (1794) and Elizabeth City (1804); perhaps the latter two names came from Elizabeth Tooley. Elizabeth City has the nickname "Harbor of Hospitality" (Wikitravel, "Elizabeth City").

The Coast Guard Air Station Elizabeth City in 1939. The Air Station Elizabeth City Wardroom in the book *Coast Guard Base Elizabeth City* identifies the northeastern part of North Carolina as the "crown jewel" of Coast Guard aviation and Elizabeth City as the "jumping point" for the Wright Brothers in 1903. The Coast Guard base in Elizabeth City continued the Wrights' emphasis on flight with its airport construction, begun in 1939.

The United States Navy operated and administered the Coast Guard base from its opening until the end of World War II. The population of the base would later reach 8,500 military personnel during World War II (Air Station Elizabeth City Wardroom, 7).

12. The Northern Tidewater Subregion

United States Coast Guard Air Base, Elizabeth City, North Carolina

The United States Coast Guard Air Base in Elizabeth City, North Carolina (Graycraft Card Company, Danville, Virginia).

The Growth of the United States Coast Guard Air Station, Elizabeth City. The United States Coast Guard Air Station, Elizabeth City, North Carolina, began on the shores of the Pasquotank River. Only 3 officers and 52 other military personnel occupied the station initially. Today it is the world's largest United States Coast Guard Station (USCGS).

With the attack on Pearl Harbor, the USCGS expanded rapidly and became a vital part of the war effort. The station served as a training base for the army and navy and as a patrol base for monitoring the coast of North Carolina. USOs became popular places (Military.com, "USCG Elizabeth City, NC").

Some Immediate Effects of World War II on Elizabeth City. World War II brought many changes to Elizabeth City. The shipbuilding and aeronautics industries, particularly, boomed with the increased emphasis on military efforts by the nation after its entry into the war.

Between 1942 and 1944, the Elizabeth City Shipyard constructed 30 111-foot SC-class submarine chasers, 4 YT-class yard tugboats, and 6 104-foot QS-class quick supply boats. Of all the U.S. shipyards during this period, the Elizabeth City Shipyard constructed the largest number of submarine chasers for the war effort. Out of the 438 total submarine chasers (SC-class ships) manufactured for World War II, Elizabeth City built 30.

The North Carolina shipyard in Elizabeth City set the construction time record for a SC-class vessel. In only 30 days the Elizabeth City shipbuilders were able to lay down the SC-740. This 30-day construction time record was not surpassed during World War II. The Elizabeth City Shipyard was still operating in June 2013 (Wikipedia, "Elizabeth City, North Carolina").

Assignments of the Air Station Elizabeth City. Located just southeast of the Elizabeth City corporate limits, the Elizabeth City air station has had several responsibilities.

    1. The base served as "a maintenance depot for flying boats." After 1945 the base found a location for an aircraft repair and supply center that was suitable at the Vultee Corporation.

    2. The base served both as a deterrent for U-boats off the coast and as an antisubmarine base. The seaplanes at the base helped provide valuable surveillance and patrol.

    3. The base was essential for search and rescue (SAR) missions—especially for those people and businesses using the nearby ocean shipping lanes. It was with the SAR that the coast guard led the way with the first use of helicopters. Elizabeth City became home to the Rotary Wing Development Squadron; Commander Frank "Swede" Erickson led the squadron (Air Station Elizabeth City Wardroom, 7–8).

    4. The base became an important aviation technical training center for enlisted aviation personnel (1978). Students who graduate from the state-of-the-art facility graduate as crew members who maintain and fly coast guard aircraft.

    5. The base operated also as a support center.

    6. The base earned the designation of Small Boat Station Elizabeth City.

    7. In addition to the above responsibilities, the base received the responsibilities of off-base National Strike Force Coordination Center of 1991. The center is in northern Elizabeth City (Military.com, "USCG").

    8. The United States Department of Homeland Security (formed after 9/11) incorporated the Elizabeth City air base and the defense contractors Diagnostic/Retrieval Systems, Inc. (DRS) into its program. The base continues to serve Homeland Security in 2014; the association of the base with the United States Department of Homeland Security results in additional local

jobs and employees, increased defense contractors to the area, and the arrival of coast guard members and their families (Wikipedia, "Elizabeth City").

The base continues to perform major depot-level maintenance for the United States Air Force helicopters and for *every* coast guard airframe.

As home to the air station, the airport executes over 1,000 Homeland Security search and rescue, and logistics missions a year. All this was done with nine helicopters and airplanes and with the C-130J Aircraft Program Office (Air Station Elizabeth City Wardroom, 8).

The Location and Duties of the Commands. The above commands—except for the National Strike Force Coordination Center that was eight miles north of Elizabeth City—were at the Support Center Complex, which was about four miles east of Elizabeth City. The Support Center still (2013) occupies and maintains 800 acres, which include runways, record offices, a medical services unit (for personnel, 500 dependents, and 700 military retirees), roadways, buildings, and taxiways.

The air station in Elizabeth City continues to perform search and rescue (S&R) missions, as needed. It also renders assistance—when appropriate—to law enforcement for drugs, for immigrants, and for fishery violations. The S&R also helps with International Ice Patrols, with District Aids to Navigation, and with cooperative flights for other local, state, and federal agencies (Military.com, "USCG Elizabeth City, NC").

Today the base still hosts several commands. These include the following:

- The Aviation Logistics Center. This command enables the execution of coast guard missions. The Aviation Logistics Center includes Depot Level Maintenance, Engineering, Supply, Procurement, and Information Services.
- The Aviation Technical Training Center. This center continues to provide safe and effective maintenance of the coast guard's aviation fleet.
- The Air Station Elizabeth City. The size of this facility has grown, its missions have changed, and the aircraft have modified with changing national priorities and national technologies, especially since World War II. A big expansion came in 1966 when it included both the Argentina and the Bermuda air stations (U.S. Coast Guard, "Air Station Elizabeth City").

With a population of 18,683 at the 2010 census, Elizabeth City and its related military personnel continue to serve the area and the nation.

The Northern Tidewater Subregion of the North Carolina Coastal Region and Its Vital World War II Efforts and Contributions: Weeksville

Weeksville is an unincorporated community in Pasquotank County. Weeksville is about eight miles from Elizabeth City, North Carolina.

Still evident is the Weeksville Dirigible Hangar, built in 1941 as the Naval Air Station Weeksville. After the United States Navy established the United States Naval Air Station Weeksville, the military was able to service and use its seaplanes and dirigibles more efficiently for surveying the eastern shores for German U-boats, the German vessels that had been targeting American ships (Wikipedia, "Elizabeth City, North Carolina").

Beginning of the United States Navy Lighter-Than-Air Stations in the United States. Before World War II began, there was only one lighter-than-air (LTA) station operated by the United States Navy in the nation. This LTA station, which had been established in 1921, was at Lakehurst, New Jersey, about 25 miles east-southeast of Trenton, New Jersey. The LTA station carried the name Naval Air Engineering Station Lakehurst.

Perhaps the Lakehurst station is most famous as being the site of the Hindenburg disaster. On May 6, 1937, at 7:25 p.m. the dirigible *Hindenburg*, which was carrying passengers from Germany to the United States, burst into flame. The accident ended 35 of the 97 lives aboard and brought an end to passenger travel in lighter-than-air crafts (About.com, "*Hindenburg* Disaster").

Lighter-Than-Air (LTA) Equipment for Surveillance. The United States Navy recognized the need to guard American shores and ships from German submarines. Locating submerged vessels from the deck of a ship was nearly impossible, but observing the U-boats from an LTA gondola was an easy task. Many of these dirigibles would later have sensors, depth charges, and weapons—including machine guns.

In 1940 the United States Navy presented to Congress its plan for a nontraditional, German U-boat surveillance program; the proposal called for the use of LTA equipment to patrol the coastlines and harbors for German U-boats. The details specified the expansion of Lakehurst and the restoration of Moffett Field in Sunnyvale, California. To carry out the project, the U.S. Navy requested also the construction of new stations: one at Cape Hatteras and others at Boston, Cape May, Georgia, Florida, Louisiana, Los Angeles, San Francisco, and Puget Sound (Wikipedia, "Naval Air Engineering Station Lakehurst").

The card shows an unidentified dirigible in flight over an unidentified location. This "Postkarte" is without company, place of publication, or date.

LTA Facility in Weeksville. In December of 1940 the United States Navy sent inspectors to the North Carolina coast to locate some flat land that was without power lines and smokestacks and that would be suitable for a base. After evaluating 43 locations, the assessors selected the ideal site for the naval station: Weeksville. Work began the following summer.

The construction of offices, storehouses, quarters, and helium and gas storage facilities began. Workers laid railroad tracks from Elizabeth City to Weeksville to transport the metal and steel components from the American Bridge Company of Ambridge, Pennsylvania; metal hangar construction often used the truss technology of bridges for design.

The proposed metal hangar would resemble an upended boat; metal trusses would help support the facility. There would be few visible, supporting columns on the 20-story building to detract from the storage space. This hangar was one of only two whose construction began before December 7, 1941.

The need for the LTA program is obvious. In the first months of 1942, 63 ships had sunk as a result of German warfare. On April 1, 1942—the day of the commissioning of the Weeksville base with its huge metal hangar—3 ships had sunk off the Carolina coast.

The airships that Weeksville serviced and housed in its 1,000-foot-long hangar were primarily K-class airships, measuring 252 feet long. The K-class ship was 60 feet longer than the Goodyear blimps of today. K-class vessels were originally constructed of rubberized cotton and filled with 425,000 cubic feet of air and helium. The sight of these huge dirigibles was impressive to U-boat crews. The navy originally planned for at least six airships to be stored in this facility (Swift).

Increased Needs for LTA Hangars in the United States. To meet the increased need for blimps, the United States Navy added 17 hangars in the United States. The navy approved one of these additional hangars at the Weeksville base almost immediately. This hangar was wooden. The wooden facility was 100 feet longer than the metal storage facility. The wood in the hangar was Southern yellow pine. The wooden hangar was the largest wooden structure in the world (National Lighter-Than-Air Historical Center; RoadsideAmerica. com).

Operating from the Weeksville base were ZNP-K patrols, named for their airships. Z was the designation for lighter-than-air. N indicated that the airship was non-rigid. P designated patrol. K represented the non-rigid, K-type airship, "the backbone of the Navy's airship fleet"; Weeksville housed and serviced primarily the K-type dirigibles. The crews "walked" the airships both in and out of the Weeksville hangar. About 40 men were necessary for docking and undocking a K-type airship (Naval History and Heritage Command).

Weeksville Hangars After World War II. After the end of World War II, the two giant hangars at Weeksville became storage units for airplanes. In 1947, new airships came to Weeksville, but the base finally closed in 1957. The use of helicopters had often replaced the use of blimps, so there was a lesser need for maintenance of the surveillance vessels.

Westinghouse Electric Corporation bought the complete base in 1966. The company found, however, that the metal facility with its high ceilings was almost impossible to heat and that the acoustics were unacceptable.

Westinghouse moved IXL, a cabinet maker, into the metal facility. A drop ceiling installed 24 feet from the concrete floor made the metal hangar more acceptable for the needs of IXL (Swift).

TCOM—a manufacturer of LTA devices and persistent surveillance systems—moved into the wooden hangar and continued its businesses in the new facilities. TCOM is still operating today and still presents itself as offering affordable persistent surveillance solutions. The fate of the wooden hangar,

12. The Northern Tidewater Subregion

however, was not as fortunate as that of TCOM or as that of Hangar No. 1—its metal counterpart still in use 70 years later (TCOM).

On August 4, 1995, things changed. A welder's torch set fire to the 50-year-old wooden hangar. The blaze was visible all the way from Weeksville to Norfolk, Virginia, a distance of more than 50 miles. Swift says that the glow from the fire was almost bright enough for people in Elizabeth City—8 miles away—to read by its light.

Evidence of the existence of the wooden hangar remained for some time after the extinguished blaze. Four columns rose 130 feet in the air. The concrete pad, which was nearly a quarter of a mile long, still remained. The wooden hangar was gone. TCOM, however, continued its testing and manufacturing operations in the Weeksville area; the company was able to operate for a while from a former KMart building until it could relocate.

In 1996, IXL moved out of the metal hangar, and TCOM moved inside. One of the first things that TCOM did was to remove the drop ceiling so that blimps and aerostats could float inside. The interest in LTAs—including the tethered aerostats—resurged.

Aerostats and Hangar 1 in Weeksville. Inside Hangar No. 1 in Weeksville today are some aerostats with new purposes. The use of some of these aerostats is to float over battlefields; a camera fastened underneath the aerostat records the scene below. Fiber-optic cables and 10,000-foot extension cords contribute to the success of their missions.

There are additional types of skins for the aerostats since the 1940s. The covering is no longer only rubberized cotton; instead the skins are a lightweight polyester laminate. With the polyester-laminate skin, the internal pressure per square inch is only two ounces; this means that a hole will result in a slow leak—not a "pop."

Aerostats can vary in size. A TCOM aerostat security model for use in Afghanistan might be only 72 feet. An aerostat for another purpose might be 243 feet long and able to lift 4 tons of freight to a height of 10,000. In 2012 TCOM had finished its largest LTA to date; the aerostat was a 351-foot whale, which could be manned and used as surveillance in the Middle East (Swift).

The United States Navy built eight hangars in 1941 for use during World War II. The Weeksville hangar is the only one of the eight still in operation today. The steel hangar is a massive 1,040 feet long by 296 feet wide. Its cost was over $6 million in the 1940s. In addition to the airdock, a mooring field for the LTAs, two runways, a seaplane launching ramp, and several mooring positions are still evident.

The effectiveness of the use of the blimps during World War II is evident. Before the operations of the LTAs at Weeksville, enemy submarines eradicated one ship every other day off the North Carolina coast; after Weeksville began its operations, enemy submarines sank one ship off the coast every two and one half months (Through the Lens, Ltd.).

The numbers above are some indications of the many contributions that Weeksville, the LTAs, and the base made to North Carolina and World War II.

The Northern Tidewater Subregion of the North Carolina Coastal Region and Its Vital World War II Efforts and Contributions: Consolidated Vultee Aircraft

Vultee Aircraft had a sizeable impact on World War II, on the nation, and on North Carolina.

Origin of Consolidated Vultee Aircraft Corporation. Gerard "Jerry" Freebairn Vultee (1900–1938) studied aviation science at Caltech from 1921 to 1923. During his time at Caltech, Vultee designed and built a full-sized aircraft.

In 1923 Art Mankey managed engineering at Douglas Aircraft. He was impressed with Jerry Vultee and hired the young man as a structural aeronautical engineer for Douglas Aircraft.

Another employee at Douglas in the early 1920s was Jack Northrop. Northrop was working on his own plan for a commercial aircraft and shared his ideas with Vultee and Alan Loughead (later spelled "Lockheed"). In 1928 Northop and Vultee together built the plane: the Vega. The plane proved very popular—especially with Amelia Earhart and Charles Lindbergh. Vultee produced many innovations, among which were retractable landing gears and large Vultee wing flaps that made reduced landing speeds possible.

When Lockheed sold out to Detroit Aircraft during the Great Depression, Vultee lost his position as chief engineer. He taught drafting and engineering at Curtiss Wright Technical and began working with Vance Breese on a six-passenger, single-engine monoplane (the Vultee–1).

In 1931 Vultee and Breese found financial backing for their plane from Errett Lobban Cord. Cord was the head of the Cord Corporation, the founder of two airlines; Cord was the owner of two aviation companies (Stinson Aircraft and Lycoming Motors), two automobile companies (Auburn and Dusenberg), two airlines, and five other engine manufacturers. Cord believed that Vultee's high-speed plane might serve to replace the Stinson tri-motors he was currently using.

In January 1932, Cord hired Vultee as chief engineer to work on the Vultee V-1 transport for a subsidiary of the Cord Corporation. The single-engine plane could reach a speed of 235 mph and was the fastest of its kind. When the federal government ruled that commercial planes be multi-engine, the V-1A was no longer viable.

When Cord faced labor problems (1932), he sold his airlines to American Airways for 7 percent of the stock of Aviation Corporation. By late 1932, Cord owned 30 percent of the stock in Aviation Corporation and gained control of the company.

After the passage of the Air Mail Act of 1934, no air mail contractor could hold interest in any aviation company. Cord had to restructure the company and get rid of American Airways, renamed American Airlines. Gerard Vultee became vice president and chief engineer of the Aviation Manufacturing Company in 1936. After further reorganization, in 1937 an independent company—the Vultee Aircraft Division—carried Vultee's name. Gerard Vultee and his wife Sylvia died in a plane crash after presenting a new plane design to the United States Army Air Corps.

The name of the plant became Vultee Aircraft, a subsidiary of the Aviation Company; Stinson Aircraft became a division of Vultee. Richard Palmer was the new president of the company. The company became Vultee Aircraft Incorporated, which became a subsidiary of the Aviation Company (1939). In 1941 Vultee became majority owner of Consolidated Aircraft Company; at their merger the new name was Consolidated Vultee Aircraft Corporation. The corporation was located at Elizabeth City, discussed above.

Vultee Plane Manufacturing. Vultee was the first major plane manufacturing plant to use powered assembly lines. The powered assembly line consisted of "an overhead oval track, located at the head of the final assembly, from which dangle twenty-five cradles fed with raw fuselage frames" (Western Museum of Flight). Vultee was able to produce more planes in a shorter time than any other similar plant.

By July 1941, Vultee was manufacturing 15 percent of the nation's military aircraft. Vultee was the first employer of women in the production of military aircraft. The Vultee company paid women the same pay for equivalent work—unusual at the time.

Consolidated Vultee Aircraft Corporation and the Military. From 1942 to 1948 Consolidated Vultee Aircraft Corporation (Convair) produced 11,537 trainers (Valiants), many PBYs (U.S. Navy patrol planes), and the largest number of B-24 Liberators (bombers) produced in the country. Convair contracted with the United States Navy for short-range missiles. Convair produced almost "every type of military aircraft from small, single engine, civilian defense trainers to huge, multiple engine land and sea bombers" (Western Museum of Flight).

When World War II began, warplanes in the United States were scarce and ill-equipped in many instances. The struggle to secure fighting equipment for the men and planes at the Coast Guard station at Elizabeth City was a fierce one. Consolidated Vultee was part of the struggle. To illustrate the frustration encountered, one might consider the following:

> Consolidated Vultee had a fleet of RCAF PBY-5s equipped with bomb racks but no bombs; the Coast Guard had pilots, the Navy Base on the other side had depth charges. The PBY-5s were frozen on the ground by commitment to the British Lend Lease Program; but owing to the efforts of Coast Guard pioneer aviator and air station commanding officer LT Richard L. Burke and a release given by Canadian and Commandant Pat Wing Atlantic Fleet, two of the frozen planes were thawed loose, depth charges were put in the bomb racks, Consolidated pilots were assembled and for the first time. Co-pilot Coast Guardsmen flew in armed planes to find the enemy, however these planes were shortly to be sent away on another assignment [U.S. Coast Guard, "Air Station Elizabeth City"].

Another instance of the difficulty of securing air power for the United States forces was a 1944 event. The Marine Bombing Squadron 6–13 received a J-model PBJ; the ability of the squad to use this plane was "virtually nil as it was immediately flown to the Consolidated-Vultee Modification Center at Elizabeth City, North Carolina for radar installation and naval modifications and was subsequently replaced with a PBJ-1H" (Marine Bombing Squadron Six-Thirteen).

Vultee did its part in preparing war-ready aircraft. The charge was not easy, but Vultee strived to fill its charge.

Vultee and the Aircraft Repair and Supply Center (Elizabeth City) After World War II. The Aircraft Repair and Supply Center received its commission in 1947 as a subunit of the Coast Guard Air Station Elizabeth City. The military sought a suitable location for the Aircraft Repair and Supply Center.

The coast guard was able to secure the facilities of the Consolidated Vultee Corporation in Elizabeth City for its Aircraft Repair and Supply Center. Consolidated Vultee Corporation (Conaire) in Elizabeth City, thus, continued to serve Elizabeth City, North Carolina, and the military even after the end of World War II (Military.com, "USCG Elizabeth City, NC").

CHAPTER 13

The Incalculable Costs of World War I and the Great Depression to the World, the Nation, the State, and North Carolinians Before World War II

The twentieth century began with presenting the United States with two seemingly insurmountable challenges: World War I and the Great Depression of the 1930s.

World War I. World War I—"the war to end all wars"—drastically changed the nation and the world. Many families had to adjust to the loss of family members.

Returning troops had to make adjustments. They found awaiting them a new era: the Roaring Twenties, the Jazz Age, a period of personal extravagance that included laborsaving devices, materialism, unwise investments, new social codes, chewing gum, motion pictures, and Prohibition, which caused many ex-soldiers to carry flasks of bootleg liquor instead of rifles.

A particular feature of the 1920s was the considerable increase in the number of automobiles. There was a jump from 548,000 registered cars in 1910 to 8,132,000 in 1920 to 21,362,000 in 1928. This meant that in 1910 about 1 out of every 36.5 households owned an automobile; by 1920, 1 out of every 3.0 households registered an automobile; by 1928 there was 1 car for every 1.4 households (Kurian 1994, 30, 267; Donovan 1965, 32, 158).

The Great Depression. Recovery from the violence of World War I had barely begun when other challenges presented themselves. On the morning of Thursday, October 24, 1929, a panic had occurred. Traders exchanged more than 12 million shares in a single day. The crash of the stock market followed on October 29, 1929—Black Tuesday; this was a 16-million-share day. Rapidly the loss became more than $30 billion. The Great Depression had begun (Davis 2003, 5).

Throughout the nation there were other indications of the problems to come. Banks began to fail. The number of households with vehicles began to decline (McElvaine 1983, 20).

Americans responded in a variety of ways. Some despondent Americans resorted to suicide. Contrary to public opinion, most of these suicides did not occur with the crash of the stock market in 1929. The Metropolitan Life Insurance Company noted that 20,000 persons took their lives in 1931 (Time-Life Editors 1969, 25). The highest suicide rate in the century occurred in the year 1932—17.4 per 100,000 as compared to 14 per 100,000 in 1929 (McElvaine 1983, 18).

Two specific events accentuated the arrival of hard times: First, in the summer of 1932 eleven thousand men assembled in Washington, D.C., to demand additional government payments from Congress for ex-servicemen (Chitwood et al. 1949, 765). Second, on the morning of March 4, 1933, America and Herbert Hoover awoke to the collapse of the banking system. This final defeat brought Hoover's remark, "We are at the end of our string." Many Americans agreed (Time-Life Editors 1969, 23). Times were hard, but even leaner years lay ahead for many.

No one lived through the 1930s without being affected by the Great Depression. With stocks dropping, banks closing, industries failing, lenders foreclosing, jobs decreasing, workloads increasing, salaries dropping, droughts and floods ravaging the land, and disease and malnutrition escalating, despair prevailed. Even the well-to-do knew of the pain and suffering about them. Hard times had come.

The Great Depression defined the nation and continues to shape current generations. The work ethics, the life styles, the values, and the traditions begun in the 1930s still remain constant in the lives of many of that generation and in the lives of their descendants. Many Americans still squeeze the last of the toothpaste from the tube and "save for hard times"; these actions remind us that the past is still with us (Davis 2003, 3).

The thirties did not clearly indicate what was to come: World War II.

CHAPTER 14

The Incalculable Costs of World War II

The first years of the twentieth century with their accompanying World War I and the Great Depression of the 1930s had brought hardship to North Carolina, to the nation, and to the world. Before the decade of the thirties had ended, however, war began in Europe. These hostilities resulted in another world war: World War II.

The surprise attack on Pearl Harbor hit the nation like a mighty blow on December 7, 1941. This plague of war would continue to impact the nation and its people for years to come.

Number of Americans and North Carolinians Who Served in World War II. Before the end of World War II, there were 16,112,566 Americans who served in the military. This number was almost four times the number—4,734,991—of Americans who served in World War I.

With 48 states in the United States, the average number of Americans serving for each state would have been 335,678. North Carolina did more than its part in World War II, however (Congressional Research Service).

Rather than contributing the average of 335,678 enlistees, North Carolina furnished 361,000 troops: 258,000 to the army, 90,000 to the navy, and 13,000 to the marines. North Carolina trained more enlisted men and women than any other state and hosted more than 20 military installations (Siniard).

World War II Casualties for the United States and North Carolina. The United States suffered an estimated 405,399 casualties during World War II. If one were to divide the 405,399 by 48 (the number of states in the 1940s), one would find that the average number of casualties would be 8,333 per state (Congressional Research Service). North Carolina gave 8,500 lives. This was more than the average 8,333 per state (Learn NC).

Of course it is difficult to write of the deaths of these North Carolinians using just numbers and without considering their lives. Each of these men was a son; many were husbands and fathers. Their deaths affected many people.

"Real Heroes." Navy Corpsman John Henry Bradley (pharmacist's mate) was a participant in the flag raisings on Iwo Jima during World War II. He continued to serve his country by participating in bond-selling events, but he did not talk much about his service to his son James Bradley or to others.

James Bradley was able to research, to talk (finally) with his father about World War II, and to write about his father's service in *Flags of Our Fathers*. John denied being a hero. James quoted his father as saying, "The real heroes ... are the guys who didn't come back" (Bradley 2000, 4).

North Carolina produced many heroes and "real heroes" during World War II. Those in service were combat engineers, paratroopers, fighter pilots, tail gunners, waist gunners, medics, infantrymen, seamen, and engineers—to name a few of their roles. They performed their appointed tasks—big and small—as they had been taught to do: to the best of their ability. Not only did these North Carolinians respond to the challenge, they excelled in their service to their country and distinguished themselves. Those in command bestowed upon the state's enlisted personnel many awards—some posthumously—including the Bronze Star, the Oak-Leaf Cluster, the Silver Star, the Soldier's Medal, the Air Medal, the Good Conduct Medal, the Expert, and the Sharpshooter Medal. Some North Carolina men received the Purple Heart. From 1932 until September of 1942, this award was for merit and for war wounds; thereafter, the award went only to those classified as KIA (killed in action), WIA (wounded in action), or DOW (died of wounds) (Davis 2003, 8–9).

The next chapter will consider the North Carolina Medal of Honor winners.

Chapter 15

The Medal of Honor

During World War II North Carolina had several Medal of Honor winners.

Definition of the Medal of Honor. The prestigious Medal of Honor is the highest military honor that the president of the United States awards in the name of Congress; the president presents the Medal of Honor only to United States military personnel for personal acts of valor above and beyond the call of duty.

The Medal of Honor is *not* the "Congressional Medal of Honor," which is an incorrect designation that some persons use. The name of the award is—correctly and simply—the Medal of Honor, or the MOH.

There is a version of the medal for the United States Army, another for the United States Navy, and a third for the United States Air Force. Military personnel of the United States Marine Corps and of the United States Coast Guard who earn the distinction receive the version of the United States Navy.

Number of Recipients During World War II. There were 464 Medals of Honor presented to military personnel who served during World War II. Of these 464 awards, 266 were posthumous.

Today, the president of the United States normally presents the Medal of Honor during a formal ceremony at the White House. The intent of the official ceremony is to signify the gratitude of the American people. If a presentation is posthumous, the next of kin usually receives the award.

United States law affords special protection to the Medal of Honor. The Medal of Honor is not to be sold or manufactured. No unauthorized adornment—including any badge or ribbon—may accompany the MOH (Wikipedia, "Medal of Honor").

Seven of the 464 World War II Medals of Honor went to North Carolinians. Some argue that the State of North Carolina should receive credit also for an eighth medal presented to the youngest American in this century to earn such an award.

Youngest American to Receive Medal of Honor. Jacklyn Lucas enlisted in Virginia, but he was born in North Carolina. The seventeen-year-old received the Medal of Honor just five days after his seventeenth birthday; he had already been in service for three years. His citation is in the accompanying list (Sterner).

Citations for the Eight North Carolinians to Receive the Medal of Honor in World War II. The complete citation of each Medal of Honor winner tells much of their story. These citations follow.

Eubanks, Ray E.

Rank and organization: Sergeant, U.S. Army, Company D, 503d Parachute Infantry.
Place and date: At Noemfoor Island, Dutch New Guinea, 23 July 1944.
Entered service at: LaGrange, N.C.
Born: 6 February 1922, Snow Hill, N.C.
General Order Number: 20, 29 March 1945.

Citation: For conspicuous gallantry and intrepidity at the risk of his life above and beyond the call of duty at Noemfoor Island, Dutch New Guinea, 23 July 1944. While moving to the relief of a platoon isolated by the enemy, his company encountered a strong enemy position supported by machine gun, rifle, and mortar fire. Sgt. Eubanks was ordered to make an attack with 1 squad to neutralize the enemy by fire in order to assist the advance of his company. He maneuvered his squad to within 30 yards of the enemy where heavy fire checked his advance. Directing his men to maintain their fire, he and 2 scouts worked their way forward up a shallow depression to within 25 yards of the enemy. Directing the scouts to remain in place, Sgt. Eubanks armed himself with an automatic rifle and worked himself forward over terrain swept by intense fire to within 15 yards of the enemy position when he opened fire with telling effect. The enemy, having located his position, concentrated their fire with the result that he was wounded and a bullet rendered his rifle useless. In spite of his painful wounds he immediately charged the enemy and using his weapon as a club killed 4 of the enemy before he was himself again hit and killed. Sgt. Eubanks' heroic action, courage, and example in leadership so inspired his men that their advance was successful. They killed 45 of the enemy and drove the remainder from the position, thus effecting the relief of our beleaguered troops.

15. The Medal of Honor

Halyburton, William David, Jr.

Rank and organization: Pharmacist's Mate Second Class, U.S. Naval Reserve.
Born: 2 August 1924, Canton, N.C.
Accredited to: North Carolina.

Citation: For conspicuous gallantry and intrepidity at the risk of his life above and beyond the call of duty while serving with a Marine Rifle Company in the 2d Battalion, 5th Marines, 1st Marine Division, during action against enemy Japanese forces on Okinawa Shima in the Ryukyu Chain, 10 May 1945. Undaunted by the deadly accuracy of Japanese counter fire as his unit pushed the attack through a strategically important draw, Halyburton unhesitatingly dashed across the draw and up the hill into an open fire-swept field where the company advance squad was suddenly pinned down under a terrific concentration of mortar, machinegun and sniper fire with resultant severe casualties. Moving steadily forward despite the enemy's merciless barrage, he reached the wounded marine who lay farthest away and was rendering first aid when his patient was struck for the second time by a Japanese bullet. Instantly placing himself in the direct line of fire, he shielded the fallen fighter with his own body and staunchly continued his ministrations although constantly menaced by the slashing fury of shrapnel and bullets falling on all sides. Alert, determined and completely unselfish in his concern for the helpless marine, he persevered in his efforts until he himself sustained mortal wounds and collapsed, heroically sacrificing himself that his comrade might live. By his outstanding valor and unwavering devotion to duty in the face of tremendous odds, Halyburton sustained and enhanced the highest traditions of the U.S. Naval Service. He gallantly gave his life in the service of his country.

Herring, Rufus G.

Rank and organization: Lieutenant, U.S. Naval Reserve, LCI (G) 449.
Place and date: Iwo Jima, 17 February 1945.
Entered service at: North Carolina.
Born: 11 June 1921, Roseboro, N.C.

Citation: For conspicuous gallantry and intrepidity at the risk of his life above and beyond the call of duty as commanding officer of LCI (G) 449 operating as a unit of LCI (G) Group 8, during the pre-invasion attack on Iwo Jima on 17 February 1945. Boldly closing the strongly fortified shores under the devastating fire of Japanese coastal defense guns, Lt. (then Lt. [j.g.]) Herring directed shattering barrages of 40mm. and 20mm. gunfire against hostile beaches until struck down by the enemy's savage counter fire which blasted the 449's heavy guns and whipped her decks into sheets of flame. Regaining consciousness despite profuse bleeding he was again critically wounded when a Japanese mortar crashed the conning station, instantly killing or fatally wounding most of the officers and leaving the ship wallowing without navigational control. Upon recovering the second time, Lt. Herring resolutely climbed down to the pilothouse and, fighting against his rapidly waning strength, took over the helm, established communication with the engine room, and carried on valiantly until relief could be obtained. When no longer able to stand, he propped himself against empty shell cases and rallied his men to the aid of the wounded; he maintained position in the firing line with his 20mm. guns in action in the face of sustained enemy fire, and conned his crippled ship to safety. His unwavering fortitude, aggressive perseverance, and indomitable spirit against terrific odds reflect the highest credit upon Lt. Herring and uphold the highest traditions of the U.S. Naval Service.

Lucas, Jacklyn H.

Rank and organization: Private First Class (U.S. Marine Corps); Captain (U.S. Army)
Place and date: Iwo Jima, 20 February 1945.
Entered service at: Norfolk, Virginia. (Some sources credit him to the State of Virginia even though he was born in North Carolina.)
Born: 14 February 1928, Plymouth, N.C.

Citation: For conspicuous gallantry and intrepidity at the risk of his life above and beyond the call of duty while serving with the First Battalion, Twenty-sixth Marines, Fifth Marine Division, during action against enemy Japanese forces on Iwo Jima, Volcano Islands 20 February 1945. While creeping through a treacherous, twisting ravine which ran in close proximity to a fluid and uncertain front line on D-plus+1 Day, Private First Class Lucas and three other men were suddenly ambushed by a hostile patrol which savagely attacked with rifle fire and grenades. Quick to act when the lives of the small group were endangered by two grenades which landed directly in front of them, Private First Class Lucas unhesitatingly hurled himself over his comrades upon one grenade and pulled the other one under him, absorbing the whole blasting force of the explosions in his own body in order to shield his companions from the concussion and murderous flying fragments. By his inspiring action and valiant spirit of self-sacrifice, he not only protected his comrades from certain injury or possible death, but also enabled them to rout the Japanese patrol and continue the advance. His exceptionally courageous initiative and loyalty reflect the highest credit upon Private First Class Lucas and the United States Naval Service.

Murray, Charles P., Jr.

Rank and organization: First Lieutenant, U.S. Army, Company C, 30th Infantry, 3d Infantry Division.
Place and date: Near Kaysersberg, France, 16 December 1944.
Entered service at: Wilmington, N.C.
Birth: Baltimore, Md.
General Order Number: 63, 1 August 1945.

Citation: For commanding Company C, 30th Infantry, displaying supreme courage and heroic initiative near Kaysersberg, France, on 16 December 1944, while leading a reinforced platoon into enemy territory. Descending into a valley beneath hilltop positions held by our troops, he observed a force of 200 Germans pouring deadly mortar, bazooka, machinegun, and small arms fire into an American battalion occupying the crest of the ridge. The enemy's position in a sunken road, though hidden from the ridge, was open to a flank attack by 1st Lt. Murray's patrol but he hesitated to commit so small a force to battle with the superior and strongly disposed enemy. Crawling out ahead of his troops to a vantage point, he called by radio for artillery fire. His shells bracketed the German force, but when he was about to correct the range his radio went dead. He returned to his patrol, secured grenades and a rifle to launch them and went back to his self-appointed outpost. His first shots disclosed his position; the enemy directed heavy fire against him as he methodically fired his missiles into the narrow defile. Again he returned to his patrol. With an automatic rifle and ammunition, he once more moved to his exposed position. Burst after burst he fired into the enemy, killing 20, wounding many others, and completely disorganizing its ranks, which began to withdraw. He prevented the removal of 3 German mortars by knocking out a truck. By that time a mortar had been brought to his support. 1st Lt. Murray directed fire of this weapon, causing further casualties and confusion in the German ranks. Calling on his patrol to follow, he then moved out toward his original objective, possession of a bridge and construction of a roadblock. He captured 10 Germans in foxholes. An eleventh, while pretending to surrender, threw a grenade which knocked him to the ground, inflicting 8 wounds. Though suffering and bleeding profusely, he refused to return to the rear until he had chosen the spot for the block and had seen his men correctly deployed. By his single-handed attack on an overwhelming force and by his intrepid and heroic fighting, 1st Lt. Murray stopped a counterattack, established an advance position against formidable odds, and provided an inspiring example for the men of his command.

Thompson, Max

Rank and Organization: Sergeant, U.S. Army, Company K, 18th Infantry, 1st Infantry Division.
Place and date: Near Haaren, Germany, 18 October 1944.
Entered Service at: Prescott, Ariz.
Birth: Bethel, N.C.
General Order Number: 47, 18 June 1945.

Citation: On 18 October 1944, Company K, 18th Infantry, occupying a position on a hill near Haaren, Germany, was attacked by an enemy infantry battalion supported by tanks. The assault was preceded by an artillery concentration, lasting an hour, which inflicted heavy casualties on the company. While engaged in moving wounded men to cover, Sgt. Thompson observed that the enemy had overrun the positions of the 3d Platoon. He immediately attempted to stem the enemy's advance single-handedly. He manned an abandoned machinegun and fired on the enemy until a direct hit from a hostile tank destroyed the gun. Shaken and dazed, Sgt. Thompson picked up an automatic rifle and although alone against the enemy force which was pouring into the gap in our lines, he fired burst after burst, halting the leading elements of the attack and dispersing those following. Throwing aside his automatic rifle, which had jammed, he took up a rocket gun, fired on a light tank, setting it on fire. By evening the enemy had been driven from the greater part of the captured position but still held 3 pillboxes. Sgt. Thompson's squad was assigned the task of dislodging the enemy from these emplacements. Darkness having fallen and finding that fire of his squad was ineffective from a distance, Sgt. Thompson crawled forward alone to within 20 yards of 1 of the pillboxes and fired grenades into it. The Germans holding the emplacement concentrated their fire upon him. Though wounded, he held his position fearlessly, continued his grenade fire, and finally forced the enemy to abandon the blockhouse. Sgt. Thompson's courageous leadership inspired his men and materially contributed to the clearing of the enemy from his last remaining hold on this important hill position.

Urban, Matt

Rank and organization: Lieutenant Colonel (then Captain), 2d Battalion, 60th Infantry Regiment, 9th Infantry Division, World War II.
Place and date: Renouf, France, 14 June to 3 September 1944.
Entered service at: Fort Bragg, North Carolina, 2 July 1941.
Date and place of birth: 25 August 1919, Buffalo, New York.

Citation: Lieutenant Colonel (then Captain) Matt Urban, l 12-22-2414, United States Army, who distinguished himself by a series of bold, heroic actions, exemplified by singularly outstanding combat leadership, personal bravery, and tenacious devotion to duty, during the period 14 June to 3 September 1944 while assigned to the 2d Battalion, 60th Infantry Regiment, 9th Infantry Division. On 14 June, Captain Urban's company, attacking at Renouf, France, encountered heavy enemy small arms and tank fire. The enemy tanks were unmercifully raking his unit's positions and inflicting heavy casualties. Captain Urban, realizing that his company was in imminent danger of being decimated, armed himself with a bazooka. He worked his way with an ammo carrier through hedgerows, under a continuing barrage of fire, to a point near the tanks. He brazenly exposed himself to the enemy fire and, firing the bazooka, destroyed both tanks. Responding to Captain Urban's action, his company moved forward and routed the enemy. Later that same day, still in the attack near Orglandes, Captain Urban was wounded in the leg by direct fire from a 37mm tank-gun. He refused evacuation and continued to lead his company until they moved into defensive positions for the night. At 0500 hours the next day, still in the attack near Orglandes, Captain Urban, though badly wounded, directed his company in another attack. One hour later he was again wounded. Suffering from two wounds, one serious, he was evacuated to England. In mid-July, while recovering from his wounds, he learned of his unit's severe losses in the hedgerows of Normandy. Realizing his unit's need for battle-tested leaders, he voluntarily left the hospital and hitchhiked his way back to his unit hear St. Lo, France. Arriving at the 2d Battalion Command Post at 1130 hours, 25 July, he found that his unit had jumped-off at 1100 hours in the first attack of Operation Cobra. Still limping from his leg wound, Captain Urban made his way forward to retake command of his company. He found his company held up by strong enemy opposition. Two supporting tanks had been destroyed and another, intact but with no tank commander or gunner, was not moving. He located a lieutenant in charge of the support tanks and directed a plan of attack to eliminate the enemy strong-point. The lieutenant and a sergeant were immediately killed by the heavy enemy fire when they tried to mount the tank. Captain Urban, though physically hampered by his leg wound and knowing quick action had to be taken, dashed through the scathing fire and mounted the tank. With enemy bullets ricocheting from the tank, Captain Urban ordered the tank forward and, completely exposed to the enemy fire, manned the machine gun and placed devastating fire on the enemy. His action, in the face of enemy fire, galvanized the battalion into action and they attacked and destroyed the enemy position. On 2 August, Captain Urban was wounded in the chest by shell fragments and, disregarding the recommendation of the Battalion Surgeon, again refused evacuation. On 6 August, Captain Urban became the commander of the 2d Battalion. On 15 August, he was again wounded but remained with his unit. On 3 September, the 2d Battalion was given the mission of establishing a crossing-point on the Meuse River near Heer, Belgium. The enemy planned to stop the advance of the allied Army by concentrating heavy forces at the Meuse. The 2d Battalion, attacking toward the crossing-point, encountered fierce enemy artillery, small arms and mortar fire which stopped the attack. Captain Urban quickly moved from his command post to the lead position of the battalion. Reorganizing the attacking elements, he personally led a charge toward the enemy's strongpoint. As the charge moved across the open terrain, Captain Urban was seriously wounded in the neck. Although unable to talk above a whisper from the paralyzing neck wound, and in danger of losing his life, he refused to be evacuated until the enemy was routed and his battalion had secured the crossing-point on the Meuse River. Captain Urban's personal leadership, limitless bravery, and repeated extraordinary exposure to enemy fire served as an inspiration to his entire battalion. His valorous and intrepid actions reflect the utmost credit on him and uphold the noble traditions of the United States.

Warner, Henry F.

Rank and Organization: Corporal, U.S. Army, Antitank Company, 2d Battalion, 26th Infantry, 1st Infantry Division.
Place and date: Near Dom Butgenbach, Belgium, 20–21 December 1944.
Entered Service at: Troy, N.C.
Born: 23 August 1923, Troy, N.C.
General Order Number: 48, 23 June 1945.

Citation: Serving as 57-mm. antitank gunner with the 2d Battalion, he was a major factor in stopping enemy tanks during heavy attacks against the battalion position near Dom Butgenbach, Belgium, on 20–21 December 1944. In the first attack, launched in the early morning of the 20th, enemy tanks succeeded in penetrating parts of the line. Cpl. Warner, disregarding the concentrated cannon and machinegun fire from 2 tanks bearing down on him, and ignoring the imminent danger of being overrun by the infantry moving under tank cover, destroyed the first tank and scored a direct and deadly hit upon the second. A third tank approached to within 5 yards of his position while he was attempting to clear a jammed breach lock. Jumping from his gun pit, he engaged in a pistol duel with the tank commander standing in the turret, killing him and forcing the tank to withdraw. Following a day and night during which our forces were subjected to constant shelling, mortar barrages, and numerous unsuccessful infantry attacks, the enemy struck in great force on the early morning of the 21st. Seeing a Mark IV tank looming out of the mist and heading toward his position, Cpl. Warner scored a direct hit. Disregarding his injuries, he endeavored to finish the loading and again fire at the tank whose motor was now aflame, when a second machinegun burst killed him. Cpl. Warner's gallantry and intrepidity at the risk of life above and beyond the call of duty contributed materially to the successful defense against the enemy attacks.

Chapter 16

The Home Front

Those at home endured hardships. Fears of the unknown and thoughts of an absent family member were never far from heart and mind.

The Blue Star Service Banner. The Blue Star Service Banner, sometimes called a service flag, often served as a reminder to others of the sacrifice that a family was making. Army captain Robert L. Queissner of the Fifth Ohio Infantry had two sons serving on the front line in World War I. He designed and patented the Blue Star Service Banner in 1917. It quickly became the unofficial symbol of having a descendent in the service.

The Congressional Record notes that a member of the Ohio Congress on September 24, 1917, read the following: "The mayor of Cleveland, the Chamber of Commerce and the governor of Ohio have adopted this service flag. The world should know of those who give so much for liberty. The dearest thing in all the world to a father and mother: their children" (Blue Stars for a Safe Return).

The Department of War specified details on the manufacture of the service flag during World War II, guidelines on who could display the service flag, and rules as to when one might fly the flag. The Blue Star Service Banner for window display was to be an 8.5" × 14" white field sewn onto a red banner. The overall size of this window banner was to be in the same proportion as that of the United States Flag (Blue Stars for a Safe Return).

Families today still display Blue Star Service Banners to honor members serving in the armed services, the national guard, and the reserves of all branches of the military. Businesses and organizations may also recognize members who are serving with a banner. Because up to five members of a family may serve, a banner may display five stars.

If a person symbolized by a blue star became a casualty while serving, the family superimposed a gold fabric star of a slightly smaller size over the blue star. The blue star formed a border. If the flag displayed multiple stars and included a gold star, to show honor the gold star was to be above the blue stars or to the right of the blue star.

Organizations such as the Blue Star Mothers and Gold Star Mothers recognize the mothers of sons in service; these groups sprang up first during World War II. A gold pin shows membership in the Gold Star Mothers Organization (Blue Stars for a Safe Return).

Religious Faith. During World War II, especially, chaplains made sacrifices in great numbers. More military chaplains gave their lives per capita than did any other military group—except for the army air corps (Velthouse).

Religious faith helped many at home—and abroad—to endure. Often North Carolina churches were open for daily prayer.

> The ringing of the church bells at noon each day is the call to prayer.... Any and all citizens are urged to share in these seasons of prayer. At that time one of the churches is open for any who will deny themselves a few minutes to come and join in the privileges of prayer. Any and all citizens are urged to share in these seasons of united prayer for our churches, our nation, our world, our fellow-citizens in the armed forces, and the coming of the King of Peace. If you care, come to the church for prayer. But wherever you are, take a few minutes immediately following the ringing of the bells for earnest, fervent prayer [*Rutherford County News*, May 11, 1944; Matthew Clark, *Daily Courier*, Vol. XIX. No. 15, 1944].

Salvaging, Rationing. Posters and the media encouraged thrift and salvaging. Metal drives were necessary and were frequent; North Carolinians saved metals for the construction of planes and ships.

Citizens also saved grease left over from cooking for recycling. These extra fats together with fabric scraps were important to munitions.

An important message that United States citizens received from posters, advertisements in newspapers and magazines, radio programs, and postcards was to be discrete and careful in whatever one said. Even children learned to be careful about sharing information with others.

Series E Defense Savings Bonds and War Stamps. On April 30, 1942, President Roosevelt announced the new Series E Defense Savings Bonds. Informally—and somewhat fondly—the public began to refer to the Series E Defense Savings Bonds of World War II as War Bonds. The original intent of the sale of these Series E Bonds was to raise money for the national defense of the United States, for American war efforts, and for the financial profit of the purchasers in the future.

This metal drive in Forest City, North Carolina, commands: "Let's stop Hitler. Put old aluminum here" (courtesy of David Daniel, Forest City, North Carolina).

Series E Defense Savings Bonds first became available to the public on Friday, May 1, 1942. President Roosevelt bought the first Series E Defense Savings Bond from United States Treasury Secretary Henry Morgenthau.

Initially, one could purchase Defense Savings Bonds through banks and other financial institutions. The Treasury Department also enabled workers to purchase the bonds through the Payroll Deduction Plan. The public soon began to refer to the Payroll Deduction Plan informally as the Payroll Savings Plan; the purchase of these investments online is still possible electronically.

War Stamps in small denominations (10¢, 25¢, 50¢, $1, $5) enabled almost any citizen, including children, to help the war effort for a dime.

16. The Home Front

This postcard postmarked October 2, 1942, urges the recipient and all who see the card to buy more War Bonds (U.S. Treasury Department, War Savings Staff).

Schools held drives to encourage the purchase of stamps in the community. Advertisements in newspapers publicized the drives.

Children and adults often hummed or sang the jingle "You get back four dollars for every three." Radio stations also played the jingle on the air, as they did Irving Berlin's "Any Bonds Today?" Through the program titled "Schools at War," the war effort purchased 90,000 Jeeps with the money from the bonds and stamps (Treasury Direct, "U.S. Savings Bonds").

Artists Who Aided the War Effort. Many artists contributed to the drive to sell War Bonds and War Stamps. Through their work they also discouraged waste and encouraged salvaging.

Roy Schatt had produced his *Harvesting Tobacco* (1941) for North Carolina's Whiteville Post Office. This work had been a product of the New Deal (Davis 2009, 185–87). Staff Sergeant Schatt continued his service to the United States government when he produced a poster for the United States Department of Agriculture in 1942. Schatt's poster, titled "Scrap," had the purpose of benefitting the military effort during the Second World War. "Scrap" shows a tall arm raised and a fist squeezing old metal farm equipment; a barn and windmill are in the background. This poster image encouraged conserving for the war effort.

Norman Rockwell, for instance, produced his oil paintings of "The Four Freedoms." These four paintings—"Freedom from Want," "Freedom from Fear," "Freedom of Worship," and "Freedom of Speech"—appeared on the covers of *The Saturday Evening Post* for February 20, February 27, March 6, and March 13, 1943. On a nationwide department store tour, these paintings raising $130 million in War Bond sales (National Archives).

Films and Songs Aiding the War Effort. Each week during World War II, ninety million Americans attended the movies. Newsreels preceded the main feature. Appeals to buy War Bonds and Stamps usually preceded the show. Occasionally a theatre would offer free admission with the purchase of a Series E Defense Savings Bond. Even the cartoons encouraged patriotism.

Besides the news updates and the cartoons encouraging patriotism, the main features often emphasized war themes. Combat action films, personal stories of war, and documentaries were well attended.

Casablanca (1942), with Humphrey Bogart and Ingrid Bergman, was a favorite story set in World War II; it won the Academy Award for the Best Motion Picture. *Thirty Seconds Over Tokyo* (1944), with Spencer Tracy and Van Johnson, celebrated the Doolittle Raid.

Even the songs of the era attempted to capture the emotions associated with war. Dinah Shore declared "I'll Walk Alone" (1944) until her love returned (from service). "I'll Be Seeing You" (1944) promises remembrances of the familiar places where the couple had been together. "I'll Be Home for Christmas" by Bing Crosby (1943) was the number one hit for eleven weeks; it promises the return of the absent sweetheart "if only in my dreams" (Wessels Living History Farm).

Film Stars Doing Their Part. Many actors and actresses contributed to the war effort in ways other than their parts in films. Bob Hope entertained the troops in World War II and for many years after.

Parades filled with stars promoted the war efforts. Star-studded shows toured, entertained, and encouraged the purchase of bonds. Mickey Rooney, Lucille Ball, and Judy Garland were among the stars who participated (Wessels Living History Farm).

Clark Gable, who starred in *Gone with the Wind*, was chair of the Hollywood Victory Committee and served as a combat pilot during World War II. Gable had enlisted in the military shortly after his third wife, Carole Lombard, died in a plane crash as she was returning from a War Bond drive. The grief-stricken Gable joined the United States Army Air Force and was off the screen for three years while he flew combat missions in Europe. Gable gave much to the war effort, as did other actors and actresses (Davis 2013, 130–31).

The Radio During World War II. The radio was important to most family units during World War II. Families regarded the radio as their primary source of immediate information. Radios across the nation turned to the news programs, and everyone gathered around the radio to keep up with what was going on across the world.

President Roosevelt used the radio for his "Fireside Chats." Roosevelt gave his series of 30 informal talks from 1933 to 1944. These speeches were on a variety of topics; the public received these radio communications well— especially those relating to World War II (History, "The Fireside Chats").

The content of the daily soap operas that many families enjoyed each day often changed with World War II. Sometimes a character would join the military in the script; the lives of those left behind would become a part of the new storyline.

With gas rationing and with family budgeting, the choice of staying at home to listen to the radio often seemed a good alternative for many people.

Radio spots reminded listeners to conserve, to purchase War Bonds and Stamps, and to speak with care.

Sentiments and Attitudes at Home in North Carolina. Posters reminded everyone, "Loose lips can sink ships." Newspaper images and post cards cautioned: "If you tell where he is going, he may never get there."

The typical sentiments of North Carolinians were that the war had to be won, that the boys had to come back home, and that those at home would do their part.

Outer Banks inhabitants observed blackouts and watched as German U-boats and Allied ships battled just offshore. People across the state and nation grew victory gardens, bought war bonds, and volunteered at USOs.

Scarcely a family in North Carolina was unaffected in some manner by the selective service. Those at home were determined to do their part to win the war and to bring those in service back home at the earliest practical moment. Women entered industry to take the place of men who had gone to war.

A shortage of workers required not only the women but also some of the retired workers to enter/re-enter the list of workers. The state's textile plants, shell plants, boat yards, and rubber plants were producing war goods and operating on full schedule. More than 20 military sites operated in the state of North Carolina, and the operations often needed the assistance of local residents. All these efforts called for many additional workers. President Roosevelt appealed to the American people, saying that the United States must be the arsenal of democracy.

The shortage of workers was keenly felt on the farms. Farmers found it necessary to increase both their acreage and their production per acre; this they managed to do, in spite of the fact that they had to achieve the increased results with less help than in the days when production was much lower. The citizens at home had to shoulder the additional load and the double production, in mills and on farms, with two men instead of eight.

But long hours of production were not the entire story. Many of these workers were connected with the various branches of the Office of Civilian Defense, which consumed what little leisure time they had (Griffin 1952, 19).

Those in service and those on the home front began making their sacrifices on the first day of the war. These sacrifices continued until Germany surrendered on May 8 and until Japan capitulated on August 14, 1945. Military casualties, however, continued throughout 1945.

Mothers and fathers never forgot their lost children; wives continued to grieve lost husbands; children grew up without their fathers; grandchildren never knew the love of a grandfather; siblings and friends mourned a lost comrade. Celebrations, however, marked the return of loved ones.

The people of the state and the nation had done their part—for God and country.

Bibliography

About.com. "*Hindenburg* Disaster." http://history1900s.about.com/cs/disasters/a/hindenburgcrash.htm.

_____. "Installation Overview: Pope Air Force Base, North Carolina." http://usmilitary.about.com/od/airforcebaseprofiles/ss/Pope.htm.

Academy of Achievement. "Stephen E. Ambrose, Ph.D." http://www.achievement.org/autodoc/page/amb0bio-1.

Air Force Historical Foundation. "Doolittle Award." http://www.afhistoricalfoundation.org/images/events/DoolittleAward-Final-Program.pdf.

Air Station Elizabeth City Wardroom. 2005. *Coast Guard Base Elizabeth City.* Charleston, South Carolina: Arcadia.

AJGA. "News and Notes." http://ajga.typepad.com/ajgablog/2012/07/news-and-notes-golf-pride-junior-classic.html#sthash.j45Qroqa.puf.

Ambrose, Stephen E. 2002. *Band of Brothers: E Company, 506th Regiment, 101st Airborne from Normandy to Hitler's Eagle's Nest.* New York: Simon & Schuster.

Ancestry.com. "U.S., World War II Draft Registration Cards, 1942." http://search.ancestry.com/search/db.aspx?dbid=1002.

Anderson, Erik. "Pearl Harbor: The Bombing." http://www.erikanderson.net/pearlharbor/casualty.html.

Ask.com. "Wilmington International Airport." http://www.ask.com/wiki/Wilmington_International_Airport.

Battleship *North Carolina.* "History." http://www.battleshipnc.com/AbouttheShip/History.

BFDC. "U-352." http://www.nc-wreckdiving.com/WRECKS/U352/U352.HTML.

Billinger, Robert D., Jr. "Nazi POWs in the Tar Heel State." http://www.amazon.com/Nazi-POWs-Tar-Heel-State/dp/0813032245

Biographical Directory of the United States Congress. "Richard Caswell." http://bioguide.congress.gov/scripts/biodisplay.pl?index=C000246.

Bishir, Catherine W., Michael T. Southern, and Jennifer F. Martin. 1999. *A Guide to the Historic Architecture of Western North Carolina.* Chapel Hill: University of North Carolina Press.

Blue Stars for a Safe Return. "History of the Blue Star Service Banner." http://bluestarsforsafereturn.com/history.htm.

Bolden, Don. 1995. *Alamance: A County at War.* Burlington, North Carolina: Times-News.

Bradley, James. 2000. *Flags of Our Fathers.* New York: Bantam.

Branch, Paul. "World War II Comes to Ft. Macon." http://www.clis.com/friends/WorldWarII.htm.

Carolina News, Fayetteville, North Carolina, and E. C. Kropp, Milwaukee, Wisconsin.

Census Viewer. "Edenton, North Carolina Population: Census 2010 and 2000 Interactive Map, Demographics, Statistics, Quick Facts." http://censusviewer.com/city/NC/Edenton.

Center for Diversity Education. "State Department Internment Camp at Montreat, NC." http://www.diversityed.org/internment-camp-amontreat-nc/.

Chacha. 2013. "Was There a Military Draft in World War II?" http://www.chacha.

com/question/was-there-a-military-draft-in-world-war-ii#sthash.feXjjQg5.dpuf.

Chapman, Reid, and Deborah Miles. 2006. *Asheville and Western North Carolina in World War II*. Charleston, SC: Arcadia.

Charlotte-Mecklenburg Historic Landmarks Commission. "Survey and Research Report on the W.P.A./Douglas Airport Hangar." http://www.cmhpf.org/S&Rs%20Alphabetical%20Order/Surveys&rwpahangar.htm.

Charlotte-Mecklenburg Story. "The Charlotte Quartermaster Depot." http://www.cmstory.org/homefront/places/qDepot.htm.

_____. "The Shell Plant." http://www.cmstory.org/homefront/places/shellplant.htm.

Charlotte Motor Speedway. "Charlotte Assembly Plant Built Ford's Model T." http://www.charlottemotorspeedway.com/media/news/549440.html.

Chen, C. Peter. "Second Happy Time." http://ww2db.com/battle_spec.php?battle_id=277.

Chitwood, Oliver Perry, Frank Lawrence Owsley, and H. C. Nixon. 1949. *The United States from Colony to World Power*. New York: D. Van Nostrand.

City of Greensboro, North Carolina. "A Brief History of Greensboro." http://www.greensboro-nc.gov/index.aspx?page=142.

City of Havelock. "Welcome to the City of Havelock." http://www.cityofhavelock.com/.

City of Wilmington, North Carolina. "Buildings." http://www.wilmingtonnc.gov/public_services/buildings.

CityTownInfo.com. "Havelock." http://www.citytowninfo.com/places/north-carolina/Havelock.

_____. "Morehead City, North Carolina." http://www.citytowninfo.com/places/north-carolina/morehead-city.

Clancy, Patrick. "US Naval Activities World War II by State." http://www.ibiblio.org/hyperwar/USN/ref/USN-Act/NC.html.

Compton. 1948. "North Carolina." In *Compton's Pictured Encyclopedia and Fact-Index*, 155. Chicago: F. E. Compton.

Congressional Research Service. *American War and Military Operations Casualties: Lists and Statistics*. http://www.fas.org/sgp/crs/natsec/RL32492.pdf.

County of Dare, North Carolina. "Dare County Regional Airport (MQI)." http://www.darenc.com/Airport/.

Craven, W. F., and I. L. Cate. "*The Army Air Forces in World War II: VI: Men and Planes*," 153–54. http://www.ibiblio.org/hyperwar/AAF/VI/AAF-VI-4.html.

_____. "Redeployment and Demobilization." http://www.ibiblio.org/hyperwar/AAF/VII/AAF-VII-17.html.

Davis, Anita Price. 2002. *Real Heroes: Rutherford County Men Who Made the Supreme Sacrifice in World War II*. Spartanburg, SC: Honoribus.

_____. 2003. *North Carolina During the Great Depression*. Jefferson, NC: McFarland.

_____. 2009. *New Deal Art in North Carolina: The Murals, Sculptures, Reliefs, Paintings, Oils and Frescoes and Their Creators*. Jefferson, NC: McFarland.

_____. 2013. *The Margaret Mitchell Encyclopedia*. Jefferson, North Carolina: McFarland.

Davis, Anita Price, and Barry E. Hambright. 2002. *Chimney Rock and Rutherford County*. Charleston, SC: Arcadia.

Davis, Anita Price, and James M. Walker. 2003. *Rutherford County in World War II*. Charleston, South Carolina: Arcadia Publishing, 2003.

_____. 2004a. *Rutherford County in World War II*. Vol. 2. Charleston, SC: Arcadia.

_____. 2004b. *Spartanburg County in World War II*. Charleston, SC: Arcadia.

_____. 2005. *Cleveland County in World War II*. Charleston, SC: Arcadia.

Davis, Anita Price, and Louise Hunt. 2008. *Women on U.S. Postage Stamps*. Jefferson, NC: McFarland.

Davis, Steve B. "Glenn Miller: Another Mysterious Disappearance." *Writings and Ramblings*. http://stamperdad.wordpress.com/category/entertainment/.

Department of the Navy, Bureau of Yards and Docks. "Building the Navy's Bases in World War II: History of the Bureau of Yards and Docks and the Civil Engineer Corps, 1940–1946." http://www.ibiblio.

Bibliography

org/hyperwar/USN/Building_Bases/bases-16.html.

Digital Forsyth. "Airports of Winston-Salem." http://www.digitalforsyth.org/photos/stories/airports-of-winston-salem.

Digital NC. "Greensboro World War II Military Base Newspaper." http://digitalnc.org/collections/newspapers/greensboro-world-war-ii-military-base-newspaper.

Discovery Diving. "Wreck Desc U-352." http://www.discoverydiving.com/index.php?option=com_content&view=article&id=241%3Awreck-desc-u-352&Itemid=158.

Documenting the American South. "S.S. *John D. Gill* Memorial Marker, Southport." http://docsouth.unc.edu/commland/monument/320/.

Donovan, Frank Robert. 1965. *Wheels for a Nation*. New York: Crowell.

Downtown Goldsboro Development Corporation. http://www.dgdc.org/demo.aspx.

Duffus, Kevin P. "When World War II Was Fought off North Carolina's Beaches." http://www.learnnc.org/lp/editions/nchist-worldwar/5908.

East Carolina University Digital Collections. "Cover of Sales Brochure for Barbour Boat Works, Inc." http://digital.lib.ecu.edu/1584#details.

11th Airborne Division. "Forming the Division." https://sites.google.com/site/seans11thairborne/Home/camp-mackall.

Ellis, M.W. "Burlington: An Ancestry.com Community." http://homepages.rootsweb.ancestry.com/~mwellis/book/chapter16.html.

Emporis. "Vanderbilt Apartments." http://www.emporis.com/building/vanderbiltapartments-asheville-nc-usa.

Everything2. "John Thomas Mackall." http://everything2.com/title/John+Thomas+Mackall.

Find-a-Grave. "Harley Halbert Pope." http://www.findagrave.com/cgi-bin/fg.cgi?page=gr&GRid=8840.

_____. "Robert Lewis Carroll." http://www.findagrave.com/cgibin/fg.cgi?page=gr&GSln=carroll&GSfn=robert+&GSmn=lewis&GSbyrel=all&GSdy=1941&GSdyrel=in&GSob=n&GRid=56108752&df=all&.

Forgotten NC. "Forgotten North Carolina." http://forgottennc.com/page/2.

Fort Bragg. "Fort Bragg History." http://www.bragg.army.mil/Pages/History.aspx.

Foxfall Medals. "Pearl Harbor Survivor's Medal." http://www.foxfall.com/fmc-phs.htm.

Fravel, Jonathan. "Alabama Legend: How Did Wallace Wade End Up at Duke?" *Bleacher Report: Alabama Crimson Tide Football*. http://bleacherreport.com/articles/465109-alabama-legend-how-did-wade-wallace-end-up-at-duke.

Freeman, Paul. "Abandoned and Little-Known Airfields: North Carolina: Greensboro Area." http://www.airfields-freeman.com/NC/Airfields_NC_Greensboro.htm.

_____. "Abandoned and Little-Known Airfields: Western North Carolina." http://www.airfields-freeman.com/NC/Airfields_NC_W.htm.

GlobalSecurity.org. "Morehead City, North Carolina." http://www.globalsecurity.org/military/facility/morehead-city.htm.

Goldsboro News-Argus. "Federal Prison Camp Will be Empty Sometime This April." http://www.newsargus.com/news/archives/2005/12/16/federal_prison_camp_will_be_empty_sometime_this_april/.

Gorman-Fancy, Emily; Rebecca Pierre; Kate Walsh, Heather D. Wilson. 2010. *Insiders' Guide: North Carolina's Southern Coast and Wilmington*. Wilmington, NC: By the Sea.

Griffin, Clarence. 1952. *History of Rutherford County, 1937–1951*, Asheville, North Carolina: Inland.

Grove Arcade. "History." http://www.grovearcade.com/history/.

Harry S. Truman Library and Museum. "Executive Order 9981." http://www.trumanlibrary.org/9981.htm.

Hickam, Homer. 1989. *Torpedo Junction*. New York: Dell.

History. "Braxton Bragg." http://www.history.com/topics/braxton-bragg.

_____. "The Fireside Chats." http://www.history.com/topics/fireside-chats.

Home Front. "A History of Morris Field." http://www.cmstory.org/homefront/places/morrisField.htm.

Horton, Ralph Terrell, Jr. Interview by the author, November 27, 2013.

iFly.com. "Pitt Greenville (PGV) Airport." http://www.ifly.com/pitt-greenville-airport#overview.

Infoplease. "Selective Service." http://www.infoplease.com/encyclopedia/history/selective-service.html#ixzz2b6waWmXV.

Information on Charles Burrington Long. Courtesy of Kristy A. Long, RA, CFM, LEED AP.

Innovateus. "What Is Isinglass?" http://www.innovateus.net/innopedia/what-isinglass.

Jordan, Robert. 2013. "North Carolina National Guard Conducts Joint Exercise with U.S. Marines for Future Missions." North Carolina National Guard. September 20. http://www.nc.ngb.army.mil/PAO/News/Pages/1-130th-USMC-Joint.aspx.

King, William E. 1997. "Wallace Wade." In *If Gargoyles Could Talk: Sketches of Duke University*. Durham, NC: Carolina. http://library.duke.edu/uarchives/history/histnotes/w_wade-bio.html.

Kure Beach. "Exploring the History of Kure Beach, N.C. from the Civil War to Today." http://www.visitkurebeachnc.com/press-releases/exploring-the-history-of-kure-beach-n.c.-from-the-civil-war-to-today/.

Kurian, George Thomas. 1994. *Datapedia of the United States: 1790–2000*. Lanham, MD: Bernam.

Langley, Joan, and Wright Langley. 1975. *Yesterday's Asheville*. Miami, FL: E. A. Seemann.

Learn NC. "World War II Dead and Missing from North Carolina." http://www.learnnc.org/lp/editions/nchist-worldwar/5889.

Lee, Bill. "The Liberty Ships of World War II: Their Union County and Other Carolina Connections," 17. http://www.jajones.com/pdf/Liberty_Ships_of_WWII.pdf.

Lefler, Hugh T., and Albert Ray Newsome. 1959. *North Carolina: History, Geography,*

Government. New York: Harcourt, Brace, and World.

Library of Congress. "The Most Famous Poster." http://www.loc.gov/exhibits/treasures/trm015.html.

Lifson, Amy. 2012. "Into the Deep." *Humanities* 33.4 (July/August): http://www.neh.gov/humanities/2012/julyaugust/statement/the-deep.

LighthouseFriends.com. "Cape Lookout, North Carolina." http://www.lighthousefriends.com/light.asp?ID=354.

Living New Deal. "Pitt-Greenville Airport—Greenville NC." http://livingnewdeal.berkeley.edu/projects/pitt-greenville-airport-greenville-nc/.

Long, Clara, and Kristy Long. 2014 Interviews, mailings, and photos.

Luebken, Uwe. "Review of *Nazi POWs in the Tar Heel State*." http://www.h-net.org/reviews/showrev.php?id=25070.

Maisel, Larry. 2013. "Museum at Ft. Johnston." http://www.southporthistoricalsociety.org/wp-content/uploads/2013/01/SHS-Newsletter-winter2013.pdf.

Mapquest. http://www.mapquest.com/.

Marine Bombing Squadron Six-Thirteen. http://www.vmb613.com/aircraft.htm.

Marines. "Cultural Resources Management: Marine Corps Base Camp Lejeune: Origins of Marine Corps Base Camp Lejeune." http://www.lejeune.marines.mil/OfficesStaff/EnvironmentalMgmt/CulturalResources/HistoryLive/HistoryofCampLejeune.aspx.

———. "Cultural Resources Management: Marine Corps Base Camp Lejeune: Tour Historic MCBCL." http://www.lejeune.marines.mil/OfficesStaff/EnvironmentalMgmt/CulturalResources/HistoryLive/TourHistoricMCBCL.aspx.

———. "Marine Corps Air Station Cherry Point, Cherry Point, NC." http://www.cherrypoint.marines.mil/Units/HHS/UnitHistory.aspx.

———. "The Montford Point Marines: A Legacy of Pride." http://www.marines.com/history-heritage/defining-moments.

Maxwell Builders. http://www.maxwellbuilders.com/our-projects/federal/.

McElvaine, Robert S. 1983. *Down and Out*

Bibliography

in the Great Depression. Chapel Hill: University of North Carolina Press.

McLaurin, Melton A. 2007. *The Marines of Montford Point: America's First Black Marines.* Chapel Hill: University of North Carolina.

Military Bases. "Fort Bragg." http://military bases.com/north-carolina/fort-bragg/.

Military OneSource. "Pope Army Airfield, North Carolina." http://www.military onesource.mil/MOS/f?p=MI:CONTENT:0::::P4_INST_ID,P4_CONTENT_TITLE,P4_CONTENT_EKMT_ID,P4_CONTENT_DIRECTORY,P4_TAB:3820,Installation%20Overview,30.90.30.30.30.0.0.0.0,1,IO.

Military.com. "Pearl Harbor: Day of Infamy." http://www.military.com/Resources/HistorySubmittedFileView?file=history_pearlharbor.htm.

_____. "USCG Elizabeth City, NC." http://benefits.military.com/misc/installations/Base_Content.jsp?id=3765.

MilitaryBases.us. "Pope Army Airfield." http://www.militarybases.us/air-force/pope-army-airfield.

Mims, Bryan. "Asheville's Fortress of Art: The Biltmore Estate." *Our State*, October 2014, pp. 40–47.

Montreat College. "About Us." http://www.montreat.edu/about-us/history/.

Moore County Airport. http://moorecountyairport.com/about-us/history/.

Morehead City, North Carolina. http://www.morehead.com/.

Morella, Michael. 2012. "How America Changed After Pearl Harbor." January 6. http://www.usnews.com/opinion/articles/2012/01/06/how-america-changed-after-pearl-harbor.

My Base Guide. "Marine Corps Air Station: Cherry Point History." http://www.militarynewcomers.com/CHERRYPOINT/resources/02_his.html.

National Archives. "The 1973 Fire, National Personnel Records Center." http://www.archives.gov/st-louis/military-personnel/fire-1973.html.

_____. "Powers of Persuasion: Four Freedoms." http://www.archives.gov/exhibits/powers_of_persuasion/four_freedoms/four_freedoms.html.

National Cemetery Administration. "Department of Veteran Affairs National Cemeteries." http://www.cem.va.gov/cems/state.asp?State=NC.

_____. "New Bern National Cemetery." http://www.cem.va.gov/cems/nchp/newbern.asp.

_____. "Raleigh National Cemetery." http://www.cem.va.gov/cems/nchp/raleigh.asp.

_____. "Salisbury National Cemetery." http://www.cem.va.gov/cems/nchp/salisbury.asp.

_____. "Wilmington National Cemetery." http://www.cem.va.gov/cems/nchp/wilmington.asp#gi.

National Geographic. "Hitler's Secret Attack on America." http://channel.nationalgeographic.com/articles/hitlers-secret-attack-on-america/.

National Lighter-than-Air Historical Center. "U.S. Naval Air Station (LTA) Weeksville." http://www.blimpinfo.com/wp-content/uploads/2012/04/NASLTAWeeksville-Comm.pdf.

National Montford Point Marine Association, Inc. "History." http://www.montfordpointmarines.com/History.html.

National Park Service. "Bodie Island Light Station." http://www.nps.gov/caha/historyculture/bodie-island-light-station.htm.

_____. "Cape Hatteras Light Station." http://www.nps.gov/caha/historyculture/cape-hatteras-light-station.htm.

_____. "Cape Lookout: Lighthouse History Timeline." http://www.nps.gov/calo/historyculture/lhouse_timeline.htm.

_____. "National Register of Historic Places: Asheville City Hall." http://www.nps.gov/nr/travel/asheville/cit.htm.

_____. "National Register of Historic Places Travel Itinerary: Asheville." http://www.nps.gov/nr/travel/asheville/bat.htm.

_____. "New Bern National Cemetery, New Bern, North Carolina." http://www.nps.gov/history/nr/travel/national_cemeteries/North_Carolina/New_Bern_National_Cemetery.html.

_____. "Oteen Veterans Administration Hospital Historic District." http://www.nps.gov/nr/travel/asheville/ote.htm.

Naval History and Heritage Command. "XI. Pre–WW II Blimps and the Evolution of the K-class." http://www.history.navy.mil/download/lta-06.pdf.

NCDOT. "Ferry Division." http://www.ncdot.gov/ferry/.

NCpedia. "World War II." http://ncpedia.org/world-war-ii-part-3-world-war-ii.

New Bern. "Havelock/Cherry Point." http://www.visitnewbern.com/havelock_museum.php.

New Bern NC Real Estate Super Site with New Bern NC Relocation, New Bern NC Retirement and New Bern Life. "New Bern North Carolina History." http://www.new-bern.nc.us/HistoryNB.

New Hanover County. "David W. Carnell Papers: The Ethyl-Dow Chemical Company Bromine Plant in Kure Beach, NC." The North Carolina Collection, New Hanover Public Library. http://www.nhcgov.com/Library/Finding%20Aids/David%20W.%20Carnell%20Papers%20The%20Ethyl-Dow%20Chemical%20Co.%20Bromine%20Plant%20in%20Kure%20Beach,%20NC.pdf.

1997 International Jewish Sports Hall of Fame. "Elected Members: Arthur 'Bluey' Bluethenthal." http://www.jewishsports.net/BioPages/ArthurBlueyBluethenthal.htm.

North Carolina Department of Commerce. "Seymour Johnson Air Force Base." http://www.visitnc.com/listing/seymour-johnson-air-force-base.

North Carolina Department of Cultural Resources. "NC State Highway Historical Marker Program: Cherry Point; ID: C-68." http://www.ncmarkers.com/Markers.aspx?MarkerId=C-68.

_____. "North Carolina Highway Historical Marker Program: Camp Butner." http://www.ncmarkers.com/Markers.aspx?MarkerId=G-105.

_____. "North Carolina Highway Historical Marker Program: North Carolina Railroad." http://www.ncmarkers.com/Markers.aspx?MarkerId=F-12.

_____. "North Carolina Shipbuilding Company." http://www.ncmarkers.com/Markers.aspx?MarkerId=D-96.

North Carolina Historic Sites. "Fort Fisher During World War II." http://www.nchistoricsites.org/fisher/ww2/ww2.htm.

North Carolina Museum of History. "NC at Home and Battle during WWII stats: World War II Figures and Facts for North Carolina." http://www.ncdcr.gov/ncmoh/NCatHomeandBattleduringWWIIstats.aspx.

_____. "North Carolina at Home and in Battle in WWII." http://www.ncmuseumofhistory.org/workshops/WWII/WWIIFigures.htm

North Carolina State Parks. "Fort Macon State Park: History." http://www.ncparks.gov/Visit/parks/foma/history.php.

Oak Island Accommodations. "Fort Caswell." http://www.rentalsatthebeach.com/OakIsland/ThingsToDo/HistoricAttractions/FortCaswell/.

OcrackokeGuide.com. "Ocracoke Attractions—Historic Sites." http://www.ocracokeguide.com/attractions/category/historic_sites/.

Ocracoke-NC. "British Cemetery-Ocracoke Island/Hyde County's Outer Banks." http://www.ocracoke-nc.com/cemetery/.

Ocracokeisland.com. "U.S. Navel [sic] Base Photos." http://www.ocracokeisland.com/navel_base_photos.htm.

Official Site of Glenn Miller. http://www.glennmiller.com/about/bio.htm.

Ohio History Central. "Burke-Wadsworth Act." http://www.ohiohistorycentral.org/w/Burke-Wadsworth_Act.

O'Keefe, Patrick. 1977. *Greensboro: A Pictorial History*. Norfolk: Denning.

Osborne, Richard. 2007. *World War II Sites in the United States: A Tour Guide and Directory*. Indianapolis, Indiana: Riebel-Roque.

OurDocuments.gov. "Transcript of Lend-Lease Act (1941)." http://www.ourdocuments.gov/doc.php?doc=71&page=transcript.

Outer Banks. "British Cemeteries." http://www.outerbanks.com/british-cemeteries.html.

Patrick, Bethanne Kelly. "Navy Captain Douglas Fairbanks, Jr." http://www.military.com/Content/MoreContent/1,12044,MLfairbanks,00.html.

PCSAmerica.net. "Welcome to Pope Air Field." http://www.pcsamerica.net/index.

cfm?fuseaction=pcsBase.baseInfo&baseID=7&baseMenu=1.

Pearl Harbor: Remembered. "USS *Arizona* Casualty List." Personal Web site. http://my.execpc.com/~dschaaf/arizdead.html.

PearlHarbor.org. http://www.pearlharbor.org/history/casualties/pearl-harbor-casualties/?do_filter=1&details=1&location=USS%20Arizona%20(BB-39%20Battleship.

Penn, Michael. 2011. "War and Roses." *Duke Magazine,* November–December 2011. http://www.dukemagazine.duke.edu/issues/111211/bowl1.html.

Phister, Jeff. 2008. *The Battleship Oklahoma (BB-37)*. Norman, OK: University of Oklahoma Press.

Pilot.com. "Cub Scout Visits Moore County Airport." http://www.thepilot.com/news/features/article_3b285dc2-1fc3-11e3-a720-0019bb30f31a.html.

Pinehurst. "At Pinehurst, an Architecture for Golf." http://pinehurstmedia.com/in_the_news.

Pitt County Government. "About Pitt County." http://www.pittcountync.gov/about/distinctions.shtml.

Pleasure Island. "North Carolina Beaches: Historic Fort Fisher." http://www.pleasureislandnc.org/fort-fisher/.

Powell, William S., ed., and Jay Mazzocchi, assoc. ed. 2006. *Encyclopedia of North Carolina*. Chapel Hill: University of North Carolina Press.

Preddy Memorial Foundation. "Major George E. Preddy, Jr." http://www.preddyfoundation.org.

Presnell, Lowell. 2005. *Mines, Miners, and Minerals of Western North Carolina*. Boone, NC: Parkway.

Raleigh-Durham International Airport. "RDU History." http://www.rdu.com/authority/history.html.

RoadsideAmerica.com. "Weeksville, North Carolina, Old Naval Blimp Airdock." http://www.roadsideamerica.com/tip/32442.

RoanokeIsland.net. "Attractions, Performances, and Events." http://www.roanokeisland.net/attractions/category/museums/.

_____. "Recreation—Flying and Skydiving." http://www.roanokeisland.net/recreation/category/flying/.

RobcoHistoryMus's Blog. "Photo of the Week: Army Santa." http://robcohistorymus.wordpress.com/category/history.

_____. "The Laurinburg-Maxton Army Air Base." http://robcohistorymus.wordpress.com.

Robertson, Mike. "A Brief History of Kure Beach Pier." http://www.kurebeachfishingpier.com/Kure_Beach_Fishing_Pier_History.htm.

Roosevelt, Franklin. 1938. *The Public Papers and Addresses of Franklin D. Roosevelt,* vols. 1–3. New York: Random House.

Roosevelt, Franklin Delano. [1941]. "Fireside Chat 19 [December 9, 1941]: On the War with Japan." http://millercenter.org/president/speeches/detail/3325.

Rosenberg, Jennifer. "About.com Guide: Pearl Harbor Facts: Facts About the Japanese Attack on Pearl Harbor, December 7, 1941." http://history1900s.about.com/od/Pearl-Harbor/a/Pearl-Harbor-Facts.htm.

S&ME Engineering Integrity. "Tryon Palace—From Superfund Site to Super Fun Site." http://www.smeinc.com/project/tryon-palace-from-superfund-site-to-super-fun-site.

St. Joseph of the Pines. http://www.sjp.org/continuing-care-retirement-community-north-carolina.php#.

Selective Service. 2013. "Selective Service." http://www.selectiveservice.us/militarydraft/7-use.shtml.

Seymour Johnson Air Force Base. "4th Fighter Wing History." http://www.seymourjohnson.af.mil/library/factsheets/factsheet.asp?id=4330.

_____. "U.S. Air Force Fact Sheet: Lieutenant Seymour A. Johnson." http://www.seymourjohnson.af.mil/library/factsheets/factsheet_print.asp?fsID=4328&page=1.

Shields, E. Thomson, Jr. 2000. "Introduction to North Carolina Studies." http://www.co.pasquotank.nc.us/History.htm.

Shipbuilding History. "Barbour Boatworks, New Bern, NC." http://shipbuildinghistory.com/history/shipyards/5small/inactive/barbour.htm.

Shmoop. "William Pitt in the French and Indian War." http://www.shmoop.com/french-indian-war/william-pitt.html.

Shute, J. Ray. "Monroe, North Carolina-Miscellaneous History: Camp Sutton." http://monroenc.blogspot.com/2012/08/camp-sutton.html.

_____. "Oral History Symposium Presented to the Old Monroe Neighborhood Association on August 17, 1980." Excerpt. Courtesy of the Union County Heritage Room in cooperation with the Carolinas Genealogical Society and the Historical Society.

Siniard, Diane. "North Carolina in World War II." http://ncwwii.lostsoulsgenealogy.com/.

Southport Times. "History of Fort Caswell." http://southporttimes.com/featured/200404.html.

Sterner, C. Douglas. "Hometown Heroes of the Tarheel State: North Carolina." http://www.homeofheroes.com/moh/states/nc.html.

Sterner, Doug. "Hometown Heroes of the Tarheel State: North Carolina." http://www.homeofheroes.com/moh/states/nc.html.

Stick, David and Paul E. Fontenoy. "Shipbuilding" in *Encyclopedia of North Carolina*. Chapel Hill, North Carolina: University of North Carolina Press, 2006.

StoppingPoints.com. "Camp Davis: U.S. 17, Holly Ridge, NC, USA." http://www.stoppingpoints.com/north-carolina/sights.cgi?marker=Camp+Davis&cnty=Onslow.

_____. "Missile Tests: Anderson Boulevard at Flake Avenue, Topsail Beach, NC, USA." http://www.stoppingpoints.com/north-carolina/sights.cgi?marker=Missile+Tests&cnty=Pender.

Sumner, Jim. "When the Rose Bowl Came to Duke." http://www.goduke.com/ViewArticle.dbml?DB_OEM_ID=4200&ATCLID=735947.

Sunken Ships of the Outer Banks. "Ships Lost in 1942." http://www.sunkenshipsouterbanks.com/ships_1942.html.

Swift, Earl. "Lighter than Air." http://www.ourstate.com/weeksville-air-station-blimps/.

TCOM. "TCOM Affordable Persistent Surveillance Solutions/Aerostat Systems." http://www.tcomlp.com/.

This Day in North Carolina History. "June 12, 2013." http://nchistorytoday.wordpress.com/tag/goldsboro/.

Through the Lens, Ltd. "History: Dirigible Hangar—TCom—Weeksville, NC." http://www.thelookinglens.com/History/Dirigible-Hanger-TCom/1850754_j2zq2P#!i=92831222&k=WjpznJZ.

Tilley, Captain Dave. "The Wreck of the SS *John D. Gill*." http://fryingpantower.com/content-print-page-34.html.

Time-Life Editors. 1969. *This Fabulous Century*. Vol. 4. New York: Time-Life.

Town of Butner. "History of Camp Butner." http://www.butnernc.org/pages/ButnerHeritage.html.

Treasury Direct. "The History of U.S. Savings Bonds." http://www.treasurydirect.gov/timeline.htm.

Trespass Against Us. "Dow Chemical's Legacy of Profit and Pollution." Environmental Health Series. http://www.trespassagainstus.com/downloads/Chapter2HouseofWonders.pdf.

Tritten, Larry. 2003. "'Black Tears' Still Shed for USS *Arizona*." *South Florida Sun-Sentinel*, December 7. http://articles.sun-sentinel.com/2003-12-07/travel/0312020501_1_pearl-harbor-battleship-arizona-monument.

Tursi, Frank V. 1994. *Winston-Salem: A History*. Winston-Salem, NC: John F. Blair.

Tyndall, Clifford. 2006. *Greetings from Camp Davis*. Chapel Hill: Chapel Hill Press.

UNC-TV. "Billy Sutton." http://wwii.unctv.org/the-participants/billy-sutton.

Union County Public Library. "Camp Sutton." http://history.union.lib.nc.us/bibliographies/CampSutton-BriefHistory-UseAsInsert.pdf.

University of North Carolina at Chapel Hill. "Lighthouses of the United States: North Carolina." http://www.unc.edu/~rowlett/lighthouse/nc.htm.

U.S. Army Medical Department. "Women in the Army Medical Department: Chapter 31." http://history.amedd.army.mil/

booksdocs/wwii/WomeninAMEDD/ WACCh31healthmedical.htm.
U.S. Census Bureau. "Elizabeth City: State and County Quick Facts." http://quickfacts.census.gov/qfd/states/37/3720580.html.
U.S. Coast Guard. "Air Station Elizabeth City." http://www.uscg.mil/d5/airstaElizabethCity/.
———. "Air Station Elizabeth City, North Carolina." http://www.uscg.mil/history/stations/airsta_elizabethcity.asp.
———. "*The Dione.*" http://www.uscg.mil/history/webcutters/Dione1934.pdf.
———. "*U-352.*" http://www.uscg.mil/history/uscghist/U352.asp.
———. "U.S. Coast Guard Beach Patrol During World War II." http://www.uscg.mil/history/uscghist/Beach_Patrol_Photo_Index.asp.
U.S. Department of Veterans Affairs. "Goldshttp://www.fayettevillenc.va.gov/locations/Goldsboro_Community_Based_Outpatient_Clinic.asp.
U.S. National Library of Medicine. "Dr. Margaret D. Craighill." http://www.nlm.nih.gov/changingthefaceofmedicine/physicians/biography_72.html.
U.S. Navy Beach Jumpers Association. "Island History: Memorial Marker for U.S. Navy Beach Jumpers Dedicated on Ocracoke." http://www.beachjumpers.com/Ocracoke/IslandPress.htm.
U.S. Office of Price Administration. 1942. *War Ration Book No. 3.* U.S. Government Printing Office.
———. 1943. *War Ration Book No. 4.* U.S. Government Printing Office.
USS *Kidd.* "Lieutenant General John Archer Lejeune [1867–1942]." http://www.usskidd.com/lejeune.html.
USS *Utah.* "Casualty List [of the USS *Utah*]." http://ussutah.org/monument.htm.
USSArizona.org. "The Alphabetical USS *Arizona* Casualty List." http://www.ussarizona.org/lists/Alphabetical_USS_Arizona_Casualty_List.pdf.
Velthouse, Lisa. "The Truth About World War II's True Shepherds." http://www.christianitytoday.com/ct/2012/november/true-shepherds.html.
Ware, Jim. "What Is the Runway that Is Grown Over at ILM? Was It Part of Bluethenthal Field?" http://www.myreporter.com/?p=15391.
Wessels Living History Farm. "Pop Culture Goes to War." http://www.livinghistoryfarm.org/farmingthe40s/life_07.html.
Western Museum of Flight. "The Vultee Aircraft Company." http://www.wmof.com/bt-13vultee.htm.
Where2Golf. "Mid Pines Inn and Golf Club." http://www.where2golf.com/north-carolina/mid-pines-inn-golf-club.asp.
Wikimapia. "Ruins of the Ethyl-Dow Chemical Plant." http://wikimapia.org/9644913/Ruins-of-the-Ethyl-Dow-Chemical-Plant.
Wikipedia. "Alamance County, North Carolina." http://en.wikipedia.org/wiki/Alamance_County,_North_Carolina#Airplanes_and_radars.
———. "Arthur Bluethenthal." http://en.wikipedia.org/wiki/Arthur_Bluethenthal.
———. "Camp Geiger." http://en.wikipedia.org/wiki/Camp_Geiger.
———. "Camp Mackall." http://en.wikipedia.org/wiki/Camp_Mackall.
———. "Cape (geography)." http://en.wikipedia.org/wiki/Cape_(geography).
———. "Cape Hatteras." http://en.wikipedia.org/wiki/Cape_Hatteras.
———. "Douglas Fairbanks, Jr." http://en.wikipedia.org/wiki/Douglas_Fairbanks,_Jr.
———. "11th Airborne Division," http://en.wikipedia.org/wiki/11th_Airborne_Division_(United_States).
———. "Elizabeth City, North Carolina." http://en.wikipedia.org/wiki/Elizabeth_City,_North_Carolina.
———. "Emblem of the 11th Airborne." http://en.wikipedia.org/wiki/11th_Airborne_Division_(United_States).
———. "File:VMSB-343 WWII Logo.jpg." http://en.wikipedia.org/wiki/File:VMSB-343_WWII_Logo.jpg.
———. "Fort Fisher State Recreation Area." http://en.wikipedia.org/wiki/Fort_Fisher_State_Recreation_Area.
———. "Greenville, North Carolina." http://en.wikipedia.org/wiki/Greenville,_North_Carolina.

Bibliography

_____. "Havelock, North Carolina." http://en.wikipedia.org/wiki/Havelock,_North_Carolina.

_____. "Jacksonville, North Carolina." http://en.wikipedia.org/wiki/Jacksonville,_North_Carolina.

_____. "The Kenilworth Inn." http://en.wikipedia.org/wiki/Kenilworth_Inn.

_____. "Laurinburg-Maxton Army Air Base." http://en.wikipedia.org/wiki/Laurinburg-Maxton_Army_Air_Base.

_____. "List of Alabama Crimson Tide Bowl Games." http://en.wikipedia.org/wiki/List_of_Alabama_Crimson_Tide_bowl_games.

_____. "List of Living Medal of Honor Recipients." http://en.wikipedia.org/wiki/List_of_living_Medal_of_Honor_recipients.

_____. "List of Space Shuttle Landing Sites." http://en.wikipedia.org/wiki/List_of_space_shuttle_landing_sites.

_____. "Margaret D. Craighill." http://en.wikipedia.org/wiki/Margaret_D._Craighill.

_____. "Marine Corps Air Station Cherry Point." http://en.wikipedia.org/wiki/Marine_Corps_Air_Station_Cherry_Point.

_____. "Marine Operational Training Group 81." http://en.wikipedia.org/wiki/Marine_Operational_Training_Group_81.

_____. "Mecklenburg County, North Carolina." http://en.wikipedia.org/wiki/Mecklenburg_County,_North_Carolina.

_____. "Medal of Honor." http://en.wikipedia.org/wiki/Medal_of_Honor.

_____. "Morehead City." http://en.wikipedia.org/wiki/Morehead_City,_North_Carolina.

_____. "Naval Air Engineering Station Lakehurst." http://en.wikipedia.org/wiki/Naval_Air_Engineering_Station_Lakehurst.

_____. "Northeastern Regional Airport." http://en.wikipedia.org/wiki/Marine_Corps_Air_Station_Edenton.

_____. "Pitt-Greenville Airport." http://en.wikipedia.org/wiki/Pitt-Greenville_Airport.

_____. "Raleigh-Durham International Airport." http://en.wikipedia.org/wiki/Raleigh%E2%80%93Durham_International_Airport.

_____. "Rose Bowl Game." NCAA Division 1 Football Records Book, 2007, 296–302. http://en.wikipedia.org/wiki/Rose_Bowl_game#cite_note-4.

_____. "Roy Geiger." http://en.wikipedia.org/wiki/Roy_Geiger.

_____. "Salisbury National Cemetery." http://en.wikipedia.org/wiki/Salisbury_National_Cemetery.

_____. "Sandhills [Carolina]." http://en.wikipedia.org/wiki/Sandhills_(Carolina).

_____. "Selective Training and Service Act of 1940." https://en.wikipedia.org/wiki/Selective_Training_and_Service_Act_of_1940#cite_note-5.

_____. "Southport, North Carolina." http://en.wikipedia.org/w/index.php?title=Southport,_North_Carolina&oldid=571835266.

_____. "Tryon Palace." http://en.wikipedia.org/wiki/Tryon_Palace.

_____. "United States Coast Guard: *Icarus*, 1932." http://en.wikipedia.org/wiki/File:USCGC_Icarus_(WPC-110).jpg.

_____. "User:Looper5920/Sandbox." http://en.wikipedia.org/wiki/User:Looper5920/Sandbox.

_____. "USS *Abele* (AN-58)." http://en.wikipedia.org/wiki/USS_Abele_(AN-58).

_____. "Wilmington International Airport." http://en.wikipedia.org/w/index.php?title=Wilmington_International_Airport&oldid=566646655.

_____. "Wilmington, North Carolina." http://en.wikipedia.org/wiki/Wilmington,_North_Carolina#World_War_II.

Wikitravel. "Elizabeth City." http://wikitravel.org/en/Elizabeth_City.

Wilbur Jones Compositions, LLC. "Witness Testimony of Capt. Wilbur Jones, Constituent Witness on behalf of HR 2717." http://wilburjones.com/world-war-two-wilmington-coalition/.

Wilson, Drew C. "Three groups trying to protect Cherry Point." Havelock News. http://www.havenews.com/news/local-news/three-groups-trying-to-protect-cherry-point-1.151761.

World War II U.S. Navy Armed Guard and World War II U.S. Merchant Marine.

"John D. Gill." http://www.armed-guard.com/item09.html.

Wunderground.com. "Weather History for Charlotte, NC." http://www.wunderground.com/history/airport/KCLT/194/12/6/DailyHistory.html?req_city=NA&req_state&req_statename=NA.

Index

USS *Abele* 136–137
ACI *see* Airports Council International
aerostats 171
Air Mail Act of 1934 173
Airports Council International (ACI) 74
Alamance County 66–68
Allied Aviation 72
Ambrose, Stephen E. 84
American Graves Registration Services (AGRS) 60
American World War II City designation 116
Anderson, Dr. Robert Campbell 65–66
Anderson, John Frankllin 23
Appalachian Hall 41, 42
Applied Physics Laboratory of Johns Hopkins University 131
USS *Arizona* 8–10
Arlington National Cemetery 26
Army Air Force Redistribution Station No.5 70
Army Air Force Weather Service 42
Army Air Forces Technical Training School, Goldsboro 94
Army Airways Communication System 42
Arrowood, 2d Lt. Dan Ray 57
Arrowood, Mary Wilson Rucker 57–58
Asheville 37, 38, 39, 42, 43, 44; axis diplomats in 36
AT&T 67
AT-21 training plane 66–67
Atlantic and East Carolina Railroad 133
Atlantic Charter of 1941 6
Atlantic (town) 14

Band of Brothers 84
Barbour, Herbert W. 135
Barbour Boat Works 135–139

Battle, Maj. Cullen A. 138
Battle of the Bulge 20
Beach Jumpers 154–155
Beaufort 148–150
Bedford, Jerrell 12
HMS *Bedfordshire* 156–158
Bergman, Ingrid 192
Berkeley, Scott 96
Bessemer Improvement Company 70
Biltmore 37, 38, 39, 41, 48–49
Blue Star Mothers 189
Blue Star Service Banner 188
Bluethenthal, Arthur ("Bluey") 119–120
Bluethenthal Air Field 119–121; and POWs 122
Bodie Island Lighthouse 159–161
Bogart, Humphrey 2, 192
Bradley, Navy Corpsman John Henry 178
Bradley, Maj. Gen. Omar 81
Bragg, Gen. Braxton 80–82
Breese, Vance 172
British Cemetery *see* Ocracoke
Brotherhood of Sleeping Car Porters 126
Broughton, James Melvin 18, 61, 75–76
Brunswick County 102
Burke Wadsworth Bill 22
Burlington Flying Service 68
Burns, Nell Daves Price 53–55
Bushong, A. B. 55
Butner, Maj. Gen. Henry Wolfe 75
Butner Training School 76

Camel City Flying Service 71
Camp Battle 138–139
Camp Butner 74–75
Camp Davis 74, 110, 129–131
Camp Geiger 125, 126
Camp Glenn 134
Camp Hoffman 82–85

Index

Camp Johnson 128
Camp Lejeune 74, 123–126
Camp Mackall 83–85, 91; *see also* Col. James Rowe Training Compound
Camp Marshall 74
Camp Sutton 62–66
Cape Canaveral, Florida 131
Cape Fear 145
Cape Hatteras 152–158
Cape Lookout 145–148
Carroll, Robert Lewis 13
Casablanca (1942) 192
casualties: American 26, 177; North Carolinians 9, 26, 177
Caswell, Governor Richard 101
Central Tidewater Subregion 135–144
Chaney, Quartermaster Edward F., Jr. 104
Chaney, Lon, Jr. 2
Charlotte 58–59, 60–62, 92, 93
Charlotte Army Air Base 60–62
Cherry Point 74, 140–143
Childes, James Madison 41
churches 189
Churchill, Prime Minister Winston 6, 156
Civilian Conservation Corps 138
Clark, 1st Sgt. Forrest S. 50
Coastal Region 100–107
Col. James Rowe Training Compound 85
Congressional Gold Medal 128
conscientious objectors 22–23
Consolidated Vultee Aircraft Corporation 172–175
Cooksey, Meg Goodwin 50–51
Cooper, Gary 2
Cord, Errett Lobban 172
Cord Corporation 172
Cosgrove, Frank, and Maisie 87
Coste, Lt. Napoleon L. 159
Craig, Stanley R. 158
Craighill, Dr. Margaret D. 105–107
Creech, Franklin 21
Croatan National Forest 144
Crosby, Bing 193
Crossing of the Rhine 20
"crown jewel" of Coast Guard aviation 164
Cunningham, Lt. Col. Alfred A. 140
Cunningham Field 140
Cushman, Col. Thomas J. 140

Dare County Airport 161–162
Davis, Maj. Gen. Richard P. 129

Davis, Thomas 72
December 7, 1941 7–9, 12
DeWitt, Lt. Gen. John 17
Dione 15, 147
dirigibles 168–169
Dönitz, German Admiral Karl 14, 150–152
Doolittle Raid 192
Dosher Memorial Hospital 104–105
Douglas, Ben E. 60–62
Douglas Airport Hangar 60
draft registration 23–24
Duke Rose Bowl (1942) 17–21
Durham, S1c William Teasdale 9

Eastern Airlines 74
Edenton 162
18th Air Support Operations Group 82
Eisenhower, Gen. Dwight D. 78–79, 90, 91, 92
11th Airborne Division 90, 91, 92
Elizabeth City 164–167
Ellington, Douglas D. 42
Erickson, Commander Frank "Swede" 166
Ethyl-Dow Plant, Kure Beach 113–115
ethylene dibromine 112
Eubanks, Ray E. 25, 186
Executive Order 6101 138
Executive Order 8802 125, 127
Executive Order 9981 128

Fair Employment Practices Commission 127
Fairbanks, Douglas, Jr. 155–156
Fairchild Field 66–68
Fairfield Aircraft 66–67
ferries 103
Ferry Division of the North Carolina Department of Transportation 134
"Fireside Chats" 193
Firestone Company 67
555th Parachute Battalion 51
Flagg, James Montgomery 24–25
Flags of Our Fathers 178
Fleet Readiness Center East 143
Fleming, Sgt. Walter W. 82
"The Flying Stovepipe" 131
For Whom the Bell Tolls 2
Ford Island 11
Forrester, Bud 17
Forsyth County 71–73

Index

Fort Bragg 74, 80–82
Fort Caswell 100–102
Fort Davis Army Air Field 121–122
Fort Dobbs 148
Fort Fisher 107–115
Fort Hampton 148
Fort Macon 148–150
43rd Airlift Wing 82
SS *Freden* 151

Gable, Clark 193
Geiger, Gen. Ray Stanley 125
George Washington Vanderbilt Hotel 39, 40
Gillette, George 129–130
Glenn Miller Army Air Force Band 89
Glenn Miller Story (1953) 89
glider training base, largest 77–80
Gold Star Mothers 189
Goldsboro 93–97
Gone with the Wind 2
Goodwin, Roger Wesley 50–51
Grapes of Wrath 2
Graveyard of the Atlantic 152–158
Great Atlantic Hurricane of 1944 109
Great Depression 175–176
Green, Dwight 10–11
Green, Margaret 10–11
Green, William Edgar 10–11
Greensboro 68, 69–70
Greenville Airport 98–99
Griffin, Mark 41–42
Griffin, William Gray, Sr. 41–42
Grove, Edwin W. 39, 43
Grove Arcade 43
Grove Park Inn 36–37, 43; *see also* Asheville
Guilford County 68–71

Halyburton, William David, Jr. 25, 119, 181
Hamrick (later Mauney), Evelyn 55
Hannah Block Building 118
Hart, Samuel C. 32
Havelock 143, 144
Headquarters Squadron, U.S. Marine Corps Air Station 140; *see also* Cunningham Field
A Hell of a War 155
"Hell on Wheels" 82
Hemingway, Ernest 2
Herring, Rufus Geddie 25, 181–182

Hickham, Homer 15–16
Hindenburg 168
Hirohito 7
Holcomb, Maj. Gen. Thomas 123
"Home of the Airborne" 82
Homosote 125
Hope, Bob 193
Horrible Headland 146
Horton Iron and Metal Company 113
Howe, Lt. Comm. Hamilton 161
Howerton, J. R. 45
Huffman Field 67–68
Huston, John 2

Icarus (Coast Guard Cutter) 151
Immigration and Naturalization Service (INS) 45
Institute of Wartime Sciences 134
Invasion of Normandy 20
Iron Dukes 18

Jacksonville 128; and Camp Lejeune 123
Jester, Lt. Maurice D. 151–152
SS *John D. Gill* 103–105
John Umstead Hospital 76
Johnson, Sgt. Maj. Gilbert H. ("Hashmark") 128
Johnson, Seymour 93, 94
Johnson, Van 192
Jones, Wilbur 116, 117, 118, 119

K-class LTA airships 170
Kahn, Albert 58
Kellex Corporation 131
Kenilworth Inn 41
Kennedy, President John F. 48
Knollwood Army Auxiliary Airfield 89, 90
Knollwood Maneuver 85, 90–92
Kure, L. C. 109
Kure Beach 107–115
Kure Beach Ethyl-Dow Plant 113–115

LaGuardia, Fiorella 61
Lake Lure 49–50
Laughlin, Joseph S. 105
Laurinburg Maxton Army Air Base 77–80
Lee, Brig. Gen. William C. 80–82
Leigh, GM3c Malcolm Hedrick 9
Lejeune, Lt. Gen. John Arthur 123, 125
Lend-Lease Act 6
Lewis, John D. 96

Index

Lindbergh, Charles 71
Lindley Field 70–71
Litwin, Cpl. Theodore ("Ted") 111
Lombard, Carol 193
Long, Bernice Burns 46–48
Long, Chaplain Charles Burrington 46–48
Long, Clara 46–48
Long, George 47
Long, Kristy 46–48
Long, Siegby 47
Lookout Bight 147
Lookout Shoals 146
Loop Shack Hill 154
LTA Facility, Weeksville 169
Lucas, Jacklyn H. 182

Mackall, Pvt. John Thomas 84–85
Mankey, Art 172
Manteo, U.S. Navy Auxiliary Air Station 162
March on Washington 126
Marine Corps Auxiliary Airfield, Atlantic 142
Marine Corps flying squadrons 99
Marine Operational Training Group 81 162
Marine Scout Bombing Squad 343 99
Marshall, Gen. George 78–79, 91
McGinnis, Lewis 71
McNair, Gen. Leslie J. 90, 91, 92
McQueen, Maj. John C. 123
Mecklenburg County 56–62
Medal of Honor 25, 179
Merchant Marines 15; Distinguished Service Medal 104
Meritorious Unit Commendation 141
metal drives 190
mica 52–53
mica mining 53
Mid Pines Inn 86–89
military service: draftees, age range 23–24; length of 23–24; number from NC who served 25, 177
Miller, Capt. Glenn 87–89
Miller Airport 71
Mitchell, Margaret 2
Model T Fords 58–59
Montford Point 125, 127, 128
Montford Point Marines, Congressional Gold Medal 128
Montreat 45

Montreat Assembly Inn 45–47
Moore Complex 51–52
Moore County Airport 92, 93
Moore General Hospital 50–51
Morehead, Governor John Motley 132, 133
Morehead City 132–133, 134
Morris, Maj. William Cobb 61
Morris Field 61
Mountain Region 36–55
Murray, Charles Patrick, Jr. 25, 119, 183–184

Nag's Head 159
"Nasty Nick" 85
National Association for the Advancement of Colored People (NAACP) 126
National Carbon Company 72
National Cemetery of the Pacific 11
National Personnel Records Center 24
National Strike Force Coordination Center 166–167
Naval Air Engineering Station, Lakehurst, New Jersey 168
Naval Auxiliary Air Station, Edenton 163
Neuse River Bridge 139
New Bern 135–139
New Bern National Cemetery 26–29, 33
New Hanover County 107–119
New Hanover County Airport 122
New River Marine Barracks 124
Norfolk Southern Railroad 133
Normandy Invasion 79–80
USS *North Carolina* 116–117
North Carolina Division of Marine Fisheries 134
North Carolina History Center 137
North Carolina Military History Museum 111
North Carolina Railroad 133
North Carolina Shipbuilding Company 116
North Carolina State Board of Mental Health 75–76
Northeastern Regional Airport 163
Northern Tidewater Subregion 159–174
Northop, Jack 172

Ocracoke Island 154; British Cemetery at 156–158
Ocracoke Naval Station 156
Ocracoke Presbyterian Museum 153

Index

Office of Civil Defense 55
Office of Flying Safety of United States Army Air Force 72
USS *Oklahoma* 8, 10–11
USS *Oklahoma* Memorial 11
Onslow County 129
Operation Bumblebee 131
Operation Drumbeat 150–152
Operation Husky 90, 91
Operation Torch 79, 85
Oregon State University 17, 18, 20
Oteen Veterans Administration Hospital 50–52

Pasquotank County 164, 168
Patton, Gen. George S. 81
Paukenschlas 14, 150–152
Pearl Harbor, casualties at 9
Pearl Harbor Medal 12, 13
Percy, Locey 17
Pershing, Gen. John J. 124
Piedmont Airlines 72
Piedmont Aviation 72
Piedmont Flight Training and Aviation Services 72
Piedmont Region 56–76
Piedmont Triad International Airport 71
Pine Needles Inn 85–89
Pinehurst–Southern Pines Airport 92
Pinkham, S2c Allen Wesley 9
Pitt, William 98
Pitt County 97–99
Pitt-Greenville Airport 99
Pocket Change 135
Pope, 1st Lt. Harley Halbert 82
Pope Air Force Base 82–83
Pope Army Air Field 82–83
POW camps: Camp Butner 75; Camp Davis 129, 130; Camp Mackall 85; first in U.S. (Fort Bragg) 81; in NC 139; in U.S. 139
POWs, German 52
Preddy, Maj. George E. 70
Price, Cpl. Arthur Fred 31–32
Price, Sgt. Falls W. 31–32
Price, Francis 41
Price, P. R. v, 54–55
Price, William 41
Prothro, Johnny 20
Psychological Warfare Center 82
"The Punchbowl" 11
Purifoy, George 152

Queissner, Robert L. 188
Quezon, Manuel 36
Quonset 125

radio 193
Raleigh Durham Airport 73, 74
Raleigh Durham Army Air Field 74
Raleigh National Cemetery 26–31, 33
ramjet-powered missiles 131
Rathke, Kapitänleutnant Hellmut 151
rations 54
Rawlings, Marjorie Kinnan 2
Resistance Training Laboratory 85
Reynolds, R J. 72
Reynolds, Richard 71
Rhodes, S1c Mark Alexander 9
Rickenbacker, Capt. Eddie 73
R. J. Reynolds 72
Robertson, Bill 109
Robertson, Mike 109
Rockwell 192
Rogers, Roy 2
Roosevelt, President Franklin Delano 2, 5, 6, 12, 13, 14, 16, 22, 23, 25, 36, 49, 81, 104, 106, 125–126, 127, 138, 189, 190, 193, 194
USS *Roper* 160–161
Rostin, Erwin 105
Rutherford County Chapter of American Red Cross 449–50
Rutherford County Library 49–50

St. Joseph of the Pines 89
Salisbury Confederate Prison 31
Salisbury National Cemetery 26–27, 31–33
Sandhills area 85–95
Sanford, Terry 21
Schatt, Roy 192
Scott, Randolph 2
Second Armored Division 82
Second Marine Aircraft Wing 143
Selective Training and Service Act (1948) 25
Senter, William 42
Series E Defense Savings Bonds 189–192
Seymour Johnson Air Force Base 96
Seymour Johnson Field 93–97; federal prison camp at 96
Shepard Point Land Company 132–133
Shore, Dinah 193
Siegfried Line Break 20

Sisters of Providence of Holyoke, Massachusetts 89
Smith Reynolds Airport 71–72
Soldier Field 17
Southern Railway 133
Southport 102–107
Southport Naval Station 102–107
Sparkman-Johnson Bill 106
Spirit of St. Louis 71
Stallings, F1c Kermit Braxton 9
Steinbeck, John 2
Stern, Bill 19
Stiner, Lon 20
Stoddart, W. L. 39
suicides 176
Sutton, Frank Howie 62
Sutton, S1c William ("Billy") H. 16, 114–115
"Swamp Davis" 129
Swannanoa 50–52
Swannanoa Rehabilitation Center 52
Swing, Maj. Gen. Joseph M. 90, 91, 92

TCOM 170–171
Tent Camp 1, Camp Geiger 125
Tent Camp 2, Camp Geiger 125
textile workers 53–54
Thirty Seconds Over Tokyo (1944) 192
Thompson, Max 25, 184
Tidewater Subregions 100–144
Tillett, Capt. J. B. "Toby" 103
Timpani Beat 150–152; *see also* Operation Drumbeat
Tingzon, Catalino 105
Titan missile 67
Tooley, Adam 164
Tooley, Elizabeth 164
Topsail Beach 131
HMS *Tormentor* 155
Torpedo Alley 14–15, 153
Torpedo Junction 16, 153
Tracy, Spencer 192
Trent River Bridge 139
Truman, President Harry S 128
Tryon Palace Historic Site 137–138
Tucker, Capt. Allen D. 103
Tufts, James Walker 86
Tussey, EM3c Lloyd Harold 9
23rd Fighter Group 82

U-85 160
U-158 103–105

U-352 150–152
"The Un-Guarded Coastline" 129
Uncle Sam Wants You 24–25
Union County 62–66
U.S. Air Force Air Mobility Command 82
U.S. Army: first airborne division 81; first black parachute unit 81
U.S. Army Convalescence Hospital, No. 12 41
U.S. Army Special Operations Command 82
U.S. Coast Guard Air Station, Elizabeth City 164–167
U.S. Coast Guard (Mounted) Beach Patrol 114
U.S. Headquarters of the Western Wing of the Flight Control Command 42
U.S. Marine Corps: and African Americans 126
U.S. Marine Corps Air Station, Cherry Point 143
U.S. Naval Ordnance Testing Facility 131
U.S. Navy Auxiliary Air Station, Manteo 162
U.S. Navy Beach Jumper Association 155
U.S. Navy LTA Station, Weeksville 168
U.S. Rubber Company 56–58
Urban, Matt Louis 25, 185–186
Urban League 126
USS *Utah* 8, 12

Vanderbilt, Edith 48–49
Vanderbilt, George 39, 48–49
Victory and War drives 35
Vultee, Gerard "Jerry" Freebairn 172–173
Vultee Aircraft Corporation 172, 174

Waco gliders 79–80; CG-4A gliders 91
Wade, Wallace 20, 21
Wallace Wade Stadium 21
War Stamps 189–191
Ward, Archie 17
Warner, Cpl. Henry F. 25, 186–187
Wayne County 93
Weaver, Gen. Walter R. 87
Weeksville 168–172
Weissmuller, Johnny 2
Western Coastal Plain 77–99, 100
Western Electric Company 67
Westinghouse Electric Corporation, Weeksville 170–171

Index

White Sands, New Mexico 131
Wilmington 26–27, 33–34, 117–118, 122; American World War II City designation 116; POW camps 118, 122
Wilmington Army Air Field 121–122
Wilmington International Airport and Space Shuttle Program 122
Wilmington National Cemetery 26–27, 33–34

Wilmington USO Club 117–118
women who served 25
Woodward, Lt. Col. Clare W. 59
Works Progress Administration (WPA) 60, 98

Yearling 2

www.ingramcontent.com/pod-product-compliance
Ingram Content Group UK Ltd.
Pitfield, Milton Keynes, MK11 3LW, UK
UKHW041957140426
5217IPUK00015B/841